Formative Media

Psychoanalysis and Digital Media Platforms

Steffen Krüger

Routledge
Taylor & Francis Group

LONDON AND NEW YORK

Designed cover image: © code_rgb (Chris Barber), *flow pt 999999*,
19 Sept. 2023

First published 2025
by Routledge
4 Park Square, Milton Park, Abingdon, Oxon OX14 4RN

and by Routledge
605 Third Avenue, New York, NY 10158

Routledge is an imprint of the Taylor & Francis Group, an informa business

© 2025 Steffen Krüger

The right of Steffen Krüger to be identified as author of this work
has been asserted in accordance with sections 77 and 78 of the
Copyright, Designs and Patents Act 1988.

British Library Cataloguing-in-Publication Data
A catalogue record for this book is available from the British Library

ISBN: 9781032308593 (hbk)
ISBN: 9781032308531 (pbk)
ISBN: 9781003307044 (ebk)

DOI: 10.4324/9781003307044

Typeset in Times New Roman
by codeMantra

Formative Media

Formative Media presents a psychoanalytic and psychosocial inquiry into the significance of the most widely used digital platforms – including Facebook, Google, YouTube, Twitter (X), and Instagram – and the relational styles that users cultivate and habituate in their interplay with these platforms.

Steffen Krüger assesses the formative effects of these platforms, considering *who we are* and *how we are becoming who we are* in relation to, as well as mediated through, digital platforms. The book considers Facebook in conversation with the Freudian theory of Eros and the Live/Love drive, then homes in on the primitive forms of orality, attachment, dependence, and symbiosis in relation to YouTube. Krüger then expands the discussion of orality with an inquiry into the notions of mastery, control, and domination that Google unfolds and activates in its search function, considers narcissism in the context of Instagram, and examines hate speech and aggression on Twitter. The book focuses on the most salient, most talked about aspects, features, and activities of commercial, corporate social media culture to inquire into the formational pushes and pulls of these activities in their contexts for our subjectivities and sense of self.

Showing in detail how digital media platforms have advanced into central "socialisation agencies," *Formative Media* will be of great interest to academics and scholars of psychoanalytic, psychocultural, and psychosocial theory, critical digital media studies, and interactional theory.

Steffen Krüger is senior lecturer in the Department of Media and Communication, University of Oslo, Norway. His research interests are located at the intersections of media studies and psychoanalysis, psychosocial studies, and critical theory.

Psychoanalysis and Popular Culture Series
Series Editors: Caroline Bainbridge and Candida Yates
Consulting Editor: Brett Kahr

In partnership with the BPC Scholars' Network

This series builds on the work done since 2009 by the Media and the Inner World research network. It aims to consider the relationship between psychoanalysis and popular culture as a lived experience that is ever more emotionalised in the contemporary age. In contrast to many scholarly applications of psychoanalysis, works in this series set out to explore the creative tensions of thinking about cultural experience and its processes whilst also paying attention to observations from both the clinical and scholarly fields. The series provides space for a dialogue between these different groups with a view to evoking new perspectives on the values and pitfalls of a psychoanalytic approach to ideas of selfhood, society, politics, and popular culture. In particular, the series strives to develop a psycho-cultural approach by foregrounding the usefulness of a post-Freudian, object relations perspective for examining the importance of emotional relationships and experience. We nevertheless welcome proposals from all fields of psychoanalytic enquiry. The series is edited by Caroline Bainbridge and Candida Yates, with Brett Kahr as the Consulting Editor.

Other titles in the Psychoanalysis and Popular Culture Series:

The American Dream and American Cinema in the Age of Trump
Graham S. Clarke and Ross Clarke

Toy Story and the Inner World of the Child
Animation, Play, and Creative Life
Karen Cross

How to be Intimate with 15,000,000 Strangers
Musings on Media Psychoanalysis
Brett Kahr

Formative Media
Psychoanalysis and Digital Media Platforms
Steffen Krüger

For more information about this series, please visit: https://www.routledge.com/The-Psychoanalysis-and-Popular-Culture-Series/book-series/KARNPSYPOP

Contents

Acknowledgements

I want to thank the people who helped me put this book together. First of all, my friend and close colleague, Jacob Johanssen, read the whole manuscript and gave me feedback on it many times over. Thanks so much, Jacob.

Thanks also to my students in my MA courses "Internet, Self and Society" and "Screen Politics," who read various iterations of my chapters and discussed issues of socio-technological development, subject formation, and socialisation with me (and many even seemed to enjoy that). Rajeev Sharma Busgeeth, Fabiola Padilla Patiño, Kaitlyn Sampson, and Ragnhild Nerheim further helped me find relevant texts. Adam Buono Glazer helped with the copy editing of the final manuscript. Many thanks!

My friend and colleague Katarina Busch from the Sigmund Freud Institute, Frankfurt, did not tire to discuss the theoretical premises of my study with me. Thank you, Katarina. Aaron Balick also put some valuable hours into giving me feedback – many thanks! And a big 'Thank You,' too, to the editors of the *Psychoanalysis and Popular Culture* book series, Candida Yates and Caroline Bainbridge, who did not need long to be sold on the project and then helped it on the way – all the way.

Susannah Frearson and Saloni Singhania at Routledge remained upbeat, no matter how annoying my questions and emails. Thanks so much! And I was fortunate to be invited to present early drafts of my chapters in the Media Aesthetic and Screen Cultures seminars in the Department of Media and Communication at the University of Oslo. Here, especially Tim Vermeulen, Andreas Ervik, Kim Wilkins, and Liv Hausken made a big difference. Many thanks!

Being part of the Screen Cultures project and MA programme throughout the past five years has offered me a frame in which I could work continually and consistently, and that has been an important catalyst for the book, even if the administrative demands in such a programme sometimes kept me from writing it. Many thanks to the Faculty of Humanities and the Department of Media and Communication here at the University of Oslo for their institutional support!

Ultimately, my kids' surprisingly mature media habits give me hope, even during the times when their parents' screen time keeps going up.

Steffen Krüger, Oslo
February 2024

Series preface

The application of psychoanalytic ideas and theories to culture has a long tradition and this is especially the case with cultural artefacts that might be considered "classical" in some way. For Sigmund Freud, the works of William Shakespeare and Johann Wolfgang von Goethe were as instrumental as those of culturally renowned poets and philosophers of classical civilisation in helping to formulate the key ideas underpinning psychoanalysis as a psychological method. In the academic fields of the humanities and social sciences, the application of psychoanalysis as a means of illuminating the complexities of identity and subjectivity is now well established. However, despite these developments, there is relatively little work that attempts to grapple with popular culture in its manifold forms, some of which, nevertheless, reveal important insights into the vicissitudes of the human condition.

The "Psychoanalysis and Popular Culture" book series builds on the work done since 2009 by the Media and the Inner World research network, which was generously funded by the UK's Arts and Humanities Research Council. It aims to offer spaces to consider the relationship between psychoanalysis in all its forms and popular culture that is ever more emotionalised in the contemporary age.

In contrast to many scholarly applications of psychoanalysis, which often focus solely on "textual analysis," this series sets out to explore the creative tension of thinking about cultural experience and its processes with attention to observations from the clinical and scholarly fields. What can academic studies drawing on psychoanalysis learn from the clinical perspective and how might the critical insights afforded by scholarly work cast new light on clinical experience? The series provides space for a dialogue between these different groups with a view to creating fresh perspectives on the values and pitfalls of a psychoanalytic approach to ideas of selfhood, society, and popular culture. In particular, the series strives to develop a psychocultural approach to such questions by drawing attention to the usefulness of post-Freudian and object relations perspectives for examining the importance of emotional relationships and experience.

Steffen Krüger's *Formative Media – Psychoanalysis and Digital Media Platforms is* a fascinating and innovative psychosocial and cultural study of our engagement with the internet. It explores our conscious and unconscious relationships to the media platforms and virtual spaces that play a central role in shaping subjectivities in a mediatised digital age. Krüger deploys psychoanalytic ideas to create a critical methodological apparatus through which to understand the design and usage of popular media platforms such as Facebook, YouTube, Instagram, Google, and X (formerly Twitter). Taking such an approach, he argues, allows us to examine the fantasies and often contradictory wishes, desires, and affects that underpin the influence and appeal of these platforms for large sections of the public who continually check in for updates, engagement with online communities, and uploading content. While never losing sight of the wider context of neoliberalism and the profit mechanisms of the digital economy, Krüger suggests that each platform taps into its own particular form of affect and fantasy structures that satisfy different impulses and drives. At the same time, however, to borrow from the language of Christopher Bollas, these structures ensure that the user repeatedly returns in search of more "psychic supplies." Krüger takes a highly original psychosocial approach to the culture and use of internet platforms, providing a very welcome addition to our book series and contributing more widely to the emerging field of psychoanalytic media and communication studies. The book charts the detailed histories of our engagement with media tools to show how they have come to exert a "formative" influence on the emotional and psychological dimensions of what it means to be human in the digital age. Often insightful, and occasionally provocative, the book maps out a compelling argument for the value and importance of psychoanalysis for understanding how and why the choices we make around engaging with media can determine sociocultural dynamics. It opens up a rich seam of thinking for anyone interested in how life online reshapes what it means to be human.

Caroline Bainbridge and Candida Yates

Introduction – the forms
of formative media

There is a genre of jokes circulating online which, working with enumerations and in typically incongruent fashion, gesture towards the main theme of the present study, specifically, the formative – subjectivising and socialising – effects of the digital media platforms of the early 21st century:

- *Instagram: My life is a party. Snapchat: My life is a quirky tv show. Facebook: My life turned out great. Twitter: We're all going to die (Mikel Jollett, Twitter, 08/01/2017).*
- *Twitter: Your jokes suck. Instagram: Your face sucks. Snapchat: Your life sucks. Facebook: Your parents love you and are also racist (Adrienne Airhart, Twitter, 29/10/2015).*
- *Facebook: Essential oils. Snapchat: I'm a bunny! Instagram: I ate a hamburger. Twitter: THIS COUNTRY IS BURNING TO THE GROUND! (Jeanne Hulme, Twitter, 28/07/2017).*
- *Facebook: My opinion is right, yours is wrong. Instagram: My flat is nice, yours is not. Snapchat: My penis is nice, but not my spelling. Twitter: F@#* your opinion, you c#*%! WhatsApp: My opinion is right, but yours is also right. Love, Mum* (unknown source).

In a few words and through the tight coordination of some of the most salient characteristics of the various platforms' use cultures, these jokes drive home in exaggerated and stereotypical ways core relational styles that have – often correctly – been attributed to them. By challenging people to make common sense of the non-sense they offer, the jokes shed light on the aspects of people's everyday media uses that are imbued with intense ambivalences – ambivalences rooted in their depending on the platforms but frequently against their will and better judgement.

Jokes such as the above have followed the spread of digital social media across the past two decades, veering between attraction and rejection and thus bringing to the fore people's intense involvement and entanglements in and with the digital in its contemporary corporate cast. Social media is like "a fridge which has something new in it every time we look", quips media critic Marcus Gilroy-Ware (2017, eBook version, n.p.), quoting a meme that has been making the rounds. However,

DOI: 10.4324/9781003307044-1

he goes on, none of the delicious things that magically appear in this fridge can satisfy for long. Rather, there is a void that media users constantly try, but fail, to fill. "*Social media is like waking up on a psychiatric ward,*" goes another joke, "*You have no idea you're committed until you try to leave.*" With each leak of internal documents at Facebook (Milmo 2021a[1]), with each closer reading of Google's engineering papers (Lewis 2018[2]), or with each internal review at Twitter (Milmo 2021b[3]), we receive confirmation of what we already know: corporate digital media platforms do not merely unfold formative powers as side-effects of their services; rather, they aim for such effects through the design and constant tweaking of their programming and algorithmic architecture.

The history of media-technological development has been closely linked to imaginaries and strategies of social engineering from the start, with the writings by Edward Bernays perhaps the best-known examples (e.g., his *Propaganda* from 1928). While earlier on, the argument goes, one could only surmise what sociocultural sense people made of the media they consumed, the deluge of datapoints their media use now produces offers detailed insight into such sense-making. In this way, the shift of such strategies toward the digital, with data mining and analysis based on automated reinforcement learning, has rung in a new paradigm (e.g., Dean 2010; Zuboff 2019; Srnicek 2017). This paradigm has begun to pose new questions to the critical branches of media and cultural studies, whose default position has been to focus and insist on the resilience and largely undeterred agency of media users in the face of the media's power to shape and frame this agency and set the users' agenda (e.g., Vanden Abeele and Mohr 2021). In this respect, digital media studies that are interested in the sociocultural shaping powers of corporate platforms are faced with a delicate balancing act. On the one hand, the field needs to continue to leave room for what Helmut Plessner (1982) has called the "eccentric positionality" of human beings – i.e., people's ability to distance themselves from their contexts of interaction and their principal ability to change their minds, no matter how strong the determining forces are that weigh in on the processes of decision making. On the other hand, media studies need to accurately describe and precisely delineate the platforms' increasing subjectifying and socialising powers. Without discarding human freedom, this study is interested in these shaping powers, tracing the technological formation (Cassirer 2013 [1930]) of relational styles and forms of relatedness (Lorenzer 2022 [1986]) that mainstream digital media platforms have been affording vast numbers of people across vast cultural spheres.

I depart from Jodi Dean's (2010) early analysis of social media along the lines of her concept of "communicative capitalism," specifically, that social media tend to hollow out structures of desire and replace them with formations of drive – "feeding frenzies, vicious circles, bubbles" (p. 30). Building from this, I follow Eugenie Brinkema (2014) in her insistence on the necessity to pay detailed attention to "the problem of form and representation" when it comes to matters of affect, the sensual and the relational. Accordingly, the central aim of the present study is to trace the development of the platforms' core formative orientations and the potential effects these have on their users. Ultimately, when Anna Kornbluh, in *The Order of Form*

(2019), defines form as "composed relationality" (p. 4) and suggests a "political formalism" as a strategy with which to evaluate "form's composedness and form's agency" (ibid), this can well be taken as a premise – motto and 'user's manual' – of my approach. Simply put, what I want to do in this book is to give an account of what have been the leading media of the early 21st century, how they were formed and with what formative influence on the people who use them.

In line with Gilroy-Ware's fridge comparison, I see notions of orality – stuffing oneself without ever filling up – and their family relations with phenomena of dependency and addiction, to be highly significant in the context of corporate digital media platforms, and I will unpack this significance in the exemplary case of the Google/Alphabet-owned video-streaming platform YouTube (Chapter 2). Yet, oral attachments are not the only ones shaping social media uses. Rather, I identify several typical attachment patterns in the make-up of digital platforms and in the social relations they foster in order to trace the interweaving of human bodies and their drives with those that platforms are facilitating and affording. In this respect, *Formative Media* draws from Freudian and post-Freudian conceptions of psychosexuality (Freud 1905a) and basic drive formations to unpack notions of Eros and the erotic in the case of Facebook (Chapter 1), forms of orality as they relate to the video streaming platform YouTube and its automatised system of video recommendations (Chapter 2). The study then revisits and re-evaluates the dynamics in arrangements of narcissism, self-love, and self-object choices on the Facebook/Meta-owned photo-sharing platform Instagram (Chapter 3), and subsequently details forms of obsessional neurosis in the history of Google Search (Chapter 4). Finally, I detail processes and dynamics of disinhibition and 'aggressivisation' in people's relation to the micro-blogging platform formerly called Twitter, now revamped as "X" (Chapter 5).

My findings aim to restate and re-evaluate widely held – at times even overused – cultural positions in digital media studies. However, while these positions might have been excessively exploited – such as the accusation of social media narcissism – this does not mean that the relational core they often entail has been sufficiently understood. In aiming at such understanding, I thus show how Facebook's orientation towards the erotic and binding has indeed turned love into labour; how YouTube can indeed be called a feeding tube, 'stilling' people with what proves most palatable to them; that narcissism *is* a ubiquitous reality on Instagram, even if it is not of the megalomaniac kind that much of cultural journalism has been decrying; how Google has indeed helped establish a culture of utilitarianism through its endeavour to make knowledge "universally accessible" (Google 2023[4]); and how Twitter must be seen as a machine for the production and circulation of aggression.

While those branches of media studies which share the present effort's critical orientation tend to prefer a focus on use cultures that *resist* the platforms' more problematic formative potentials, I hold that it is important not to avoid these troubling aspects. Rather, I want to face them head on – with clarity, but also with empathy so as to unfold the conflicts, contradictions, and dilemmas that drive them. Doing this might at times mean emphasising negative human capacities – e.g., inclinations towards dependencies, towards impaired capabilities to act, and towards inhibitions and disinhibitions, compulsions, and the irrational. Yet, this does not mean that human beings are *only* or *necessarily* characterised by these negatives. Whereas the resounding critiques of the Frankfurt School (Horkheimer and Adorno 1994) – for example, by Stuart Hall (1980) and John Fiske (1989) – have been ruling out attempts at taking seriously notions of impaired media user agency, *Formative Media* reengages with many of these more formalist positions in order to reintroduce the uncomfortable truths they hold to current debates in the field. It is thus from a formative perspective that I return to some of the most discussed aspects of corporate social media culture – searching, liking, bingeing, commenting, sharing, pranking, shitstorming, etc. – to offer a critical psychoanalytic re/construction of their formative potentials and effects and to give a realistic analysis of the resulting forms of subjectivity. The subject I see as arising from the era of platformed digital media is one whose opportunity for object-relations is being reduced and whose commitment to a shared notion of social reality becomes weakened. Again, this does not mean that this is necessarily so in the case of all people using digital media platforms; however, it means that the forms of socialisation and subjectivation afforded by these platforms clearly point in the direction of such a weakening.

If the predictions of influential media critics are anything to go by, the era of corporate social media that is at the heart of this book's inquiry might be slowly coming to an end, or at least to a major turning point. Facebook is now regularly ignored when major institutions compose their social media strategies; since Elon Musk acquired the platform, Twitter/X has received serious competition in the field of microblogging; and Google Search is faced with an impending paradigm change brought about by Microsoft's incorporation of Open-AI's Chat-GPT into its own search engine, Bing. Hence, at a point in the development of social media platforms at which a sense of change is pervasive, the term *Formative Media* also refers to the ways in which these era-defining platforms, by having become prosthetic and integral dimensions of human subject formation, are being productive for *how we have become who we are.*[5]

As critical scholars of the digital (e.g., Chun 2021; Cheney-Lippold 2017; Finn 2017; Greenfield 2017) have pointed out, the subjectifying 'pushes and pulls' of digital media are distributed and stacked (Bratton 2015) – i.e., spread across networks and built into layers of design and programming – and extend well beyond their users' immediate contact and direct possibility of observation. Frequently, such influence can only be inferred through speculative analysis of exemplary incidences, such as Facebook's experiments on emotional contagion (Stark 2018), or from interface design choices (Krüger and Spilde 2020). Much of the algorithmic governance (Rouvroy and Stiegler 2014) that is brought to bear on users, however, remains part of the platforms' trade secrets, with troves of data and analytic sophistication far beyond users' – as well as cultural analysts' – access and comprehension. In this context of one-way mirrors (Zuboff 2019), our skin and body cannot be understood as the boundaries of our being; instead, as Cheney-Lippold (2017) and Olga Goriunova (2019), amongst others, hold rightly, subjectivities extend far beyond the users' skin, across vast information networks and into the various data centres in which their use and meta-data are being analysed and turned into "measurable types" (Cheney-Lippold 2017, 24), designed for the use by interested third parties which then *re*-present these versions of 'people-like-ourselves' back to us and our demographic neighbours in order to create affective resonance with a brand, product, service, or cause. Nevertheless, despite bits and pieces of our subjectivities having begun to permanently circulate and mutate according to the multiple contexts in which they are relevant, I argue that this relational and distributed conception of subjectivity (cf. Braidotti 2013) always harks back to, aims to become reinscribed in, and ultimately shows on the body and its life praxis in relevant ways. As Deborah Lupton (2020) states poignantly, "… not only do human-data assemblages configure and materialise certain dimensions of human embodiment and selfhood, they also have material effects on humans in recursive ways" (p. 17). It is in the context of such recursiveness that a psychoanalytic perspective promises significant critical knowledge gains. Specifically, this perspective offers theories of human interaction and experience that are sensitised towards the automaticity of learned expectations and towards those rationalities in human behaviour that show their social character in their specific forms of compromise, adaptation, and makeshift solutions for unsolvable conflicts. And while the wide distribution of that which seeks to resonate with embodied subjectivity makes it necessary to open the view towards knowledge from other spheres, detailed analyses of the ways in which social media platforms afford social interaction promise important insights into how the sphere of digital platforms has been affecting subjectivity and sociality, and with what political consequences.

--

As I have begun to sketch out, this is the context in which the present study operates and the basic knowledge that readers need to take with them when entering into the main chapters of this book. The chapters are case-based and constructed to shed light on the forms of the relationships that have gone into the respective platform's making and the particular formative forces that these platforms afford their users in turn. Hence, while I focus on the most prevalent of these characteristics of each platform, these are by no means exclusive. On the contrary, similar relationships and formative constellations can be found across the entire field of platformed digital media. In this way, what I work out in my chapters are relational and affective forcefields that need to be seen as being held in constantly varying interplays with each other and where, for example, the erotic demands of flirtation afforded by one service might become enacted through, or defended against, the attempt to master or dominate an object relation afforded by another.

For those readers who would like the theoretical and methodological apparatus behind this study's understanding of formative media fleshed out in more detail, please follow me through the rest of this introduction, where I turn to the notion of the media "platform," to my peculiarly caricaturing method of cultural analysis, to the concept of the "formative" as this study's central metaphor, as well as to the intricacies of a psychosocial theory of digital subject formation with a psychoanalytic orientation. I will round off this introduction with a brief literature review, positioning my work in related traditions, and a summary of the main chapters.

Platformed economy – platformed sociality

As Slavoj Žižek (2008 [1989]) has rightly diagnosed, contemporary forms of ideology lie less in what people know, think, and say, but much rather in what they actually *do* – which frequently flies in the face of the former. For example, the more we proclaim to people around us how idiotic make-over tv-shows are, the more we seem to give ourselves licence to watch them. This ideological form continues to thrive on corporate social media platforms, where a generation is currently coming of age who use and experience these privately owned, corporate services as central conduits of both their private and their public lives (and all shadings in between) and, thus, as conventional, perfectly normal, and 'second-natural' environments for their everyday interactions. The circumstance that they might harbour strong ambivalences against these platforms, or even resent them and resent themselves for their dependency on them, in no way weakens these ties; rather, like the relationship that young adults have towards their parents, ambivalence must be seen as an inevitable by-product, and even necessary lubricant for, the vitality of every close relationship.

This ambivalence between users and platforms also becomes relevant in another way that is yet more complexly entangled with the platforms' business model. Already in 2010, Tarleton Gillespie observed how the word "platform" was taken up by the owners and operators of corporate social and content-sharing networks at the very point at which they put their focus on how to monetise the vast amount of activity on their sites. In this respect, the term "platform" turned into a discursive tool with which the networks could depict themselves as at a certain – innocent – distance from the inter- and transactions performed on them by and between various user groups and private businesses. YouTube, for example, after having been bought by Google in 2006, used the "platform" label to distance itself from its users publishing videoclips that had been produced by mainstream media outlets on its site so as to reject claims of copyright infringement from the film and television industries (Gillespie 2010). By describing its services as merely offering people a platform, i.e., an elevated position facilitating these people's views, work, skills, interests, etc., YouTube attempted to clear itself of all culpability (see Johanssen and Krüger 2022, 111).

However, as Nick Srnicek (2017) argues, digital platforms have never been as neutral as they attempt to appear. Drawing on Rochet and Tirole (2003), he suggests that the idea of the platform as an intermediary between two or more groups and as the ground upon which the interactions between these groups take place has become the central business model of the digital era. This is echoed by the German sociologist Philipp Staab (2019), who sees the platform model of digital capitalism to ring in the end of the neoliberal era (p. 44ff). Facilitating and affording specific activities in specifically designed ways, the platform channels, funnels, tracks, and archives these activities and harvests the connection data resulting from them, which it then renders into financial profit, as for example in the case of Google's AdWords, by selling the 'findability' of something or someone in association with specific search terms to the highest bidder.[6] The more users the platform draws onto itself, the longer these users remain on it, and the more interactions these users produce, the better the platform will be able to customise its services and to tailor them to the demands, needs and desires of its users, the more ingrained the platform will become in the lives of its growing user base, the stronger its opportunities for financialisation and profitmaking will become, the stronger its market position – and the more powerful will its formative potential be in relation to its users. By offering users entire "sociotechnical ecosystems" (Dolata 2015; Staab 2019, 38), markets are no longer monopolised by powerful players, but the most powerful players turn themselves into the markets. This idea had been programmatically promoted by the media-trend agency O'Reilly Media for the creation of what would be called "Web 2.0" (O'Reilly 2007; Fuchs 2012). At the level of the users, this means that people become increasingly enveloped in arrangements that, while not directly perceivable to them, ensure that each interest they have, each interchange they enter into, and each question they put in a search bar are responded to in a way that addresses them, not only as a person with a desire for knowledge about the world (to remain with the search bar example), but also as a potential customer and buyer of commodities. This again has potential effects on what users expect of their environment and themselves. If we feel we are customers, we might expect prompt and exacting service and want results fast. With only a handful of extremely powerful, globally operating corporate platforms, their formative powers are immense. And while there are clear signs of the monopolistic standing of the US corporations Alphabet, Meta, Amazon, and Apple being on the wane – with Chinese, state-protected companies on the rise in many parts of the world – it is hardly plausible that the formative influence of the US platforms on Western countries, while it will surely change in form, will be totally diminished any time soon.

In this continuing context of user surveillance and data analysis for the purpose of matching people with goods and services and profiting from the commission fees, ambivalence becomes relevant once more. For not only is it understandable that users are ambivalent to the platforms they have come to depend on; rather, an increased understanding of the platforms' business model also shows an inherent ambivalence on the part of the platforms towards their users. Whereas the platforms' serviceability is first and foremost geared towards gaining and capturing the largest possible number of users and keeping them on the platform for as much time as possible (Seymore 2019, 64) so as to gain an advantage over the competition in the endeavour of monetising personal use data, this inherent selfishness and competitiveness must still be turned 'altruistic' to a significant degree in that it must offer people a valuable service. Platforms need to *love* and *care for* the people they interact with, but this love can never be entirely genuine and exclusive, because (a) the platforms' function as facilitators of exchanges means that there is always at least one more party who craves to be nurtured and (b) with the platforms seeking to profit from these exchanges, the care for their users necessarily oscillates between empowerment and arrest, between making people independent enough to enter into exchange relations with others and keeping them dependent enough not to leave the services behind that the platform offers. Hence, rather than the metaphor of the elevated platform, corporate social media might be better captured as a sandbox filled with playing toddlers, with a caregiver watching from the side. It is this notion of the caregiver, with its stereotypically maternal connotations – a caregiver who hovers over every action, who constantly observes, controls, and weighs in on interactions – which connects my take on the platform with Lacanian and Žižekian (1998) notions of a psychotic state of reality itself. In such a state, as Dean (2010) put it, "the Other is both missing and fully, over-whelmingly present" (p. 8).

What is entailed in the ambivalence of the platform can be seen to amount to one of the main contradictions of society under capitalism, specifically that of the particular and the universal. As Christian Fuchs (2016) explains for the case of Google:

> Google stands at the same time for the universal and the particular interests on the Internet. It represents the idea of the advancement of an Internet that benefits humanity and the reality of the absolute exploitation of humanity for business purposes.
>
> (Fuchs 2016, 149; see also Chapter 4)

In other – more general – words, on the corporate, platformed internet, notions of use and exchange, production and surplus, private and public, and the universal and the particular are all folded into one another. This has concrete consequences for the formation of subjects who are asked to grow, but not grow up, expand their horizons, but not beyond the nodes of the network, and develop their personalities, but not to the detriment of the platform's third parties. Networks, writes Wendy Chun (2018), "because of their complexities, noisiness, and persistent inequalities, foster techniques to manage, prune, and predict" (p. 61), and, while pruning is a term from gardening which means to channel and trim and bring about the desired kind of growth, it is the gardener who does the pruning while the plant still needs to do the growing.

--

There is one more aspect of the platform economy that is important to touch upon here. As digital media scholars have pointed out, the core propositions of the big corporate platforms are usually only the tips of the icebergs, i.e., they are the most visible and engaging parts of much larger and more diverse, horizontally and vertically integrated corporate structures. Google, or Alphabet, as its holding company, is not merely a search engine, but also runs a mobile operating system (Android) and builds laptop computers (Chromebook) and a myriad of other applications (YouTube, Gmail, Google Maps, Google Health, Google Drive [i.e., cloud service]). Facebook/Meta does not merely consist of a social network, but at least *three* such networks, with its high-profile acquisitions, Instagram and WhatsApp, becoming increasingly integrated into its core service, but Meta has also become an internet provider for smartphone users in many developing parts of the world, and also its notion of the "Metaverse" (e.g., Stokel-Walker 2022) continues its vision of growing a web within the web.

José van Dijck and colleagues (2018) differentiate in this respect between *sectoral* platforms, "which serve a particular sector or niche, such as news, transportation, food, education, health, finance, or hospitality" (p. 13), and *infrastructural* platforms, which span multiple aspects at once, such as "search engines and browsers, data servers and cloud computing, email and instant messaging, social networking, advertising networks, app stores, pay systems, identification services, data analytics, video hosting, geospatial and navigation services" (ibid). Since my interest lies in the major formative influences of social media platforms, this study is limited to the best known, core sectoral aspects of those giga-platforms that otherwise display infrastructural ambitions, too, as is clearly the case with Google/Alphabet and Facebook/Meta. On the one hand, this limitation finds its justification in the persistent salience of these platforms' core functions and their importance for the formation of expectations and habits that inevitably unfold a basic subjectifying force. On the other hand, as I will turn to in the following, my method of analysis has been relying not merely on a vast number of existing studies on the functioning of platforms, but also on inquiries into the platforms' own development – their 'formative years,' so to speak. Accounts on the rise of social media have been written almost exclusively with a focus on the major platforms, with these accounts often taking the form of heroic myths and rags-to-riches stories. Despite such ideological biases, a psychoanalytically oriented reading, I argue (and demonstrate in the chapters), can regularly point to central conflicts and deadlocks in the development of a service. It is these conflicts, I claim, that continue to exert a formative charge on the significant forms of the service's usage.

The caricaturing method

The major methodological influence on *Formative Media* could not seem further removed from contemporary digital culture: the works on classical portrait caricature by the Viennese art historian and psychoanalyst Ernst Kris (1936; 1951; cf. Krüger 2011). Kris's theory of caricature amounts to a visual equivalent of Freud's (1905b) theory of jokes. Mediating between the intersubjective construction of reality on one side and individual – yet historically and culturally shared – unconscious dynamics on another, Kris saw caricatures as putting the primary process of the unconscious into the service of the ego, and hence the reality principle. Successful caricatures, he held, are not merely subjective distortions of someone's likeness, in which an aggressive charge is turned into visual form, but rather the condensation of a person's likeness up to the point at which this condensation becomes affectively endowed with an entirely new vision (Krüger 2012). In this way, aggression becomes sublimated into creation.

Figure I.1 Honoré Daumier (1834), "Les poires", caricature series of King Louis-Philippe (1830–1848).

Kris and his younger colleague Ernst H. Gombrich (1938) used Honoré Daumier's gradual transformation of King Louis-Philippe into a pear (Figure I.1) as exemplary for their psychosocial methodology of a caricaturing, creative method of symbolisation. Along the lines of this caricaturing process, Kris would in his media-related works of the early 1940s, in exile in the UK and later in the USA, trace the intentions and motives that informed National-Socialist (NS)-German propaganda (e.g., Kris 1941). The success of these studies, which he conducted for the British Ministry of Information and in collaboration with the communication studies group, headed by Harold Lasswell at the New School for Social Research in New York, is still a strong testament to the epistemic prowess of research with an orientation towards form (cf. Krüger 2012; 2021).

For the study of formative digital media, I have followed Kris's caricaturing strategy of layering and condensing critical perspectives on digital platforms to bring forth a vision of them creatively derived from their inherent functional logic. For these perspectives, I have drawn on relevant academic and journalistic literatures, including analyses of the platforms' functionality and design features, their programming and algorithms, their economic rationale and profit strategies, their use cultures and cultural significance, the aesthetics of their user-generated contents, more fine-grained observations on user interactions, advertisements, online debates, and several generations of the platforms' "About" pages, as well as biographical and autobiographical texts by/about the inventors, developers, engineers, and investors of the platforms. These sources have then been committed to both a synthesising interpretation, which allowed for the most central formative tendencies of the platforms to emerge, and an analytical interpretation in which these central tendencies were given room to unfold. When Kornbluh (2019), in referring to Clifford Geertz, suggests that working with forms should proceed via "models," writing that "we build models in order to learn, criticize, build, and rebuild" (p. 10), this again characterises the present project well. Furthermore, as Florian Cramer (2018) has remarked about processes of hermeneutics and interpretation in the field of digital media, artificial intelligence, and data analytics: "Historically, there may never have been as much interpretation going on as there is in the age of analytics, yet this paradoxically coincides with a blindness for the subjective viewpoint involved" (p. 36). In line with this claim, I argue that it is on the basis of a condensing heuristic of form – a caricaturing hermeneutic that spans from the biographical to the algorithmic in order to synthesise these perspectives – that such a "subjective viewpoint" can be re-injected into our field of experience and knowledge development.

In this mode of production, then, what I work out in the coming chapters are – highly objectivated and, at the same time, highly idiosyncratic – visions of corporate digital platforms that depart from the latter's most salient characteristics and functions. In this approach, Facebook emerges as an Eros machine (Chapter 1) that strives to synthesise ever more entities into a single whole, denying questions of death in the process; YouTube comes forth as a feeding tube (Chapter 2), with its default "Autoplay" function suggesting a constant flow of nourishment. Instagram unfolds its credentials as a "narcissising" machine (Chapter 4), whose tripartite functionality of instant imaging, publishing, and editing falsely promises to close the gap between ego and ego ideal; Google, in turn, arises as an "anal-ising" (sic) machine (Chapter 3), with its archive being not only about 'world knowledge' but also, significantly, about knowledge on the relevance and usefulness of this knowledge for its users. Finally, Twitter/X comes to the fore as a channel for the flow of aggression (Chapter 5). Its emphases on brevity, currency, and wit might allow us to trace both regressive *and* sublimated ways of acting upon the world, of maturation and change, if its cascaded logic of seduction were not to close down this possibility. Following a remark by my colleague Aurora Hoel (private communication), what I am thus working out in these distinct, yet overlapping, chapters are "forms of interaction" (Lorenzer 2022) that emerge within the affective forcefields of major digital actors and that can best be captured in neologistic verb-coinages, such 'eroticising' (Facebook), 'oralising' (YouTube), 'narcissising' (Instagram), 'analysing' (Google), and 'aggressivising' (Twitter). As I unpack further below, it is in the facilitation, structuring, and modulation of these basic human dispositions that the formative tendencies of digital media platforms can be identified.

The field of the formative

With "formative" being the central concept of this publication, some explanations of the notion are in order. The English word "formative" is in relatively frequent use today, where it is commonly used in turns of phrases, such as the "formative years," or "formative influence." According to the Oxford English Dictionary,[7] "formative" stems from the Latin verb "formare," to form, and was introduced into English via old French, with the earliest detected written uses dating back to the 15th century. Already in the 16th century, phrases such as "the formative power of the parents" were in use, and it is this straightforward meaning of the word as "having the faculty of forming or fashioning"[8] that I want to bring to bear on the field of corporate digital platform culture. In their constant striving to turn their services into ever more present, ever more relevant and reliable, as well as ever more active parts of our lives (e.g., Krüger and Ni Bhroin 2020) – to make them seamless, effortless, convenient, comfortable, and intuitive to use, to smoothly fit them into and enrich with them our everyday routines, to make us experience these services as magically efficient and elegant, and to have us imagine these qualities to rub off on ourselves – digital platforms need to be conceived along the lines of what critical feminist scholar Ulrike Prokop (1976) has called "socialisation agencies."

Following the psychoanalytic tradition of Frankfurt School thought, the specific twist of Prokop's conception of the "socialisation agency" is that it does not first and foremost refer to *cognitive* functions – such as the geolocation functions on our smartphones that tell us exactly where we are in the world and where to get, say, our next double cappuccino. While platforms as socialisation agencies do that, too – no doubt they inform and orient us – what is more significant from both Prokop's perspective and the present study's formative one are the intricately relational and developmental qualities that our interactions with the digital produce. Hence, while, on a cognitive level, an online service might help us find relevant information about, say, a job that we might consider applying for, on the formative level what is of interest are the relational, affective, and emotive dimensions of this experience. In this respect, the way in which the digital service informs us about the job offer – or, indeed, that it does inform us about it in the first place – might be (experienced as) activating, motivating, and empowering, or angering, disquieting, and anxiety provoking, or calming, supporting, soothing, and reassuring, or a mixture of these.

Along these lines, my interest in the formative is to a certain extent defined by its difference to the informative. However, this difference is an artificial one and exists on an analytic level only. For example, whenever I am prompted by the commercial digital platform for academics, Academia.edu, to leave a message to the author of a paper I am downloading, this is not only meant as informative – *Hi, I am very interested in the issue of "digital labour" too! –* but also as formative – *Very much looking forward to reading your text! Keep up the good work in the field! –* which, in the current example, means having a positive, productive, and encouraging effect on this author and their work in the field of digital labour (and in this way, making this author become further implicated in the contradictions of this kind of labour).

This notion of encouragement, in turn, points to the second central aspect of the formative, specifically "the developmental." With this aspect, *Formative Media* harks back to a discussion that has a long tradition and history within cultural studies. Already in the 1930s, Erich Fromm (1989 [1929]) linked the question of "what influence the growth of technology [...] has on the psyche of the individual" to "an ever-increasing gratification, or a decreasing deprivation, of the instincts" (p. 38) and hence to a formative concern (see also Kühn 2019). Likewise, Herbert Marcuse, in *One-Dimensional Man* (1986 [1964]), held that "advanced industrial society is confronted with the possibility of a materialisation of ideals" (p. 58), which he saw as holding a distinctly negative potential for the members of societies. To these perspectives and their focus on cultural change, I would like to add that of Ernst Cassirer, who in his seminal "Form and Technology" (2013 [1930]) insisted that such changes could only correctly be perceived and understood if one paid detailed attention to the formation of technology itself. "The world of technology," he writes, "begins to open up and to divulge its secrets only if we return from the *forma formata* to the *forma formans*, from that which has become to the very principle of becoming" (Cassirer 2013, 276).

In the field of sociology, important impulses for my understanding of "formative media" have come from Georg Simmel's (e.g., 1972) sociology of social forms, where Simmel understands the social as based on "inter-individual as well as inter-group relations" that nevertheless receive "relatively stable external form[s]" (p. 351), with one weighing in on the further development of the other. Another point of orientation for the formative in this study has come from Norbert Elias (e.g., 1991) and his sociology of processes and "figurations." About his notion of "figuration," Elias explains that:

[i]t is only through a social moulding process within the framework of particular social characteristics that a person evolves the characteristics and modes of behaviour that distinguish him or her from all the other members of his or her society.

(Elias 1991, 59)

In media studies, Andreas Hepp and Nick Couldry (2017) picked up on Elias's term of "figuration" to describe the "variety of ways in which *possible* orderings of the social by media are further transformed and stabilized through continuous feedback loops" (p. 4, emphasis in the original).

In film studies, it was first and foremost Jean-Louis Baudry (e.g., 1975) who reignited the debate about the formative powers of the cinema as an "apparatus" along the lines of Louis Althusser. Whereas Baudry saw cinema's power to lie in a nourishing-like function in which the spectator becomes latched on to the screen like a baby to a breast, putting them in a somnambulist state, Christian Metz, who built his argument in *The Imaginary Signifier* (1977) on Baudry's work, saw the influence of cinema to lie in a slightly later developmental stage, specifically that of identification. Characters on screens, he held, are frequently offered to movie goers like (improved) stand-ins for their own mirror image. Laura Mulvey, in her famous interventionist essay "Visual Pleasure and Holly-wood Cinema" (1975), would again build on Metz's model of "primary cinematic identification" to articulate her critique of the hetero-sexist way of looking – the well-known concept of the "male gaze" that suggests for men to be the active lookers and for women passive objects to-be-looked-at – which she saw as baked into both the *modes* and the *relations* of production of classic Hollywood movies (see Johanssen and Krüger, 2022, and Paasonen et al., 2021, for further developments of this theme).

Implicitly, *Formative Media* picks up on this psychoanalytic tradition with in-depth and detailed studies about the ways in which digital platforms seek to establish very specific formative relationships with the people that use them daily. Not all of the relational qualities that digital platforms are geared to facilitate might be equally conductive of what one might consider a positive and progressive formation of one's personality. However, it is easily comprehensible, I hope, how each of the qualities, in case they are encountered frequently and regularly, can prepare and unfold a habitual effect that goes beyond the merely cognitive and takes on something more engraining and subjectifying.

The interest in the formative is thus closely aligned with habits and the habit-ual, and, in her study on "habitual new media", Wendy Hui Kyong Chun (2016) rightly calls habits "the productive nonconscious" (p. 7) – i.e., automatisms and embodied interactional scripts that *can* relate to what psychoanalysis calls the (re-pressed) unconscious, i.e., forcefully forgotten or systematically unsymbolisable interactional patterns, but can just as well refer to preconscious thoughts, which are principally available to consciousness, but not activated in a given moment. Crisscrossing my differentiation between the informative and the formative, Chun sees the workings of digital networks to lie in their enabling of "a form of cognitive mapping" (p. 17), i.e., a form of ordering the world in relation to the subject that offers security through anchoring and spatialisation, although such cognitive maps, she writes, always remain painfully incomplete and unstable.

Already Fredric Jameson (1990) had evoked the term "cognitive mapping" which he conceived of as a critical practice with which to "expand our sensorium and our body to some new, yet unimaginable, perhaps ultimately impossible, di-mensions" (p. 39). This expansion, Jameson hoped, was to make us receptive to our new global and hyper-capitalist environment. For the case of network science, Chun (2018) asserts that digital networks, too, function as cognitive maps "by revealing the links between the individual to the totality in which she lives" (p. 69). However, as Chun drily remarks, in contrast to Jameson's hopes, the maps supplied by digital platforms are "hardly socialist or empowering"; rather, they "contract the world into a map" (p. 70).

Translated into the formative paradigm of the present study, one can say that, while platforms are designed to have strongly supporting – soothing, anchoring, orienting, securing, protecting – functions that are comparable to what Donald W. Winnicott (1960) has called the "holding environment" which the primary caregiver provides to their child during infantile development, this experience of being held becomes inevitably associated with ideas about the world that the platform articulates as self-evident. For example, on the dating app Tinder, the submenu where one can retrieve those other users that one has 'liked' by swiping over the smartphone screen from left to right is at exactly *that* place on the app's interface where online shopping websites usually have their 'basket' or 'trolley' (cf. Krüger and Spilde 2020). For the case of the dating app, then, this design solution not only makes those contacts easily findable, but it also suggests a certain ease in handling and managing the people represented and deposited in this way that is suggestive of their being turned into commodities.

The cognitive map of digital platforms thus entwines the informational and formational into an anchoring experience, and the more its design taps into widespread conventions, the more intuitive it weaves a plethora of cultural and ideological connotations into its users' self-understanding. Hence, when Jameson (1991) brings the notion of the cognitive map in contact with Althusser's definition of ideology as "the representation of the subject's *Imaginary* relationship to his or her *Real* conditions of existence" (Althusser in Jameson 1991, 51), the entwinement of the (Lacanian) imaginary with the real, of fantasy with the body, the social-relational with the psychic, and the cognitive with the emotive comes poignantly to the fore. In this sense, the ways in which we experience and act upon how information is made available and relevant to our lives in the digital become formative not merely for us as subjects, but also – via aggregated processes of subject formation – for the field of the social itself. To remain with Althusser, we are not only *interpellated* as subjects by our social, digital surroundings, rather the subjectivities that are arising from the dynamic interplay on digital platforms must also be expected to become *interpellating* for these surroundings in return (Jefferson 2008).

The decentred subject

As stated above, *Formative Media* is working from out of a critical-theoretical and psychoanalytic paradigm and, in so doing, it aligns itself with efforts in media studies and the humanities and social sciences that seek to counter an ongoing trend of depreciation and turning away from the humanistic, pragmatic, interactional, and historical-materialist positions of the 20th century (cf. Chun 2018, 89–90; Flisfeder 2021). When inquiring into the reasons for this trend, Cramer's (2018) observation of the unwillingness of media theory and related fields to even engage with the notion of "subjectivity" offers a first indication. Overlooking theoretical developments in the 20th century, Cramer (2018) states:

> [A]ny inclusion of 'subjectivity' in 'terms of media' – or more precisely, in information technology – seemed to be an oxymoron, since rejection (or at least criticism) of the humanist subject has been a common denominator of cybernetics, poststructuralism, and most schools of materialism and feminism.
>
> (Cramer 2018, 44)

These anti-humanist currents have been strong in all of the humanities. As Rosi Braidotti observes in *The Posthuman* (2013), the trend to leave the notion of human subjectivity behind arose, because this "… [s]ubjectivity is equated with consciousness, universal rationality, and self-regulating ethical behaviour" (p. 15). All too frequently, such a purified vision of human subjectivity has been used as a tool to wield and legitimise social, epistemological power on the basis of which others have been judged as inferior – "sexualized, racialized, and naturalized others, who are reduced to the less than human status of disposable bodies" (ibid).

This turn away from considerations of subjectivity has continued in new-materialist theories, where the critique of the human subject has been taken further so as to allow not only 'other human others' to step out of its shadow, but non-human others as well. "[O]bjects", writes Steven Shaviro (2014) by way of defining his theory of speculative realism, a variation of new materialism, "are irreducible to simple presence" (p. 51). This irreducibility, he holds, is particularly perceivable in the instances in which tools, or other objects, break or "fail to function as expected" (p. 50). In a bow to Heidegger and Whitehead, what Shaviro sees in these failures are moments of the object's uprising or unveiling – moments in which these objects become alive (ibid). This aliveness, this anthropo*morphic* quality, which at the same time points beyond the anthropo*centric*, not only puts them on an equal footing with the humans who use them but also transcends all notions of a principal difference between the human and the non-human. Shaviro evokes a poetics of object-orientation to make this point (2014):

> I do not come to know a world of things outside myself. Rather, I discover – which is to say, I feel – that I myself, together with things that go beyond my knowledge of them, are all alike inhabitants of a 'common world'.
>
> (Shaviro 2014, 3)

Another example for the turning away of contemporary social theory from the notion of subjectivity returns us to the field of digital media studies. Here, the decentralised network architecture of the internet and the dynamic ways in which content travels, multiplies, and metamorphoses from one node to the next have led to a revival of Gabrielle de Tarde's (2003 [1890]) social philosophy of imitation and contagion, together with Gilbert Simondon's (2012 [1958]) thoughts on individuation, and Gilles Deleuze and Felix Guattari's (1983; 1987) theory of assemblages and the rhizomatic, modular shifting of affective intensities between forcefields at the pre-subjective level. A central point in these approaches is that the embodied subject, bounded by their skin, is not a necessary unit for the understanding of figurations of the social anymore. As Latour et al. (2012) put it in the context of digital data analysis: "once we have the experience of following individuals through their connections […] it might be more rewarding to begin navigating datasets without making the distinction between the level of individual component and that of aggregated structure" (p. 591).

This vanishing of the subject as a relevant category for media-sociological research is taken further in Deleuzian orientations. In his book on *Virality* (2013), the media theorist Tony Sampson follows the "monadological understanding of social relationality" (p. 3), explaining that:

> *Virality* is […] located in an epidemiological space in which a world of things mixes with emotions, sensations, affects, and moods. In this space is a continuous "generation of neurophysiological ecosystems" boosted by the "cultural amplifiers" of objects and commodities, such as "caffeine, sentimental novels, and pornographic works," that can adapt the social in novel and unpredictable ways. This is a world awash with hormones and consumer goods, making people happy or sad, sympathetic or apathetic, and a space in which affects are significantly passed on, via suggestions made by others, more and more through networks.
>
> (Sampson 2013, 5)

To a degree, I can side with the above approaches, not least since their political orientations are vastly compatible with my own critical-theoretical outlook. As Flisfeder (2021) comments rightly, the posthuman moralism of "flat ontology" is "certainly understandable given the naïve and perhaps ignorant fashion with which humans have acted upon the nonhuman" (p. 19) – or upon other humans, for that matter. And yet, like Flisfeder, I am not prepared to give up on a focus on the bounded, embodied subject – not because I insist on this subject being the measure of all things; not because I want to play out the universalist tendencies baked into notions such as "possessive individualism" against others who do not seem to fit the "conception of the individual as essentially the proprietor of his [sic] own person or capacities" (C.B. Macpherson 1962, quoted in Hayles 1999, 3); and surely not because I want to believe that social change starts in the ways in which individuals are "evolutionarily hardwired" (Sampson 2013, 11). If anything, we know now that such "hardwiring" is more of a "live-wiring" (Eagleman 2021) in that brain function adapts with astonishing plasticity to given environments, conditions, and situations. Rather, I insist on a human subjectivity centred on the body, because I hold that the specific forms of human interacting and experiencing and the patterns that emerge from the dynamics of human relatedness still play the most fundamental part in the process of 'hardwiring' both the individual psyche and the societal whole. In this respect, specific, cultural-historically derived forms of acting upon and interacting with the world still offer the most exquisite instruments for the diagnosis of the constitution of the social. As Braidotti rightly remarks:

> [A] focus on subjectivity is necessary because this notion enables us to string together issues that are currently scattered across a number of domains. For instance, issues such as norms and values, forms of community bonding and social belonging as well as questions of political governance both assume and require a notion of the subject.
>
> (Braidotti 2013, 42)

While Braidotti holds that this notion of the subject must be seen as scattered across various domains, my focus on this subject's body should be seen as an attempt at tracing how these scattered and distributed fragments of subjectivity register in and hark back to the human body, as well as what this body makes of them. It is in this way that this study can be seen to hold on to an idea of the 'centrality' of the human subject. In other words, while for currently dominant theories of the social, the notion of subjectivity might have run its course, I still see in it a privileged site with which to (a) bring the shifts and movements of the social, political, economic, and cultural into view and (b) flesh them out and make them plausible and understandable in the first place. It is in the tensions and interplays between the distributed and the embodied, the pre-subjective and the subjectivised, or in Deleuze and Guattari's (1983) terms, the modular and the molar, I hold, that forms of existence in the digital need to be described.

Psychoanalytic realism

Hence, when it comes to the question of the forms of human relationality, which to my mind is still one of the most fundamental and exquisite questions we can ask when inquiring into the social, I argue that psychoanalysis has more to offer than any other theory in existence. Its focus on the individual human subject, no matter how distributed this subject needs to be seen, does not result in a grandiose vision of self-determination, but in one that sees human beings as fundamentally decentred and constantly struggling to keep an illusion of self-determination and self-centredness alive, inventing ever new contraptions with which to keep the truth about the make-shift status of their existences at bay. Recently, philosopher Amy Allen (2021) has given powerful new urgency to the question of *Why Critical Theory Needs Psychoanalysis*, arguing that what psychoanalysis offers is a *realistic* conception of subjectivity. Defining this realism, she sums up the smallest common denominator for critical theory as follows:

> By highlighting the irrational and unconscious forces that motivate us to act in ways that we do not fully understand and that remain stubbornly resistant to rational reflection, psychoanalysis serves as a realistic check on the tendencies

toward excessive rationalism and idealism that might tempt the critical theorist qua normative theorist.

(Allen 2021, 4)

Whereas Freud's thinking was still mostly oriented towards an individualised notion of subjectivity – with His/Her "Majesty the Baby" embarking on its developmental journey in originary psychic isolation – most of the major advances in post-Freudian psychoanalysis have been made in an object-relational, intersubjective, or interpersonal paradigm, with many of the complex and delicate intra- and inter-subjective dynamics etched out in hour after hour of clinical practice, infant observation, cultural analysis, psychosocial and social-psychological studies, and, since the 1990s, also increasingly in neuroscientific, neuro-psychoanalytic research. Along with Lacanian advances, which are reasonably well established in media studies (e.g., Dean 2010; 2016; Flisfeder 2021; 2022; Rambatan and Johanssen 2021), it is especially these relational paradigms, I argue, that can be applied to research on digital culture (see Johanssen and Krüger, 2022, for an overview of the field of psychoanalytic media studies). Specifically, if one works from the premise that the relational styles of corporate digital platforms amount to a resurrection and simulation of a dyadic, primary function of care, as this study does, this premise opens for a heuristic and tentative use of psychoanalytic theory for the issue of the digital 'platforming' of subjectivity.

By the same token, however, such a use of psychoanalysis needs 'checks and balances.' Not every aspect of the process of digital platforming can be understood through the psychoanalytic lens. Already in 1929, Erich Fromm cautioned against the "mistake of wanting to give psychoanalytic answers where economic, technical, or political facts provide the real and sufficient explanation of sociological questions" (1989, 37). Rather, the psychoanalytic perspective needs to constantly be opened out and brought into play with other academic fields and disciplines – a principle that is at the core of psychosocial studies (Frosh 2010). To quote Fromm once more: "the individual person [of Freudian psychoanalysis] in reality exists only as a socialized person" (p. 38). In this respect, I am following the example of my colleague Jacob Johanssen (2019) and take a dialogical and conversational (p. 1) approach to combining psychoanalysis and digital media studies.

It is from out of this dialogical mode, too, that I am taking a broad – but not eclectic – approach to psychoanalytic theory with respect to the digital – from Freudian, Lacanian, ego and self-psychological, as well as in-depth hermeneutic approaches, to object-relational, Winnicottian, and relational ones – frequently finding formulations in one idiom that, while theoretically consistent, would not have been as adequate to a phenomenon in another. The theory, however, that has been opening the most productive pathways into understanding digital culture for me is Alfred Lorenzer's historical-materialist and interactional translation of Freudian theory into a sociological and critical-theoretical frame – a theory which is fundamentally based on a logic of reciprocity and the gradual patterning of specific forms of interaction (cf. Rothe, Krüger and Rosengart 2022).

Corroborating the basic outlines of Lorenzer's theory, Viviane Green (2003), in an overview of the status of psychoanalytic knowledge in neuroscience, states that "it has long been axiomatic that early experiences have a formative impact on later development" (p. 4). For example, neuroscience has shown that "early relationship experiences are laid down in procedural memory as an encoding of the implicit 'rules' of relating" (p. 5). The "implicit-procedural memory" (Shore 2003) and the rules of relating it generates tie in well with Lorenzer's (2022) definition of the unconscious as a pre-verbal register of embodied, interactional, and affective experience, which becomes inscribed in the body in the form of social, relational scenes crystallising into specific forms of interaction. From a neurological perspective, this can be explained through differences in the states of involvement of the brain's frontal cortex and hippocampal regions in the storing and recalling of experiences. Hence, especially childhood memories, which are laid down when the frontal cortex, which is "crucial for the retrieval of memory in a *realistic, rational* and *orderly* way" (Turnbull and Solms 2003, 74), is still poorly developed, are difficult to recall in a sensible way later on. This is so, since "[i]f something is encoded in one form, it is more difficult to retrieve it accurately in another" (p. 75). In the case of grown-ups, indications are that what psychoanalysis conceives of as "repression" has to do with the impairment, or uncoupling, of hippocampal functions during stressful experiences, which makes traumatic memories, for example, significantly less available to consciousness (p. 69). In general, what neurological research shows consistently is that people's conscious and unconscious lives are shaped by people interacting with their world and, while the brain displays most plasticity during infancy and early childhood, it retains this ability to adapt to new circumstances to an astonishing degree throughout life.

The relational, interactional paradigm of the unconscious connects well with the study of digital media. Especially Lorenzer's conception of the unconscious as a learned and patterned, yet not fully symbolisable interactional response to specific social scenes shows striking commonalities with the algorithmic embedding of human subjectivity in the digital. As Chun (2018) writes by drawing on the works of Antoinette Rouvroy (2011): "If Big Data [...] devalues human language by privileging bodily actions over narratives, it does so via capture systems that [...] translate our actions into 'grammars of actions' [...]. Our silent – or not so silent – actions register" (p. 67). Therefore, when Lorenzer understands the unconscious as a "not so silent" register of embodied forms of interaction and Chun understands technosocial capture systems as analysing such interactional registers with the aim of exploiting them, this offers a productive way of coordinating psychoanalytic theory with the sociotechnical attempts at capturing subjectivity. And whereas the therapeutic direction of clinical psychoanalysis is still well-articulated in Freud's "Where It is, I shall be," a rephrasing of this credo along the logic of corporate digital platforms might be: "Where It is, We shall be, granting You access." Leo Löwenthal's (in Adorno 1954, 223) poignant critique of advertising as "psychoanalysis in reverse" thus articulates what I see as one of the central formative orientations of digital platforms. Ultimately, when Chun (2021), despite her critique of psychoanalysis, suggests that "[t]he relationship between network science, psychoanalysis, and ideology critique [...] enables the kinds of unconventional interdisciplinary work needed to tackle behavioralist exploitation" (p. 244), I hope that my present study makes a positive contribution to this work.

--

One more thing about the status of psychoanalysis is important. Specifically, and despite my broad interest in psychoanalytic theory, I have been drawn particularly towards those theoretical aspects in Freud's writings that have become increasingly difficult to digest, especially for readers not versed in psychoanalytic thought. These aspects encompass the stages of psychosexual maturation (Laplanche 1999), and here particularly the oral and anal stages (for the latter, see also Krüger 2020). Furthermore, I revisit in this book psychoanalytic theories of narcissism, aggression, and ambivalence, as well as Freud's later metapsychological conception of Eros, i.e., his heavily criticised ideas of the life (and death) drives. However, I will not apply an orthodox understanding of these theories to the field of the digital, but rather bring them in dialogue with post-Freudian reformulations and modifications and use them as heuristic devices to more fully account for the relational dimensions articulated and contained in the digitally platformed relational styles.

What I find productive about these theoretical positions are the ways in which they allow me to conceive of the social circulation of forms of affect and relatedness – between people and institutions, technologies, commodities, etc. – as involving and resonating in specific ways with people's *erotogenic zones*. As human centres of somatic stimulation – centres of specific human vulnerabilities as well as intense pleasures – these zones are anthropological receptacles for the movements of affect in the social, which I define as paradoxically active-passive, self-other processes of transmission-reception, and in-between phenomena (see Johanssen 2019 for an elegant summary of psychoanalytic and other positions on affect). While I thus come close to Deleuze and Guattari's conception of affect as a force *between* objects in the world, including people, my interest in the de- and reterritorialising effects of such circulation nevertheless remains focused on – and repeatedly departs from as well as returns to – human bodily forms and functioning: mouth-ingestion, lips-sucking, teeth-biting, skin-feeling, eyes-ogling, bowel movements, erections, and excitations, as well as all the libidinal, erotic, and creative (re)appropriations and repurposing of these zones and their suggested functions via the process of anaclisis (Laplanche 1999). Such a psychoanalytically informed focus on human bodily form, function, excite- and affectability I see as being productively open towards both a construction of what Deleuze and Guattari (1983) call the molecular, centripetal, and deterritorialising lines of flight and, on another, more traditionally psychoanalytic level, the molar, centrifugal, and reterritorialising re-erections of familial structures and forms as well as the redrawing of cultural-political borders and boundaries (Kornbluh 2019).

Psychoanalytic media studies – brief literature review

While many of the formative influences that have gone into the present study have already been mentioned – e.g., Alfred Lorenzer, Jodi Dean, Ernst Kris, and Wendy Chun – others still need to be given credit. Hence, at the juncture between psycho-analysis, psychosocial, and media studies, the works of Sherry Turkle are still a fixed point of reference. When Turkle starts her foreword to Margaret E. Morris's study *Left to Our Own Devices* (2018) by stating dryly that "we all talk back to technology. Or want to," this gives an indication of how much the present study's focus on the formative is indebted to her work. Aaron Balick's *Psychodynamics of Social Networking* (2014), in turn, has been the first in-depth study of digital media from an intersubjective, relational psychoanalytic perspective and has also been an important influence. More recent publications by Jacob Johanssen (2019), Greg Singh (2019), Matthew Flisfeder (2021; 2022), and myself together with Johanssen (2021; Johanssen & Krüger 2022) have added more critical perspectives to Balick's primer which the present study has been in close, ongoing dialogue with.

Media studies-based work in digital culture by Jose van Dijck, Nancy Baym, dana boyd, Alice Marwick, Jean Burgess, Crystal Abidin, and Katrin Tiidenberg has informed this project all the way, even though I have frequently found my assessments to take a more pessimistic turn.

Furthermore, psychoanalytic and psychosocial works on media and popular culture (Bainbridge and Yates 2014; Richards 1996; Bown 2018; Walkerdine 2007; Blackman and Walkerdine 2002; Prokop and Jansen 2006; König 2008; Rohr 2014; Yates 2019) have been important signposts in the development of the overall outlook of the book. In Germany, the writings of Vera King, Benigna Gerisch, and Hartmut Rosa (2019) on strategies of (self-) optimisation and perfection have likewise been important sources for my conception of the social-psychological context of corporate digital media culture.

Dean's writings on communicative capitalism and the concepts of drive and capture have been instructive for the present advances into the concept of the formative (see also Giraud 2015). Key to Dean's (e.g., 2010; 2015) argument of communicative capitalism is that "Lacan's version of the psychoanalytic concept of drive expresses the reflexive structure of complex [digital] networks" (2010, 30). "Communicative capitalism," Dean argues, "thrives not because of unceasing or insatiable desires but in and as the repetitive intensity of drive" (ibid). Flisfeder (2021), in contradistinction, holds that desire, and here particularly the desire of the Other, is still the dominant paradigm.

> In the context of social media, we see how we perform, not necessarily for our own sense of self – we curate our identities, not to satisfy our own desire, but to satisfy the desire of the Other in the form of likes, shares, comments, follows, and so forth.
>
> (Flisfeder 2021, 67)

In this debate, I tend towards Dean's side; and readers who would like a straight-forward answer as to why, please hop directly to the book's conclusion. What the chapters in the book's middle part show in much detail, however, is how the major platforms' orientations, their design and programming, frequently make objects and the desire for them recede into the background, with drive taking over; in other instances, objects of desire are provocatively 'dangled in front of users' noses' but kept out of reach, so that desire again becomes drive, etching out those patterns of interactions that repeatedly breathe new life into the networks we should leave behind.

The chapters

Chapter 1, "Outrageous growth and the Eros of Facebook", starts from a discussion of Facebook in conversation with the Freudian theory of Eros and the Live/Love drives, which serves as a specific form of what media studies have frequently captured in terms of "social contagion" and "virality" (Stark 2018). As psychoanalyst Nicola Abel-Hirsch (2010) has written lucidly, interpretations of the Life and Death drives have often been oversimplified, with the implication being that "the life instinct is 'good' and the death instinct 'bad'" (p. 1055). Much rather, she holds, it takes an imbrication and implication of the two to strike a healthy balance between binding and unbinding, construction and destruction, in the course of human life. As I gather from a plethora of programming and design features, as well as from a vast number of statements by key corporate representatives, Facebook has repeatedly ignored – *denied*, really – this insight, with the result being that libido has run rampant on/via the platform and unfolded a thanatotic tendency of its own. I trace the rise and development of the libidinous and erotic on and in Facebook and connect its unbridled kind of love to the curse of digital labour, where people become ever-more enmeshed in relationship maintenance chores that are not sustainable in the long term.

Chapter 2, "*The feeding tube* – YouTube, oral cravings, and the question of addiction", homes in on the primitive forms of orality, attachment, dependence, and symbiosis in relation to the video-sharing service YouTube. It is particularly the platform's recommender system, which keeps selecting videos that, in default app settings, start playing automatically, which is of interest when it comes to YouTube's formative dimension. The relational orientation of this system has been sharply critiqued – and that particularly in culinary and oral metaphors. In my analysis of Google's engineering papers on recommender systems, I follow the psychoanalytic literature on the oral phase, eating and ingestion, interpersonal needs, attachment and attunement, as well as addiction, to critically inquire into the platform's 'feeding practices' and their formative effects. I argue that YouTube's recommender system, in tandem with Alphabet/Google's immense wealth of user data and analytic prowess, might indeed have the potential to provide a nourishing holding environment, simulate a "good enough mother" (Winnicott), and provide the optimal distance between gratification and frustration that people need to be well-functioning, well-reasoning, and empathic beings. However, its orientation towards maximising its users' "time on device" (Seymore 2019, 64) turns it into a feeding tube that has no realistic strategies of detachment and weaning built into its conception.

Chapter 3, "*Anxious narcissism* – Instagram, self-image practices, and the persistent question of narcissism," continues the inquiry into foundational processes of becoming as they are adapted, simulated, and appropriated by the digital with a focus on narcissism, which I will unfold in relation to the photo-sharing platform Instagram. Instagram is firmly associated with the pejorative effects of digitally facilitated self-image practices. The accusation of a web-based culture of narcissism through which troves of internet users turn into self-absorbed and self-obsessed beings, who have lost all empathy towards others, has for the past ten-or-so years been directed at Instagram (now TikTok gradually takes this place), with broad-ranging studies into the mental health of teenagers and young adults finding Instagram still to be the most problematic online service in existence (e.g., Macmillan 2017[9]). Following these imaginaries, the chapter coordinates the analysis of the platform's conception, design, and programming with the most salient use cultures relevant to self-image making on Instagram, as well as existing research on mental health. The coordination of these dimensions is then brought into dialogue with the tradition of psychoanalytic thinking about narcissism and related phenomena. From its inception in 2010, Instagram has supported its brand image of artistry, embellishment, and promotion by offering photo filters and the possibility of touching up and editing photos before publishing them on the network. These filters, frequently offered by third parties, have increasingly been directed towards automated augmentation effects – i.e., at optimising facial and bodily features, removing blemishes and visible pores, modifying the position and size of the eyes, modulating cheekbones and chins, etc. In psychoanalytic terms, these functionalities have been explained and advertised as bridging the gap between the ego and the ego ideal. However, whereas Lacan rightly holds that this gap is unbridgeable and the divide between these two poles formative of human development per se, Instagram's filtering logic literally *stuffs* this gap with calls to self-work and commands at self-improvement and optimisation. Promising technology with which to close this gap, augmentation filters make the inevitable existence of the gap all the more persecutory. Along these lines, I develop the notion of an "anxious narcissism". Instead of social media users showing tendencies of self-obsession due to an inflated sense of grandiosity, a trend towards constantly surveying one's outer appearance can be traced back to a fundamental, existential insecurity that can be summed up in the anxious questions of: *Am I alright? Is this ok? Am I worthy of love in this way?* (cf. Balick 2014, 81).

Chapter 4, "*Compromised formations* – Google, obsession, and the desublimation of knowledge," offers an inquiry into the notions of mastery, control, and domination that Google unfolds and activates in its search function, which moves this function into direct proximity to notions of obsessional neurosis and a regression to the anal phase of psychosexuality. Cultural analytic assessments of Google have invariably pointed to the knowledge and consciousness-forming dimension of the platform's search function. John Durham Peters (2015), for example, writes poignantly that: "Google inherits the narrative of the priestly class that discerns the universe, renders order out of chaos, answers our entreaties, and invites us to take in mantic acts of divination" (2015, 333). Siva Vaidhyannathan (2013), in turn, has polemically written about the *Googlisation of Everything*, and, in my chapter, I am tracing the salient form that this Googlisation has taken. As Shoshana Zuboff (2019, 63) has worked out in detail, the universal access Google promises to provide is attached to an exchange economy of gifts. By tracing what people do with (Google's organisation of) the world's knowledge, the company has been able to, in its own words, "gather large volumes […] of *relationships* of interest" (in Zuboff 2019, 65, my emphasis). It is this knowledge about the relationships of interest that Google has been refining ever since, and in so doing it has organised information increasingly so as to be able to monetise it on the basis of these relationships. Along these lines I analyse in this chapter Google's strategies and practices of information management and the structuring of knowledge, including related issues, such as the debate on the "Right to be forgotten" (e.g., Meg Leta Jones 2016). Ultimately, when Freud (1913a) conceives of the drive to knowledge (Wißtrieb) as the sublimation of the sadistic component in compulsive phenomena, calling it "a sublimated offshoot of the instinct of mastery" (p. 324), what needs to be asked is whether the conflation of the drive to knowledge with that of usurpation, as is clearly the case in Google's gift economy, does not present us with an incident of what Herbert Marcuse (1986 [1964]) called "repressive desublimation."

Chapter 5, "The joke that isn't funny anymore – Twitter, aggression, and the perfect shitstorm," focuses on a central formative dimension of object-relations, specifically that of human aggression, which is conductive of both libido and subject development. Apart from Facebook, whose entanglement with the destructive I approach via the erotic in Chapter 1, the social media platform that has received the most critical attention for the presence of hate speech on its network is Twitter/X. In this chapter, I am assessing Twitter's central characteristics from the perspective of the formative to work out why and how the platform has created such a marked disposition towards aggression in a significant number of its posts. What comes to the fore in this respect is a mix of design and programming choices that repeatedly suggest the circulation of – albeit mild – forms of aggression, as well as a persistent ambiguity and ambivalence about the platform's social orientation. While one of the founders, Jack Dorsey, conceived of the service as an ambiently personal news-ticker that would narrow-cast people's mundane everyday life moments to family, friends, and acquaintances, another founder, Ev Williams, saw its importance to lie in the public sphere and in its potential for the distribution of news. I approach the issue of aggression on Twitter by departing from psychoanalytic theories of jokes and the comic. According to Freud's (1905b) original formulation, particularly tendentious jokes amount to small, triangulated acts of aggression. By cleverly hiding in plain sight thoughts, wishes, and desires that would be off-limits and taboo in less symbolically refined form, the teller of a tendentious joke seduces an audience to join in an assault against an object that is thus turned into the butt of the joke. It is this relatively simple, dynamic model of seduction that, read in tandem with psychoanalytic works on mass/group psychology (Freud 1921; Nitsun 2015; Rosenfeld 1971), provides a productive blueprint for the understanding of the manifestation, escalation, and cascading of aggression on Twitter. Particularly, the colloquially dubbed "shitstorm," which is characteristic of the platform, can be explained along the lines of a tendentious joke that fails to provoke laughter in its audience. In such a case, the form that such rejection takes is usually harsh, because what is rejected is not merely a claim or statement, but literally the attempt at seduction, which jokes represent in relation to their audience. Due to Twitter's affordances and genre expectations, the rejection of the initial joke can be expected to again take the form of a joke. In this way a dynamic is set in motion that at bottom consists in a *seduction to a refusal of being seduced – a seduction to a shared ressentiment.*

The book's conclusion offers me the opportunity to give the study's findings a final synthesising push in an attempt to etch out the overall figuration of the subject as it emerges from its 'primary digital relations'. As I argue, this subject is one not merely characterised by its drives, but one *characterised by drive*. It is a subject that tends to become stuck in circuits of self-reflection and self-doubts and inhibited by the precariously flirtatious – uncommitted, unbinding, unactual – forms of relationships afforded by the – in the strict sense – "virtual reality" of the platforms (see "Conclusion"). This subject tends to veer between intense attachments and dependencies and aggressively defensive acts of affirming its independence, in this way driving on a process of loosening object-relations and ties to a shared notion of social reality.

Notes

1 https://www.theguardian.com/technology/2021/oct/25/facebook-revelations-from-misinformation-to-mental-health (accessed 28/06/2023).
2 https://www.theguardian.com/technology/2018/feb/02/how-youtubes-algorithm-distorts-truth (accessed 28/06/2023).
3 https://www.theguardian.com/technology/2021/oct/22/twitter-admits-bias-in-algorithm-for-rightwing-politicians-and-news-outlets (accessed 28/06/2023).
4 https://about.google/ (accessed 28/06/2023).
5 For another, related take on this theme, please consult the study *Becoming Human Amid Diversions*, by my colleague Andreas Ervik (2022).
6 In this respect, Google is a peculiar case of a media platform in that its core search function has more or less made the World Wide Web its platform. The many changes to its search algorithm, which have often dire consequences for webpages and the businesses they represent, need to be seen as attempts at curating the modes of presentation of content on this 'platform.'
7 https://www.oed.com/view/Entry/73452?redirectedFrom=formative& (accessed 24/06/2021).
8 ibid.
9 https://time.com/4793331/instagram-social-media-mental-health/ (accessed 28/06/2023).

Chapter 1

Outrageous growth and the Eros of Facebook

The following quotation takes us about one third into a – by now infamous – internal memo that Andrew Bosworth, one of Facebook's (now "Meta's") head engineers and currently its Chief Technology Officer, wrote and circulated amongst Facebook's staff in 2016:

> The ugly truth is that we believe in connecting people so deeply that anything that allows us to connect more people more often is *de facto* good. It is perhaps the only area where the metrics do tell the true story as far as we are concerned.
>
> (Bosworth 2018 [2016])

Bosworth's memo is reported to have caused strong and polarised reactions, and, when it was leaked and published by the entertainment and journalism website Buzzfeed in 2018, Mark Zuckerberg, Facebook's co-founder and CEO, needed to make one of his many public apologies: "Boz is a talented leader who says many provocative things. This was one that most people at Facebook including myself disagreed with strongly" (Zuckerberg, quoted in Burch 2018).

Even if one does not doubt that this apology was made in good faith and believes that most Facebook staff will not have surrendered to Bosworth's suggestion of ends justifying means, Facebook, whose entire business operations have now been repackaged into "Meta," an umbrella term meant to spell out a vision for a fully digitised future in virtual reality (VR), was geared toward such growth from the first. Hence, even if one grants that Bosworth's rhetoric had merely overshot its mark, as Zuckerberg emphasised, the principal equation of growth=good is one that has been holding true of the entirety of Silicon Valley start-up culture. "Scaling," writes Katherine Losse (2012) in her memoir as an early Facebook employee (the second woman to be hired), "was the fetish of the valley. [...] Things were either *scalable*, which meant they could help the site grow fast indefinitely, or *unscalable*, which meant that the offending feature had to be quickly excised or cancelled" (p. 6). Facebook, which relocated to 'The Valley' soon after its founding by students at Harvard University, is the most successful, paradigmatic instantiation of the drive toward scale. As Bosworth continues in a less spectacular passage in his memo:

DOI: 10.4324/9781003307044-2

I know a lot of people don't want to hear this. Most of us have the luxury of working in the warm glow of building products consumers love. But make no mistake, growth tactics are how we got here. If you joined the company because it is doing great work, that's why we get to do that great work. We do have great products but we still wouldn't be half our size without pushing the envelope on growth. Nothing makes Facebook as valuable as having your friends on it, and no product decisions have gotten as many friends on as the ones made in growth. Not photo tagging. Not news feed. Not messenger. Nothing.

(Bosworth 2018)

From a psychoanalytic perspective, coordinating the company's orientation toward growth with the activity of connecting people and with notions of warmth ("glow") and friendship ("having your friends on it"), as Bosworth does, evokes Freud's definition of Eros and the Love/Life Drives in a precise and straightforward manner. Centrally defined as one of the two general drive groups – inherent not merely in all people but in all living matter, as Freud held – Eros binds living substance and connects and combines it into ever-larger, ever more complex units. As Losse (2012) remembers, late in her Facebook career, which lasted from 2005 to 2010, "Mark told me that his dream for Facebook was […] to make us all cells in a single organism, communicating automatically in spite of ourselves, perhaps without the need for intention or speech" (p. 166). One will be hard-pressed to find a formulation that brings Freud's concept of Eros closer to online social networking than this.

However, as Freud also held, the relentless orientation towards adhesion on the part of Eros needs to be positioned in a continuous interplay with its opposite, the Death Drive, which is geared towards cutting off the connections that Eros makes and towards bringing all binding movement to a halt. As psychoanalyst Nicola Abel-Hirsch (2010) rightly points out in her work on "The Life Instinct,"[1] interpretations of Freud's concept of the Life and Death drives have tended to oversimplify their relationship with each other, with the implication being that "the life instinct is 'good' and the death instinct 'bad'" (p. 1055). Freud, however, is clear that: "Neither of these instincts is any less essential than the other; the phenomena of life arise from the concurrent or mutually opposing action of both" (Freud 1933, 209). In other words, Abel-Hirsch cautions against the conflation of what Freud refers to as "the phenomena of life" with Eros and the Life Drives, as this robs the theory of the paradoxical truth that also death and cessation of movement make a 'vital' contribution to life. As psychoanalyst John Steiner (1997) holds: "Not only are these two great primordial forces in opposition to each other but they also stimulate each other, and if ever one gains too dominant an advantage, the other is provoked into action" (p. 5; quoted in Abel-Hirsch 2010, 1055). Accordingly, what Abel-Hirsch seeks to work out in her article is the movement of Eros becoming deadly in its own right when left unchecked, or as she puts it: "a pathological variation of the life instinct in which binding is without the negation, rest, limit or end provided by the 'opposing action' of the death instinct" (ibid). The striking aspect in Bosworth's memo is that it explicitly points to this pathology while at the same time refusing to consider alternatives: "Maybe someone dies in a terrorist attack coordinated on our tools. And still we connect people" (Bosworth 2018).

That there is a specific *erotic* at work in the way that Facebook has been facilitating user interactions is easily corroborated. The proverbial Facebook Friend, the Like button, and the various mission statements of making the world "more open" and bringing people "closer together" (Newton 2017)[2] are only a few examples that point to the centrality of love in its various forms and intensities for the platform's operations. However, to my knowledge, there is very little academic work that has attempted to analyse Facebook/Meta from a theoretical perspective that puts the notion of love at its centre. To be sure, there are a vast number of publications inquiring into practices of friending, dynamics of socialisation, and the qualities of, say, strong and weak ties *on* the platform. But framing the platform itself – the intentions going into it, the programming of its functionalities, the interface design and affordances – in terms of love has hardly been attempted.[3] This is relatively understandable, since this perspective must appear naïve, seemingly ignoring the many infidelities Facebook has committed to the detriment of its users. Indeed, when it comes to these infidelities, works by Jose van Dijck (2014; van Dijck et al. 2018) and Taina Bucher (2018; 2021) cover them dexterously. In this respect, Kevin Healey and Richard Potter's "Facebook and the ethics of psychoanalysis 'outside the clinic'" (2018) deserves explicit mentioning as it unpacks the strained relationship between the company's ethical mission "toward closeness […] which is more than connectedness" (Healey and Potter 2018, 664, quoting Nieva 2017) and its commercial orientation in psychoanalytic terms. Closer yet to the present effort is work that Jacob Johanssen and I (Johanssen and Krüger 2022, 161ff) have recently done, in which we focus on the sexualities of digital platforms.

My chapter is related to these efforts but takes a distinct path. Specifically, what I intend to show is that the Freudian notion of Eros, which has not found many adherents amongst psychoanalytic theorists (see Loewald 1988; Lear 1996; and Aarseth 2016, for exceptions), offers a conception of love that is wide, paradoxical, and dialectical enough to capture the core operational logic of Facebook in its very contradictoriness. Hence, in what follows, I inquire into the history and formative development of Facebook/Meta from the vantage point and through the prism of Freud's theory. Applying Abel-Hirsch's (2010) term of "outrageous growth" – an orientation towards growth without "the capacity to reject, limit or bring something to an end" (p. 1060) – I argue that what is being repressed and denied in Facebook's erotic mission of bringing the world together is the very dialectics in the relations between Eros and Thanatos that Freud put at the centre of his late drive theory. As much as Eros pertains to life, creation, synthesis, and unity, it needs the "work of the negative" (Green 1999) as a throttle, modification, and correction so as not to switch into its lethal opposite. In this respect, it is *The Boy Kings*, Katherine Losse's (2012) critical account of her years at Facebook – first as a customer care staff, then in engineering-related tasks – that builds the backbone of this chapter's argument, not merely because her critique of Facebook brings the theme of love into focus, but also because this critique is delivered with the right degree of love mixed in. Thus, whereas Bucher (2021) has rightly argued that Facebook as an object of study has outgrown any dimension at which one could still bring it under one overall defining label (p. 21), I argue that the vantage point of Eros and notions of love nevertheless offer a productive means with which to identify an overall tendency in its architecture and in the directedness of the many activities that the company facilitates; this tendency is of a love that stops at nothing.

I commence this chapter with a discussion of Freud's notion of Eros to then turn to the history of Facebook, which I analyse in four steps, roughly following a chronology of the company's different phases of development that I interpret in terms of shifts in its libidinal economy.[4] In psychoanalytic fashion, my focus is on the platform's early years, and hence, in Phase 1, I take a detailed look at the application's invention and early dissemination. This phase I see as dominated by a raw, aggressive libidinal energy on the part of the creators – a primitive kind of love that is devouring and poorly differentiated from its negative, hate – which becomes channelled into a flirtatious handling of people's relational needs so as to optimise the overall dynamics of forging ties on the platform. This primitive libidinal form of love is what I see at the core of Facebook as a formative medium.

Phase 2 sets in with the gradual recalibration of the service from a mere facilitator to an active pusher of ties. In this phase, a constant stream of innovations aiming at the expansion of connections is being punctuated by apologetic responses to user protests against Facebook's "outrageous growth." Beginning with the introduction of News Feed in 2006 and characterised by the launch of the "Like" button in 2009, this era in the company's development can be seen to have lasted up until the political scandals of the late 2010s, with that of Russian Campaign meddling and the Cambridge Analytica data leak bringing this phase to its end.

The public reckoning that needed to follow – including several hearings in front of major political bodies in the USA and Europe – marks Facebook's third phase, which stretches roughly from 2017 to 2021. This phase is marked by changes to the algorithmic feeding of news to users, from political content back to more family- and friend-related posts, and an overall change in Facebook's mission, from "making the world more open and connected" to "giv[ing] people the power to build community and bring the world closer together" (Zuckerberg 2017).[5] While these changes were meant as deft responses to the company's increasingly poor reputation, an analysis of the new rhetoric of the "power of community" shows that the orientation towards outrageous growth has remained largely untouched. As technology journalist Sarah Frier (2020) writes rightly: "The people thinking about fixing the product had an incentive not to fix it too much, at least not to the point where it would jeopardize Facebook's business" (p. 260). As I work out in detail in the chapter on YouTube, this fetishist attitude is one that Facebook has shared with other corporate digital platforms.

This third phase of atonement is ongoing by the time of writing but has become partly supplanted by a yet more far-reaching business relaunch when it was announced in late 2021 that the Facebook app/platform family would change its name to "Meta".[6] This announcement marks the start of the latest, fourth phase in Facebook's development. "Meta," as a short handle for the "metaverse," is the *chiffre* for a long-term plan to integrate the several Facebook-owned services – Facebook, Instagram and WhatsApp – as well as a wide variety of third-party offers, in one expansive media ecology in the form of a VR environment. Here too, Facebook's erotic mission of binding finds an undeterred continuation in the planned integration of people's interpersonal ties in one online simulation of social life itself.

Overlooking Facebook's development from the perspective of Eros, one can say that all phases in Facebook's development have been characterised by a primitive form of love which initially appeared to have successfully become sublimated into *caritas* (love admixed with care), but time and again lapses back into a more outrageously expansive form of *amor* which threatens to kill off the very objects it seeks to bind (cf. Benvenuto 2016, 10). In this respect, I argue that Facebook's continuous denial of the negative in human life as a necessary counterpoint to its totalitarian ideas of harmony is one of the root causes for the social pathologies that the company has helped exacerbate in western societies and beyond. Specifically, this entails a neoliberal work ethic that collapses life and work and prompts people to love their work as much as their lives. In parallel, the dialectic of Eros is to assimilate so much life, to accumulate so much living matter, that the principle of homeostasis, to which Freud saw all drives obeying, can only be reached by bringing all of life under its aegis.

The dialectics of Eros

Freud's late revision of his theoretical apparatus unfolded in a tentative and searching process (Löchel 1996), resulting in major reshufflings of his work up to that point. In *Beyond the Pleasure Principle* (1920), where Freud introduced the two major drive categories for the first time, he also introduced the idea of repetition compulsion and made major advances in trauma theory by returning to the idea of the "protective skin" of the ego whose function is to regulate exposure to stimulus. Leaning on Ernest Jones' (1953) biography of Freud, the psychoanalytic scholar Gerhard Zenaty (2022) emphasises the shock that Freud's profound reworking of his theory must have caused his colleagues and followers, observing that the subsequent polarisation still reaches into more recent theoretical discussions (Aichhorn 2006; Löchel 1996).

In his "Outline of psychoanalysis," Freud (1938) gives concise definitions of the Love/Life and Death drives: "The aim of the first [Eros] is to establish ever greater unities and to preserve them thus – in short, to bind together; the aim of the second is, on the contrary, to undo connections and so to destroy things" (p. 148). Whereas the Death Drive must have appeared as a radical innovation in a theory that had earlier focused on the powers of unconscious wish fulfilment, introducing a deluge of dark matter (such as narcissism and masochism) into it, Eros has remained pale and ill defined. As Laplanche and Pontalis (1988 [1973]) point out, the latter only comes to the fore through its opposition to the former (p. 218). What has seemed most problematic with Eros, though, is that the field of sexuality, which had theretofore been characterised by its disruptive potential, was now to be grouped under the Love/Life drives of Eros, with its harmonising connotations of binding and uniting. In this respect, many psychoanalysts after Freud were particularly concerned that this might rob the theory of its subversive edge. Roland Gori (2005), for example, writes: "Such an Eros is no longer a troublemaker, a divisive agent that disturbs the mental apparatus. It is the power of creation, of reproduction; it makes existence possible and postpones the return to an inorganic state" (p. 513). Laplanche and Pontalis (1988) voiced a still stronger critique, bemoaning that:

> Up until this point, sexuality had played the part of an essentially subversive force, represented by the first components of the major antitheses recognised by Freud: free energy as opposed to bound, primary as opposed to secondary processes, the pleasure principle as opposed to the reality principle and – in the 'Project for a Scientific Psychology' (1950a [1895]) – the principle of inertia as opposed to the principle of constancy. With the advent of the final instinctual dualism, the death instinct takes over as the 'primal,' 'demoniac' force which is of the essence of instinct, while sexuality – paradoxically – goes over to the side of the binding process.
>
> (Laplanche and Pontalis 1988, e-book version, n.p.)

However, this claim of a blunted sexuality – the concern of which I otherwise share – becomes complicated to a degree in various places in Freud's later texts. For example, when, in the "Outline," Freud (1938) states that the "contrast between the instincts of self-preservation and the preservation of the species, as well as the contrast between ego-love and object-love, fall within Eros" (p. 148), this indicates that the conflict potential of sexuality is by no means cancelled out through its inclusion into Eros. Rather, since these contrasts have the power to develop tensions up to the point of turning into contradictions – for example, ego/self-love can easily curb and mar the love we develop towards objects/others (cf. Freud 1914, 85)[7] – Freud seems to have built such contradictions and dialectical switches directly into his conception of Eros itself. When André Green (2008 [2000]) proposes that "sexuality, now considered as a function with its sign, libido, is what is perceptible of the phenomena of Eros, and gives us an idea of its functioning beyond our consciousness of it" (p. 115), this casts a wide enough net to cover its various, at times contradictory and paradoxical, articulations. Hence, when Laplanche and Pontalis point out that Eros goes against the most basic principle of a drive, namely the "restoration of less differentiated, less organised forms" (n.p.), it is my hunch that this regressive character, which Freud attributed to all major drives, is achieved in the case of Eros through its very relentlessness. By gathering, accumulating, combining, and expanding relentlessly, the ultimate aim of the drive is to reach a resting point where all living matter is brought into unity. In that conception, Eros is just as lethal as the Death drive taken by itself alone, only that its danger is the rigidly affirmative one of a constant and never-ceasing process of loving. As stated above, this dialectic of Eros is captured poignantly by Abel-Hirsch (2010) in her work on the pathological Life-drive function of binding without negation.

Abel-Hirsch turns to Freud's (1925) article on "Negation" to make her point. Here, Freud defines the "creation of the symbol of negation [as] a first measure of freedom from the consequences of repression and, with it, from the compulsion of the pleasure principle" (p. 239). While Freud suggests further that "the 'negativism' shown by some psychotics is probably 'a sign of a defusion of instincts that has taken place through a withdrawal of the libidinal components,'" Abel-Hirsch (2010) continues his line of thinking by proposing that "life instinct functioning – when defused from the death instinct – could lose the capacity to reject, limit or bring something to an end" (p. 1060). In this way, whereas Laplanche and Pontalis see Freud's new metatheory move away from the folkloric juxtaposition of love and hunger towards that of love and discord (1988),[8] I suggest that the functioning of hunger within the new frame is no less productive. By making hunger part of the contrasting and contradictory field of Eros, hunger might just become so strong as to consume love.

Flirtation and the erotic of Facebook

"'What does poking mean?' was a question asked hundreds of times a day," writes Losse (2012) of her experience as an early Facebook customer care staff:

> We always responded innocently, "It's just a way to get someone's attention," knowing full well the range of childish and sexual connotations in play. Being coy, not admitting the libidinal urges driving so much of the site's usage, was professionally necessary, a way to differentiate Facebook from the cheap and overtly sexual vibes of MySpace. Being coy was also part of the fun, part of the illusion we as a company were constructing that life on Facebook, unlike in reality, was always safe, easy, playful, free, void of cost or obligation. As Dustin Moskovitz, Mark's Harvard roommate and Facebook co-founder, said over lunch in the office that fall, with his dry, practical intelligence, "Everything on Facebook is flirty." He was right. Facebook, like flirting, was a fun way to present yourself lightly and attractively to the world, with no downside, and no commitment.
>
> (Losse 2012, 10–11)

I quote this passage at length because it holds an important key to Facebook's success in user uptake throughout its existence. Writing from her early experiences, what Losse describes as a customer care staff's central skill is to perform a ritualistic act of fetishistic denial – where a specific erotic 'truth' is as much negated as it is maintained. Distributed between platform creators/staff and customers/users, this act becomes constitutive of Facebook itself. In this respect, the notion of flirtation holds specific relevance in understanding the libidinous basis upon which Facebook is built.

In her study *The Play of Political Culture, Emotion and Identity*, the psychosocial scholar Candida Yates (2015) similarly points to flirtation's associations with "coquetry, dalliance and play; it connotes a lack of seriousness or intention, as in the refusal to commit romantically, or as Georg Simmel (1984 [1909]) reminds us, the desire to move between different opinions and ideas" (Yates 2015, 22). When digital media scholars throughout the past two decades discuss virality in terms of forcefields of affect and affect as a pre- and proto-emotive intensity which pushes and pulls people from and/or towards things, what becomes easily overlooked is that, in the case of Facebook as *the* paradigm of Web 2.0 virality, this affective intensity is based on and built from a specific play of flirtation, a specific erotic of offering and withholding.

Additionally, when Yates emphasises the relevance of flirtation for studying forms of masculinity, this points further towards inquiring into flirtation's productiveness for understanding Facebook and its immense success. Flirtation, Yates argues, can represent either a desire for defensive, "retrosexual fantasies" of masculinity, or "the wish for more progressive, playful and creative modes of masculinity" (Yates 2015, 24). In this light, what is striking when going through the literature capturing the atmosphere in which the platform was created is just how "retrosexually" masculine this atmosphere was. And yet, the product outcome, I argue, has been much more ambiguous and vaguer in its sexual charge and promise, much harder to pinpoint and significantly more allowing of playful and creative modes, not so much of masculinity, but of sexuality per se – or better: of a sexual humanity, or: *Eros*. In other words, what becomes central in an inquiry into the inception of Facebook from a perspective of Love/Life drives is how the platform managed to transcend a white, elitist and upper (middle) class, hacker, and frat boy masculinity into a set of applications oozing a flirtatiousness that attracted the widest possible range of people. And yet, despite this general appeal, I argue that Facebook's flirtatiously erotic charge remains attached to its early retrosexual roots. Operative underneath its veneer of sublimating raw libido into ties of friendship lies a decisively more primitive and hungrily devouring love. Facebook, goes my argument, thus channels its progressive orientations through its retrograde sexuality. Consequently, its enactment of progress in the form of "outrageous growth" results in a retrogradation of the very progress it seeks to bring about.

Phase 1: raw libidinal energy – the erotic roots of virality

The beginnings of Facebook in Zuckerberg's spiteful programming of the "Facemash" application in a Harvard University dorm room are a vital part of 21st-century internet folklore. They have been served to a global audience in David Fincher's 2010 movie *The Social Network*, which in turn took its inspiration from

Ben Mezrich's dramatisation in the book *The Accidental Billionaires* (2009). David Kirkpatrick's (2010) rendering of the saga, in turn, is sufficiently sober and informed to be served here:

> Facemash gave the Harvard community its first look at [Zuckerberg's] rebellious irreverent side. Its purpose: figure out who was the hottest person on campus. Using the kind of computer code otherwise used to rank chess players (perhaps it could also have been used for fencers), he invited users to compare two different faces of the same sex and say which one was hotter. As your rating got hotter, your picture would be compared to hotter and hotter people.
> (Kirkpatrick 2010, 23)

To be sure, the "Hot or Not" game, facilitated with clumsy freshmen pictures that Zuckerberg grabbed from Harvard University websites, included students of male and female genders. Yet, whereas Zuckerberg denies that he created the application in response to having been rejected on a date with a young woman (Levy 2020, 6), he nevertheless veered its intentions clearly towards the male gaze (Mulvey 1975). Hence, when Losse (2012) quotes from a report on early Facebook user behaviour, finding that "Men prefer looking at women they don't know, followed by men looking at women they do know," as the two biggest segments of viewing behaviour (p. 89), this sheds light on both the conservative – indeed, reactionary – masculinity of the "Facemash" prank and how this masculine eroticism would become successfully reproduced on Facebook.

When it comes to unpacking the 'retromasculinity' that went into Facebook's making, the tech journalist Adam Fisher (2018) does this in admittedly shrill colours, assembling a pastiche of voices involved in Facebook's founding in a mode it calls "brogrammer 'tude" (p. 349). Unsurprisingly, this erotic is time and again likened to the escapades of college dorms, fraternities, and undergraduate student culture (p. 363). Nearly all of Facebook's early hires were recruited from the Ivy League institutions from which Zuckerberg and his roommates-cum-co-founders also hailed (albeit as dropouts). "For the first few hundred employees, almost all of them were already friends with someone working at the company, both within the engineering circle and also the user support people. It's a lot of recent grads," remembers programmer Ezra Callahan (in Fisher 2018, 362).

By way of fleshing out the Facebook frat culture, people remember vast amounts of gadgets and toys – robots, Legos, Play Stations, Nerf guns – scattered across old couches, with blankets in corners making clear: "people were sleeping there" (Fischer 2018, 358). Indeed, some employees recall sleeping at the office two to three nights a week; others remember coming in their pyjamas "and that would be totally fine" (p. 359).

Katherine Losse, too, is made to feed into the chorus of admirers of Facebook's "retrosexuality" when she is quoted comparing Facebook with "really normal American activities – like beer pong" (in Fisher 2018, 362). Indeed, alcohol is shown to have played a key role in shaping this young, sheltered elite group's sense of disinhibited corporatism. Callahan states: "There would be mornings when I would walk in and hear beer cans move as I opened the door, and the office smells of stale beer and is just trashed" (p. 358).

How this laddish party and drinking culture translated into heterosexual relationships with women is indicated in the graffiti that street artist David Choe made for Facebook's first office spaces.

> The office was on the second floor, so as you walk in you immediately have to walk up some stairs, and on the big ten-foot-high wall facing you is just this huge buxom woman with enormous breasts wearing this Mad Max-style costume riding a bulldog. It's the most intimidating, totally inappropriate thing.
>
> (Callahan in Fisher 2018, 357)

Inappropriate as it might have seemed, this image, which blended Japanese Manga comic style and pornography, was very much in line with the form of male sexuality celebrated in hacker, nerd, and cyberpunk culture, which received one of its central hubs, 4chan, at exactly the time when Facebook was funded, in 2004.

The mural thus propagated an idea of sexuality that invited men to surrender women to their gaze, albeit in an immature and 'not-quite-phallic' manner (cf. Johanssen 2022; Krüger 2020; and Johanssen and Krüger 2022, for an analysis of online male subcultures). As Losse (2012) remembers, struggles over the control of the gaze were as central to Facebook's in-house culture (p. 52) as they were to its online service itself. Yet, as she also suggests, a willing surrender to the male gaze on many women's parts is itself a widespread aspect of the US dorm room culture: "American college women, after all, are known to kiss each other at parties for male attention" (Losse 2012, 78).

Whether one was oblivious to the heavily gendered tones of the corporate culture or not, working at Facebook was said to take on such centripetal, heavily binding force, that, with staff recruitment already based on a friend-of-a-friend basis and people frequently crashing at the office, in-mating became inevitable and omnipresent: "You're hanging out. You're drinking with your coworkers. People start dating within the office," Callahan explains matter-of-factly. And Sanghvi adds: "We found our significant others while we were at Facebook. All of us eventually got married. Now we're in this phase where we're having children" (both in Fisher 2018, 359). Programmer Katie Geminder, in turn, adds a darker note to this all-pervasive sexual drive:

> If you look at the adults that worked at Facebook during those first few years – like, anyone over the age of thirty that was married – and you do a survey, I tell you that probably 75 percent of them are divorced.
>
> (ibid)

Now, if this handling of sexual tensions seems immature, this is not far off the mark, since, as Geminder emphasises, "literally they [the Facebook founders and early employees] were kids" (in Fisher 2018, 359). In 2005/6, roughly the years to which this quotation refers, Zuckerberg and co-founder Dustin Moskovitz were merely 21 years old, the age at which it is first legal in the USA to purchase alcoholic beverages. Even Zuckerberg referred to himself as a "kid" when talking about the house-share from which they operated Facebook after moving to Palo Alto in 2004, emphasising the unsupervised, uncontrolled, and unregulated nature of their childlike state:

> Most businesses aren't like a bunch of kids living in a house, doing whatever they want, not waking up at a normal time, not going into an office, hiring people by, like, bringing them into your house and letting them chill with you for a while and party with you and smoke with you.
>
> (in Fisher 2018, 355)

This renegade image is again evoked when Sean Parker, co-founder of the early peer-to-peer file-sharing application Napster, remembers his chance encounter with the Facebook founders by way of "this group of kids walking toward me – they were all wearing hoodies and they looked like they were probably pot-smoking high school kids just out making trouble" (p. 354). Whereas this gang-like, misfit image was central to Facebook's hacker ethos, it also gestures towards the gaping social divide existing between the risks and possibilities of these *white* hoodie-wearing 'new kids on the block' compared with potential *non-white* hoodie-wearers in the same neighbourhood. As Losse emphasises in a polemic against the start-up ethos of disruption (2013a), just a few kilometres down the road from where Parker will have met the white Facebook gang, in East Palo Alto, chances are that if "you decided to walk across the 101 freeway to University Avenue […], you'd be taking a risk, but not one likely to be rewarded" (Losse 2013a, n.p.).

Move fast and break–repair–roll back things – the hacker ethos revised

Contrasting sharply with Zuckerberg's origin myth of 'a bunch of slacker kids doing whatever they want,' technology designer Aaron Sittig remembers being "really impressed" with the focused atmosphere in the Palo Alto house-share: "[F]or the most part they spent all their time sitting at a kitchen table with their laptops open […,] working, constantly, to keep their product growing" (in Fisher 2018, 354). This impression of focus and dedication casts a different light on a time that is mostly romanticised for the founders' rumbustiousness. Rather, it points to a dynamic where a constant striving for product growth might well have been applied to counter and drown-out vexing questions of legitimacy. In his study about Freud's notion of Eros, psychoanalyst André Green writes that Eros binds together "the ego and the object, *as far as is allowed by the intervention of the super-ego, which will set the limits of that relation, making sure that it is, so to speak, 'legitimate'"* (Green 2000, 114, emphasis added). From this perspective, Zuckerberg' emphasis of a state of unsupervised immaturity on the one hand, and the utmost focus on product growth on the other hand, gestures towards how super-egoic questions of legitimacy will have been handled, specifically, through the single-minded dedication to the flow state of developing code (cf. Levy 2020, 20ff).

This active suppression of any sense of conscience or guilt is also what defines the hacker ethos and the work process based on it. When Facebook's office spaces would be covered with posters proclaiming "Be Bold," "Move fast and break things," "Done is better than perfect," and "What would you do if you weren't afraid?" (Frier 2020, 93), this is in line with Facebook's attempt at maintaining this hacker ethos as part of the company's philosophy. Particularly "Move fast and break things," which served as the unofficial company motto, is based on an aggressiveness that is not so much derived from modes of resistance and defence, but again from a drive towards unfettered productivity and creativity, liberated from caution, safety procedures – and the law.

In his famous treaty "Conscience of a hacker," better known as the Hacker Manifesto (1986), Loyd Blankenstein, aka the Mentor, ritualistically refers to himself as a "Damn kid" so as to evoke the scorn of his social surroundings. Furthermore, he rhetorically repeats the phrase "… and you call us criminals" as an evocation of the lack of social appreciation: "We explore... and you call us criminals. We seek after knowledge... and you call us criminals" (Blankenstein 1986). Similarly, in the film *Hackers* (Softley 1995), which was a major source of inspiration for Facebook's engineering staff (Losse 2012, 108), a small group of young genius misfits spends long nocturnal hours breaking into company computer networks and enmeshing themselves in the ephemeral beauty of computer code. When towards the end of the film the 'hackers of the world' literally unite, it is to show the world the difference between their hacking practices, which are depicted as innocent transgressions and almost noble forms of sportsmanship, from fully fledged internet crimes and terrorism, as performed by the film's evil security officer, Eugene 'The Plague' Belford.

In keeping with this hacker ethos of transgressive playfulness and playful transgression, Facebook's workday proper would not start until relatively late in the evening, when, after some heavy afternoon drinking, new functions would be added to the service without any significant testing in advance. "There was an absence of process that was mind-blowing," remembers Geminder, "There would be engineers working stealthily on something that they were passionate about. And then they'd ship it in the middle of the night. No testing – they would just ship it" (in Fisher 2018, 360). As Jeff Rothschild corroborates: "That's the hacker mentality: You just get it done" (p. 361). Yet, as he admits, this process started to grind when the company grew: "[I]t worked great when you had ten people. By the time we got to twenty, or thirty, or forty, I was spending a lot of time trying to keep the site up" (in Fisher 2018, 361).

At this point, while minor things might have been allowed to break in minor ways, the overall working of the site needed to be maintained at all costs, and this gradually turned the process of 'moving fast and breaking things' into an often painful one of moving fast, breaking things, then trying to repair things and, ultimately, if this failed, rolling things back. Max Kelly remembers: "If four a.m. rolled around and we couldn't fix it, I'd be like, 'We're going to try and revert it'" (p. 361). Hence, despite it becoming obvious that the passionate erotic of the "hacker way" stopped working, the company was curiously slow in responding to this insight; rather, what comes forth in people's recollections is a pattern of "reversal," in which, as Freud (1909) writes about the phenomenon, an obsessive act unfurls in two successive stages, "of which the second neutralises the first" (p. 192). When Freud then continues that such compulsive acts are "a representation of a conflict between two opposing impulses of approximately equal strength: [...] love and hate" (ibid), this indicates indeed that what is banished in insisting on a creative process of pure passion is the creeping sense of a fundamental ambivalence at its core.

This insistence on a process of pure passion has been formative of Facebook's business ever since and has recently taken on increasingly messianic overtones: "Ultimately, that's the unique thing that Facebook was put on this Earth to do," Zuckerberg said in an interview about Facebook's mission of connecting people. And no matter how often the company has needed to row back and apologise for the features it added, it has stuck to its principal formula of unmodulated growth. When Steven Levy, in his *Facebook: The Inside Story* (2020), sums up his findings by stating that: "Virtually every problem that Facebook confronted [...] had been a consequence of two things: the unprecedented nature of the mission to connect the world, and the consequences of its reckless haste to do so" (p. 16), this captures the gist of my overall argument well.

Total commitment

In line with Freud's notion of obsession, the amount of work that was required to expand Facebook and both warrant the service's functioning and maintain its hacker-way of creation seemed all consuming. "I only own a mattress," Zuckerberg stated, and this frugality served as the counterpoint to the regressively playful partying culture that was celebrated at the office. Especially the lesser paid Facebook staff, who, in the autumn of 2006, were financially incentivised to move within "the mile" – i.e., to live no more than a mile from Facebook's offices – often could not afford much more than a mattress either. Yet, even Losse (2012) admits to relishing this frugality as a sacrifice to what owners and staff alike saw as their mission: "to bring everyone on board the social network" (p. 87). In an interview with technology critic Noah Kulwin (2018), she returned to this sense of mission: "The thing that makes Facebook different [from] even some of the other tech platforms [...] was that there was this very moralistic sense of the mission: of connecting people, connecting the world" (Losse in Kulwin 2018). And elsewhere she concedes: "that early feeling of intensity was pretty exciting; [...] there's something delicious and hypnotic about being all in it together and counting on each other" (Losse in Casserly 2012).

What could be binding Facebook's staff more intensely to its operations than the utterly positive mission of binding people together in one expansive community? On the surface, it must have appeared that the team practised what the company preached: love and togetherness. While I will look into Freud's *Group Psychology and the Analysis of the Ego* (1921) in more depth in the chapter on Twitter, suffice it to point out here that when Freud explains the relational mechanism of "suggestion" as an individual ego's surrendering of itself for someone else's sake – or as the German original has it: "ihnen zu Liebe" ("for love of them", p. 92)[9] – this seems to be a poignant way of spelling out what Losse (in Kulwin 2018) refers to as "the universally, at least on its face, positive motive," that Facebook was able to harness. Indeed, founders and staff, as well as early users, were willing to surrender significant parts of their control to Facebook's adhesive mission. However, when Freud in "Instincts and their vicissitudes" (1915) observes that, in the oral phase, love is coextensive with aims of devouring and incorporation and that, in the anal phase, it is still "hardly to be distinguished from hate in its attitude towards the object" (p. 138–9), this suggests that Facebook's mission might not have been as soundly moral as could be framed in the discourse of openness and togetherness. Rather, along the lines of the concept of Eros, notions of hunger, mastery, and domination would become mixed into it.

Zuckerberg had a "fanboy affinity with the emperor Caesar Augustus," writes Levy (2020), "a brilliant conqueror and empathetic ruler who also had an unseemly lust for power" (p. 31). Especially when it comes to Facebook's demands on its staff and its relation to competitors, the kind of love that it was pursuing proved a conquering and domineering one. Accordingly, as Losse (2012) points out, Facebook "was looking for soldiers, not journeymen" (p. 74). Relatedly, Callahan recollects that: "We had company parties all the time, and for a period in 2005, all Mark's toasts at the company parties would end with 'Domination!'" (in Fisher 2018, 368).

Tellingly, Zuckerberg, upon being interviewed about his fierce competitiveness, said, half evadingly, "there's a natural zero-sumness" to his way of leading Facebook (Zuckerberg in Osnos 2018). In this remark, he comes closer than usual to acknowledging the thanatotic elements that arise as a necessary by-product of an erotic, unfettered drive towards binding. After all, what Facebook has once bound and brought under its spell is bound so entirely that, as long as the network is healthy, it cannot be claimed by others. In this way, the erotic charge of the company becomes coextensive with its authoritarian potential. These tendencies come to the fore in another of Losse's recollections. In a biting critique of the postfeminist currents in *Lean In*, the self-help book for businesswomen by Facebook COO (between 2008 and 2022) Sheryl Sandberg (2013), Losse (2013b) writes that "I decided to leave Facebook because I saw ahead of me, by Zuckerberg's and Sandberg's own hands, an unending race of pure ambition, where no amount of money or power is enough and work is forever" (n.p.). What Losse argues readers could learn from Sandberg's book is "how one transforms one's life entirely into work" (ibid). If work is indeed love made visible, as an old say-ing has it, then the totality of work that is Facebook is an adequate articulation of the company's conception of love.

Translating beer pong into code – early Facebook user experience

The origins of Facebook's corporate culture thus hail from an immature male sexu-ality which depends on rhythms of cathexis and catharsis, inhibition and disinhibi-tion, and regression and recreation, to unfold its drive towards a mode of binding that needs to dominate and a form of domination that wants to dissolve in love. But how about the users' side? How did they experience the service in its early itera-tions? And, asked from the perspective of Eros, how might one conceive the erotic form of this experience?

As stated above, what tends to recede in the background in the (albeit often ironic) celebrations of Facebook's retro-masculinity is that its unruly-seeming li-bido became transformed into code that afforded well-restrained flirtatious play. However, while this restraint in the service's design points to an impressive act of sublimation, I will show how this sublimation ultimately remains stuck in the limit-lessness of drive. This fixation already shows in Facebook's adherence to hacker culture and its orientation towards gaining access – first and foremost to data, but, via data, to information, goods, services, and people. Strikingly, what Facebook's engineers realised is that, in order to obtain optimal access to people and their rela-tions, it was first and foremost necessary to *limit* people's access to the service and to each other.

Hence, the way in which Facebook managed to throttle, modulate, and refine the libidinal charge of its makers and attach it to more refined aims can best be unpacked when comparing it with its forerunners: Friendster and MySpace. With Friendster founded in 2002 and MySpace in 2003, both these services were para-digmatic of online social networking. They converged on the basic functions of affording people to (a) create a profile page and (b) build a network of related profile pages by connecting with them, so as to (c) "view and traverse their list of connections and those made by others within the system" (boyd and Ellison 2007, n.p.). Friendster had originally been conceived as a dating site and designed "on the assumption that friends-of-friends would make better romantic partners than would strangers" (boyd and Ellison 2007, n.p.). However, whereas its radius of potential contacts was restricted to four degrees (i.e., friends of friends of friends of friends; boyd 2006, n. p.), this was still a very large, vastly uncontrollable amount of people that each user would receive access to and, vice versa, be accessible to. Furthermore, whereas Friendster's user uptake had already been significant before traditional broadcasting media started to report on it, the tidal wave of new users that came as a result of this reporting "upset the cultural balance" on the page (ibid) and caused the service grave technical problems, slowing it down and often causing it to crash. As boyd and Ellison (2007) report, "Many early adopters left because of the combination of technical difficulties, social collisions, and a rupture of trust between users and the site" (n.p.).

MySpace, in turn, was partly conceived to offer a home to those Friendster users that either abandoned the platform or were rejected by it. As danah boyd (2006) writes:

> While Friendster was irritated by fake Profiles, MySpace embraced this practice. One of MySpace's early strategies was to provide a place for everyone who was rejected from Friendster or who didn't want to be on a dating site. Bands who had been kicked off of Friendster were some of the earliest MySpace users.
>
> (boyd 2006, n.p.)

Especially smaller indie bands flocked to the network, and even though the service had not been specifically designed to facilitate connections between bands and their fans, this turned out to be one of its main drivers of network expansion. However, because the music fans were often underage, MySpace changed its terms of service to admit minors. After the site had then been bought by Rupert Murdoch's NewsCorp for more than half a billion dollars in 2005, it was soon confronted with legal charges of sexual assaults on minors. And even though these were occurring to far lesser degrees than the moral panic around it suggested (Bahney 2006), further safety and privacy issues, a significant amount of unsolicited pornographic materials and the site's overall cluttering with ad banners and chaotic page designs, meant MySpace's eventual demise.

Compared with these significantly raw attempts at networking libidinal energy – attempts that by no means would have seemed uncharacteristic of Facebook's partying hacker fraternity – Facebook itself managed to attract early adopters with its reduced and discreetly ad-free design.[10] As Losse (2012) writes, it was "minimalist to the extreme. It was strikingly clean, and novel in its simplicity, lacking the gaudy advertisements and spammy content that were inevitable elsewhere on the Internet" (p. xv). Aaron Sittig agrees: "I was really impressed by how focused and clear their product was. Small details – like when you went to your profile, it really clearly said, 'This is you,' because social networking at the time was really, really hard to understand" (in Fisher 2018, 353). When Sittig goes on to remark that "there was a maturity in the product that you don't typically see until a product has been out there for a couple of years and been refined" (ibid), this impression of maturity once more gestures to the astonishing sublimation of an emphatically immature charge.

Indeed, what is astonishing about early Facebook, particularly against the background of the many data leaks and scandals that have implicated the company in recent years, are the strong privacy features it had. The service started exclusively as a Harvard University student network, and this did not merely entail an aspect of elite exclusivity, but also made it a closed off and intimately private space. It was this exclusive privacy that was then exported to other universities. As boyd and Ellison write: "To join, a user had to have a harvard.edu email address. As Facebook began supporting other schools, those users were also required to have university email addresses associated with those institutions" (2007, n.p.).

Going hand in hand with the requirement of university email was that of signing up with one's real name. And whereas this real-name policy received a substantial amount of critique across the years (e.g., Hogan 2013), it helped Facebook avoid its networks being spammed with porn in the way MySpace was (Zuckerberg in Fisher 2018, 352). Again, Losse's (2012) experience is valuable here:

> Visiting Facebook's rudimentary privacy page, which had just a few drop-downs that offered options to make your profile visible either only to your school or only to your friends, I realized that it was possible, for the first time on the Internet, to protect my profile from being visible to anyone outside of my immediate group of acquaintances.
>
> (Losse 2012, xv)

Importantly, what Facebook's early limitation to university and school campuses warranted was that all people who were available to users online were so too offline, and this availability was at the centre of the flirtation that Facebook was geared towards. As Dustin Moskovitz sums up a central pillar of this appeal: "Back then there was a really common problem that now seems trivial. It was basically impossible to think of a person by name and go and look up their picture" (in Fisher 2018, 351). In this respect, Facebook in its early form would have the feel of "a richer, more playful form of email" – with pictures – and "the option to post public messages onto people's walls" (Losse 2012, xxiii). When, a few years later, Sherry Turkle (2011) would observe with an acute sense of melancholy that "we look to the network to defend us against loneliness even as we use it to control the intensity of our connections" (p. 13), this balance, which Facebook would go on to export into most parts of the world, struck a powerfully erotic chord in the context of university campuses. Here, as in many other contexts initially, it meant a welcome increase in loving bonds of communal connectedness:

> Facebook had miraculously solved the biggest social problem that plagued Hopkins [university campus; S.K.] and had led to its low rankings in student satisfaction. The campus had no public space aside from the library [...]. In an instant, Facebook had created a public space, albeit a virtual one, that was accessible at any time, from anywhere.
>
> (Losse 2012, xii)

That this "public space" was privately owned (Klein 1999) would only unveil its problematic sides further down the line. Hence, with a Facebook profile merely consisting of a relatively small portrait photo and a limited set of profile fields that the user could fill out or leave blank meant that users indeed had a form of control over the intensity of their connections that had been lacking on similar networks.

This relative feeling of safety and control proved to be the ideally facilitating, formative environment for users to make themselves available to others in their network as well as to the network itself. As investor Mark Pincus recalls about his accessing Facebook for the first time: "[I]t was amazing. People are putting up their phone numbers and home addresses and everything about themselves and I was like, I can't believe it! But it was because they had all this trust" (in Fisher 2018, 351).

In summary, Facebook's early user experience took on the form of an exciting 'possibilisation,' and the flirtatious offer to gain access and become accessible to potentially all others in one's immediate physical and institutional surroundings, within a sheltered, quasi-communal space. Virtually mapping the actual territory of its users' lives, Facebook's flirtatiousness lay in this very virtuality of a myriad of relationships lying dormant and with the potential to be actualised 'in real life,' but in ways and to degrees that seemed controllable. And whereas MySpace, with its focus on bands and music, was still based on the logic of pushing products onto people (Chmielewski and Sarno 2009), Facebook was focusing exclusively on ties between people. Again Losse (2012) captures this poignantly when writing that, in 2006, "The Internet was heading in the direction of replicating not just individual identities but the relationships between individuals […] and Facebook was already doing that better and more comprehensively than any other service" (p. 94).

Neutralising Eros in homophily

Returning to Yates's (2015) take on flirtation, one can say that the retrosexual fantasies of Facebook's makers had indeed been sublimated into "progressive, playful and creative modes" of human relations (p. 24). Yet, that this sublimation might not have been based on solid foundations already shows in the programming staff's disregard of their service's users: "'[O]ur users are stupid.' Literally those words came out of somebody's mouth," recalls Katie Geminder (in Fisher 2018, 366). In this respect, the hacker orientation towards gaining access ties in well with early 20th-century notions of social engineering as "the conscious and intelligent manipulation of the organized habits and opinions of the masses" (Bernays 2005 [1928], 9). Hence, what becomes apparent in Facebook's strategy of engineering flirtation for optimal access is a strongly instrumental current running through the service which was threatening to cancel out its progressive orientations from the start. This counterpoint found an early paradigmatic expression in the "Facebook friend."

Already with respect to Friendster, boyd (2006) had observed that, "[a]s people began using the site, they overloaded Friends to mean more than simply a representation of friendship" (n.p.). Rather, beyond actual friends, the category came to entail acquaintances, family, work colleagues, and superiors, as well as everybody else whose request one did not want to reject. Friending would serve a cataloguing function in case one needed a contact at a later point, an access function in case people's profiles were closed to non-friends, and a decorative function since many considered having lots of friends indicated popularity. Even though Facebook paid close attention to hindering the 'friendships' fostered on its own platform from becoming devoid of meaning, the inflationary and devaluing effects of socially networked 'friending' were eventually ascribed to Facebook as well (e.g., Lewis and West 2009).

A frequently used explanation for this hollowing out of the notion of friendship has been found in the workings of the digital per se, which is seen to neutralise human ties in the binary of connection/no connection. Indeed, when Bucher (2018) quotes from Facebook's patent application that "The term friend […] simply implies a connection in the social network" (2018, 9), this presents a strong case in point for this neutralising effect. Another case is made by what Robert W. Gehl (2012) has called "real software abstraction," that is, "an architecture, waiting for a user to realise it with content" (Gehl 2012, 107). However, while the distinction between architecture and (user-generated) content holds true for all social media, what is particular about Facebook is how well it has managed to gear its architecture towards nudging users to produce specific kinds of content and foster specific kinds of connections. Hence, in the case of Facebook, the moment of instrumentalisation of its erotic function should not be seen as simply lying in an inevitable digital effect of neutralising connections. I argue that the hollowing out of friendship and other sublimated forms of loving ties is not so much driven by their digital affordances per se, but much rather by the specific understanding of love as infinite expansion that has become programmed into Facebook's architecture. In the case of the function of friending, this understanding becomes articulated in exactly the attitude that Bosworth captured in his brutal equation of growth=good (see above), which can be paraphrased as *a love of all loving ties*.

Wendy Chun's (2018) work on networked homophily, i.e., a networked love of sameness, pertains to this brutal conception of Eros. When she writes that "Homophily launders hate into collective love" (p. 62), this connects well to the undifferentiated kind of love that I see in Facebook's design. Her argument can be unpacked with what Robert W. Gehl (2012) refers to as "Facebook's openness" (p. 108). Using Satanism as his example, Gehl observes that "the Facebook Satanist page, like all Facebook pages, is so aesthetically clean it renders the content in the frames nonthreatening" (Gehl 2012, 107). Again, however, this should not be seen as a process of neutralisation; rather, it is a lovingly formative process that Facebook is algorithmically geared to administer to all.

And not only that. As has been widely discussed, Facebook's algorithm traces and identifies other 'satanists like you,' who can then be connected with 'you,' thus perpetuating bias and inequality "in the name of 'comfort,' predictability, and common sense" (Chun 2018, 62). In 2017, for example, a ProPublica inquiry showed that "the world's largest social network enabled advertisers to direct their pitches to the news feeds of almost 2,300 people who expressed interest in the topics of 'Jew hater'" (Angwin et al. 2017). Facebook's love seems endless in that everybody can realise their passion there, be it the members of a university's chess club, satanists, or worse.

Phase 2: "don't ask for permission, ask for forgiveness" – unfettered expansion

At this point in the chapter, I have spelled out the main gist of my argument of "outrageous growth" as the primitive conception of love that Facebook's mission of connecting the world is suffused with. In what follows, I cast individual spotlights on how this ideology and practice of "outrageous growth" become reproduced in Facebook's consecutive developmental phases, from its expansion into the entirety of the internet, via the Like button, to its consecutive turn towards community and its more recent venture into the metaverse.

When technology critic Kara Swisher (2018) asked Zuckerberg apropos disinformation campaigns on Facebook whether he simply does not see "that side of humanity," she put her finger on the sore spot in Facebook's design that a focus on Eros points towards, specifically, the absence of any notion of negativity or 'badness' which is dialectically needed to balance off the forces of good from turning bad themselves. In his response, Zuckerberg concedes that: "In retrospect, I do think it's fair to say that we were overly idealistic and focused on more of the good parts of what connecting people and giving people a voice can bring" (Zuckerberg in Swisher 2018, n.p.). However, while Zuckerberg surely has a point when he goes on to emphasise the corporate response – "we're a profitable enough company to have 20,000 people go work on reviewing content" (ibid)[11] – it becomes clear from overlooking the further development of Facebook's business practices that the drive towards limitless binding has never been significantly reigned in. True to Zuckerberg's hacker motto "Don't ask for permission, ask for forgiveness," Facebook's second phase thus can be – indeed has been (e.g., Fowler and Esteban 2018) – characterised as one long line of excuses and apologies for the often-illegal amassing of ever-more connections which has been the company's undeterred goal.

Consequently, what becomes characteristic of Facebook's second phase is a change of the service from a mere facilitator of people's 'loving ties' to an *active pusher* and creator of them. Whereas this change was introduced with the launch of "News Feed" in late 2006, its central articulation is the "Like" button. I will discuss these in turn.

As Losse (2012) explains:

> Before News Feed, Facebook had been a comparatively discreet book of profiles, maintained and updated individually by each profile owner. News Feed introduced a new homepage where any and all updates to a friend's profile might appear as a broadcast story, with a headline and accompanying photographs. Your friends' activities on Facebook were now news, and your homepage was a kind of social newspaper.
>
> (Losse 2012, 90)

Who in your network had befriended whom? Who amongst your friends had broken up with whom? Who had posted on whose wall? Who had changed their relationship status to what? On 5 September 2006, without prior notice, "users faced a start page that listed every act undertaken by their Friends within the system," writes boyd (2008, 13) about what she called the "Facebook privacy trainwreck": "None of the information displayed through this feature was previously private per se, but by aggregating this information and displaying it in reverse chronological order, News Feeds made the material far more accessible and visible" (ibid). Yet, despite the loud protests online and offline, what Facebook's engineers saw just days after News Feed's launch was that usage of the service increased manifold. Max Kelly remembers: "Even the same people who were telling us that this is terrible, we'd look at their user stream and be like: *You're fucking using it constantly! What are you talking about?*" (in Fisher 2018, 367, emphasis in the original).

Moskovitz claimed that "News Feed is the concept of viral distribution, incarnate" (in Fisher 2018, 365) and, indeed, this virality-in-spite-of-the-users shows that, in terms of Eros, the very irresistibility of the Life drives can come into stark opposition to "the phenomena of life" themselves (Freud, see above). "Creepy" was a word used with increasing frequency in relation to Facebook in this phase,[12] and this must be seen as symptomatic of this opposition. Defined as an unwanted closeness and intimacy – a closeness that is "creeping up" on people – the term captured Facebook users' increasing sense of their service's exploitative attitude towards them. This attitude, in turn, is poignantly captured in José van Dijck's (2013a) differentiation between "connectedness" and "connectivity," which she unfolds with reference to Facebook's affordance of "sharing" things:

> From a technological point of view, the two meanings of "sharing" relate to two different types of coding qualities. The first type relates to *connectedness*, directing users to share information with other users through purposefully designed interfaces. [...] The second type of coding features relates to *connectivity*, as they aim at sharing user data with third parties, such as Beacon (now defunct), Open Graph, and the Like button.
>
> (van Dijck 2013a, 46–47)

Facebook itself does *not* acknowledge this differentiation. As Healey and Potter (2018) observe, the company regards its social mission and commercial motives as mutually compatible. Zuckerberg, they write rightly, "argues that commercial organisations are the key to stabilising 'our social fabric'" (p. 665). Already in 2007, Facebook invited private businesses and companies onto the platform, offering them to become regular members, just like every other user.[13] In this respect, News Feed would prove only the first in a long line of addendums and tweaks to dial up the binding power of the service – in the service of third parties. As that, News Feed prepared the introduction of all advertisement on the platform. The infamous "Beacon" application was introduced (and soon after rolled back due to user protests) in its wake, automatically posting people's online purchases to their friends' News Feeds (Boulton 2007). Two years later, Facebook used the introduction of its timeline to set all existing and newly opened accounts to a default "public" setting, making all profiles visible to any and everybody else on Facebook (van Dijck 2013b); it took five years of protests until the company set the default back to "friends" in 2014.

This "opt-in by default" strategy took on decisively more sombre forms still in Facebook's expansion into developing countries. Infamously, this happened in Myanmar, where Facebook spread fervently from 2014 onwards by offering cheap mobile internet access via preinstalled Facebook apps and accounts on newly bought smartphones – often "equipped with pre-installed friends, and in many cases celebrities and a collection of hot girls" (Bucher 2021, 27). When Facebook then left the wave of incendiary posts against the country's Rohingya Muslim minority largely unmoderated, it made itself complicit in the mass violence and murderous attacks against this minority at the hands of Buddhist ultranationalists.

Yet, the most characteristic representation of Facebook's libidinally expansionist scheme is the Like button. Other social buttons had been introduced to the internet before it; Reddit, for example, had designed buttons that could be added to other websites, thus popularising "the acts of sharing and recommending content" (Gerlitz and Helmond 2013, 1351). However, it speaks to Facebook's overall erotic mission that its own button's main function would not be 'bookmarking' or 'recommending,' but a simple, positively relational 'like.' Following its patented definition of "friend" as a mere connection in the network, the Like button was designed to expand Facebook's binding logic across the whole of the internet. As Anne Helmond and Carolin Gerlitz (2013) observe, Liking was initially put forward as a social activity *within* Facebook – a shortcut for "short affective statements like 'Awesome' and 'Congrats!'" – which could be "performed on most shared objects within Facebook, such as status updates, links or comments" (p. 1352). In 2010, Facebook followed this up with the introduction of an external Like button: "a plugin that can be implemented by any webmaster, potentially rendering all web content likeable" (ibid). In this respect, the Like button has been an important part of an overall strategy "in which web users can engage with potentially all web content outside of the platform through Facebook-based activities such as liking, sharing or commenting," thus following the plan "of 'building a web where the default is social'" (Zuckerberg quoted in Gerlitz and Helmond 2013, 1352).

It is remarkably consistent with this chapter's theme of "outrageous growth" (Abel-Hirsh 2010) that Facebook for a long time ignored ever-louder user complaints and requests for a "Dislike" button. When a negative-sentiment option finally arrived, it was in the form of cute emojis, expressing sadness and indignation in the nonthreatening way that Gehl (2012) argues is characteristic of Facebook's overall interface design. Cuteness, states Sianne Ngai (2010), is a "domestic and commodity-oriented aesthetic" (p. 125). And Gerlitz and Helmond (2013) follow this argument when observing how the infrastructure of the Like button "is turning user affects and engagement into [...] objects of exchange" (p. 1361). Yet, when Bonni Rambatan and Jacob Johanssen (2021) add that cuteness online "masks a form of violence through which the Subject is turned into sanitised images, data points, and flat signifiers" (p. 8), this points to an even more fundamental struggle, namely, that between life and death. Hence, approached from Freud's drive theory, the claim of the turning of "social interactivity […] into valuable consumer data" (Helmond and Gerlitz 2013, 1349) might be paraphrased thus that Facebook's incessant colonisation of the internet with Life and Love ultimately saps the life out of its objects and creates only 'dead ends' by infusing all ties with a relentless spirit of production.

Phase 3: "a responsibility to do even more" – Facebook's community spirit

It was in light of the political scandals of Russian meddling in the 2016 US presidential election and the manipulation of nearly 90 million user profiles by Cambridge Analytica that Zuckerberg's public apologies could no longer absorb the widespread exasperation at the indiscriminate and exuberant ways in which Facebook sought to connect the world. A more decisive change in business orientation was needed, and Facebook sought to bring this about by recalibrating its News Feed algorithm and rewriting its overall mission statement. While the company claims to have reset the algorithm to funnel more posts from "closer ties" – the fabled "family and friends" – to users and thus deprioritising political news, the mission statement was changed from "making the world more open and connected" to giving "people the power to build community and bring the world closer together" (e.g., Constine 2017). And yet again, when Facebook sought to drive home its new-found allegiance to the power of community by organising a Facebook community convention, Zuckerberg's inaugural address inevitably gravitated towards the ideology of unlimited binding:

> Right now, I think the most important thing we can do is bring people closer together. It's so important that we're going to change Facebook's whole mission to take this on.
> For the past decade, we've focused on making the world more open and connected. We're not done with that. But I used to think that if we just gave people a voice and helped them connect, that would make the world better by itself. In many ways it has. But our society is still divided. Now I believe we have a responsibility to do even more. It's not enough to simply connect the world, we must also work to bring the world closer together.
>
> (Zuckerberg, 22 June 2017)

Instead of announcing more substantial changes and making concessions – for example, to the effect that Facebook itself might have contributed to social divisions – Zuckerberg's rhetoric barred the possibility that these divisions had anything to do with his company. Rather, when he bemoans that "society is still divided," this suggests that these divisions exist *despite* his platform's social achievements. Accordingly, the political crises in which the platform has been involved are seen as having come about *not due to a 'too-much' of Facebook, but because of a too little*, hence the need to do "even more."

In turn, the implications of Zuckerberg's assertion that "It's not enough to simply connect the world, we must also work to bring the world closer together," could already be glimpsed when, in 2014, emotional contagion experiments (Kramer et al., 2014) caused a public outcry. "[W]e were concerned that exposure to friends' negativity might lead people to avoid visiting Facebook," the study's main author tried to apologise in a post, framing the research "as motivated by 'care about the emotional impact of Facebook and the people that use our product'" (Stark 2018, 205). However, while most protesters were rightly concerned with notions of manipulation and "mind control" (ibid), what shows in hindsight is that Facebook considered countering negative expressions already at this early point. Hence, as early as 2014, it was no longer enough for Facebook to "simply connect the world,"; rather, it also became increasingly important *to control the nature of these connections.*

This logic, which represents a further expansion of Eros into Facebook's relational work, seems to have become increasingly important for the company's conception of "community." When, in his testimony to the US House of Representatives in 2018, Zuckerberg spells out his vision of community, he again comes worryingly close to suggesting the straightforward suppression of negative content:

> It's not enough to just connect people, we have to make sure those connections are positive. It's not enough to just give people a voice, we have to make sure people aren't using it to hurt people or spread misinformation. It's not enough to give people control of their information, we have to make sure developers they've given it to are protecting it too. Across the board, we have a responsibility to not just build tools, but to make sure those tools are used for good.
>
> (Zuckerberg, quoted in Timberg and Romm 2018)

As the evolution of the platform has shown, the ways in which Zuckerberg's 'desire for good' is being implemented have unerringly tended towards repressive dynamics in which anything that does *not* pertain to positive growth is rendered non-existent. Consequently, attention needs to turn to the question of where, when, and in what forms this repressed returns on the platform. And while the deluge of hate speech offers one place to start such an inquiry, Losse's (2012) thoughts on the widespread practices of trolling amongst Facebook's engineers offer another. "[T]rolling […] is a kind of admission that we can't win online as our true selves, that authenticity online makes us too vulnerable," she writes, adding that, despite Facebook's business needs, "Neither Mark nor any of the boys said anything that particularly revealed their emotions" (p. 206). Losse herself reports that she developed a particular kind of trolling response that affirmed Facebook's demands in a markedly overblown and exaggerated way: "'<333333333333333333333,' I posted as my status regularly, sometimes <3-ing particular things and people, with an exuberance that seemed infectious" (Losse 2012, 206). This, I argue, can be read as a symptomatic response to Facebook's mantra of Eros in that even its makers were prompted to articulate this 'message in reverse' (Lacan 1999 [1972–1973], 139–40).[14]

Phase 4: "cells in a single organism" – binding life in the metaverse

Finally, I want to indicate how this mantra of pure Eros has carried over into what is currently being framed as "the metaverse."[15] Whereas some technology critics see Facebook's recent turn towards this metaverse as a sign of a wider process of reorientation, away from politics and towards becoming a facilitator of an extended private sphere, Meta's grand ambitions in the field of VR are still very much aligned with Facebook's traditional mission of binding. Accordingly, in this latest phase of the company's development, Eros is transposed onto a new digital plane of reality.

Hence, what Zuckerberg imagines becoming possible in VR is to capture "a whole experience," as he explains. "I do think that we're gonna move towards this world where eventually you'll be able to capture a whole experience that you're in and be able to send that to someone. I think that that's just gonna be an amazing technology for perspective taking and putting yourself in other people's shoes," Zuckerberg told Kara Swisher (2018). Again, the field of Eros is expanded and deepened: from its beginnings in flirtation, via the ambition of making the entire internet social, and from the engineering of communal sentiment to the *programming of empathy itself.*

Swisher is taken aback: "I'm not sure you can give people empathy though. You can see people, the world through people's eyes, but you can't understand their experience, necessarily," she contends. Zuckerberg, however, seems so animated by the idea of VR's empathic potentials that he lets his enthusiasm spill over into another talking point of the metaverse, specifically, that of equal opportunity:

> [O]ne of the biggest issues economically today is that opportunity isn't evenly distributed. You get all these people have to move to cities, and then the cities get to be way too expensive, and if you have a technology like VR where you can be present anywhere but live where you choose to, then I think that that can be really profound.
>
> (Zuckerberg in Swisher 2018)

This idea of battling inequality with the equalising powers of VR has been circulated under the label of "Reality Privilege" by Facebook-cum-Meta affiliates ever since the company's relaunch. Borrowed from the VR developer Beau Cronin, Facebook visionaries have been elaborating the concept far beyond Cronin's scope (Pogue 2022, 40–1). The journalist James Pogue quotes from comments that Facebook's board member Marc Andreessen made in an interview in 2021:

> A small percent of people live in a real-world environment that is rich, even overflowing, with glorious substance [...]. Beautiful settings, plentiful stimulation, and many fascinating people to talk to, and to work with, and to date. [...] Everyone else, [...] the vast majority of humanity, lacks Reality Privilege – their

online world is, or will be, immeasurably richer and more fulfilling than most of the physical and social environment around them in the quote-unquote real world.

(Andreessen quoted in Pogue 2022, 41)

This then is the way that Facebook intends to push its erotic mission further in the metasphere, specifically, by replicating the social world in VR in a way that will be so loving and life-affirming that a critical mass of people will migrate there, leaving the material world and its inequalities and injustices behind. In this way, the metaverse is intended to continue the eradication of negativity in a vastly positive community on another level of reality. However, as Pogue (2022) observes rightly, "with investors already moving into the market, it may soon be as difficult for a young person to imagine buying a house in Decentraland [i.e., one of the current metaverse applications; S.K.] as in the real world" (p. 42).

Conclusion – the cruel optimism of Facebook love

"How to destroy the world, one solution at a time," is how Wendy Chun entitled the introduction chapter of her study *Discriminating Data* (2021), and this title offers an apt way of returning to this book's overall theme of formative media. In turn, when Losse (2012) admits that, despite her harsh critique of Facebook, she always felt "sympathetic and almost protective" of Zuckerberg, this ties in well with the witticism in Chun's title. As stated, Facebook's love has never been a kind and caring one, and when it now threatens to 'kill the world with kindness,' we need to keep in mind that its love was always one of domination, and its form of connectedness always tinged with connectivity (van Dijck 2013a). While this chapter has largely focused on Eros as the formative principle of Facebook as a company itself, I want to use the chapter's conclusion to home in on the formative effects that the platform's mode of outrageous expansion has on its users.

In this respect, Marcuse's writings on *Eros and Civilisation* (1987 [1956]) are informative. Whereas his positive suggestions for a fully rounded, self-sublimated state of socio-erotic being might have lost some of their plausibility since their publication in the mid-20th century, his critique of the existing conditions of his time has not. Hence, when he writes about "the release of constrained sexuality within the dominion of [...] institutions" that "libido continues to bear the mark of suppression" and "strengthens rather than weakens the roots of instinctual constraint" (p. 202), this anticipates what I see as the effect of Facebook's 'endless love' on its users. Put differently, the loving ways that Facebook affords its users to relate to each other seem by no means conducive of the "spread [...] of libido" and the "erotizsation of the entire personality" that Marcuse saw as a utopian societal state (1987, 201) and that Facebook has been gesturing towards ever since the change of its mission statement in favour of the power of community. Instead, what the company has produced on the users' parts are inhibited and constrained attempts at maintaining social capital – attempts for which notions of work and labour are central (Johanssen and Krüger 2022, 95ff).

"The Facebook product itself made staying on task difficult," Losse (2012) remembers apropos such work, "With the steady stream of pictures flowing down our pages, how could we be expected to focus on anything but planning our next photo opportunities and status updates?" (Losse 2012, 193). This anecdotal dig at the company's work culture ties in seamlessly with the intricate and problematic interlacing of work and leisure activity, as well as free digital labour performed by the platform users, which has been debated for nearly two decades (Terranova 2000; Krüger and Johanssen 2014). In this respect, the relational work that people perform on Facebook clearly bears the mark of the limitlessness that the platform's understanding of love itself entails. There are always new people to be in touch with and old friendships to maintain, always achievements to acknowledge, birthdays to remember, and arrangements to endorse. Yet, since these expressions of relationships invariably bear the mark of productiveness, they indeed strengthen the "roots of instinctual constraint," as Marcuse (1987, 202, see above) put it.

Jacob Johanssen and I (2022) have used Otto Fenichel's (1939) notion of the counter-phobic attitude to capture the constant state of anxious alert that characterises current work in the digital. This mental state of precarity, I think, is a fitting picture of the dialectical switch from unlimited love to something decisively more deadly. It is that which I have sought to work out in Facebook's operational logics (cf. van Dijck and Poel 2013). Furthermore, when I compare this state of excessive love with a retrogradation of progress, this reverberates with Lauren Berlant's (2011) theory of *Cruel Optimism*. "A relation of cruel optimism exists when something you desire is actually an obstacle to your flourishing," goes the first sentence in her well-known study (p. 1). Hence, optimism turns cruel when "the object that draws your attachment actively impedes the aim that brought you to it initially" (ibid). Love understood as Eros – as a movement towards binding and combining – is akin to optimism in Berlant's definition, as "the force that moves you out of yourself and into the world" (p. 1). What turns Facebook's love cruel, in turn, is the very overflow of its offering, facilitating, and pushing of ties – *Connect with this. Befriend these. Follow those. Relate to that!*

When Hans Loewald (1988) sees in Eros the "perpetuation of tension" and the maintenance of "the excitation inherent in living substance" (p. 30), Facebook tends to dial this tension up to a degree at which it risks becoming painful for users, with burnouts a widespread form of digitally induced *jouissance*. Similarly, when Abel-Hirsch (2011) speaks of the "'little death' of orgasm" as "a workable limit" to the life drives of Eros (p. 1059), this points to the taboo of the consumption of love on Facebook since this would mean the engineering of a pause and break in the endless renewal of tension. As Losse (2012) writes, "[F]rom sex – the true, physical, total interlacing of bodies – you cannot go back to the virtual. [...] Real intimacy is the third rail of a publicity-driven, virtual society. We must avoid it at all costs" (p. 213–4). In 2010, at the height of her Facebook career, Losse decided to no longer avoid it: "I wanted – I needed to try to kill it. I felt a sudden urge to destroy this – the tension, the war, the endless battle to be loved and liked – once and for all," she writes (2012, 214).

A few weeks later Losse quit the company, sold her stocks, moved states, and started writing her behind-the-scenes book. Following Zuckerberg's motto, "Don't ask for permission, ask for forgiveness," she did "what Silicon Valley leadership really loves," specifically, she became "the person who leaves you and builds something else" (Losse in Kulwin 2018). Yet, by enacting this radical split, she chose the only negative stance towards the company that is available to staff and users alike. The erotic drive towards binding units into ever greater entities could not be lessened, abated, negotiated, or tempered with; rather, it could only be radically cut off and abandoned.

Notes

1 Freud's term "Trieb" has erroneously been translated as "instinct," a word that corresponds to the German "Instinkt," which Freud defined as closer to biology. Trieb ("drive") represents a concept of a phenomenon mediating between the biological and psychological. I will use the term "drive," but will leave quotations as they are.
2 https://www.theverge.com/2017/2/16/14642164/facebook-mark-zuckerberg-letter-mission-statement (accessed 14/04/2023).
3 See Cross (2017) and Lopato (2016) for notable exceptions.
4 These four phases I have constructed independently from Helmond, Nieborg, and van der Vlist's (2019) work on the evolutionary phases of the platform. The latter find four distinct phases in Facebook's evolution as well but base their suggestions on an analysis of the platform's development of "boundary dynamics" – i.e., the launch, gradual expansion, and modification of its developer platform, partnership programmes, and marketing tools. Apart from their analysis commencing with Facebook's launch of the developer platform in 2006 and, hence, at a later point than the present one, their historisation shows clear similarities. What I cover as phases two and three in this chapter prove relatively coextensive with Helmond et al.'s (2019) four phases of Facebook's political-economic paradigm shifts. Rightly, they take the period around Facebook's IPO (initial public offering) in May 2012 as a distinct phase of "infrastructural ambitions," which renders the periods from 2006 to 2010 (expansion) and from 2014 to 2018 (solidification) separate.
5 https://epublications.marquette.edu/zuckerberg_files_transcripts/720
6 https://about.fb.com/news/2021/10/facebook-company-is-now-meta/
7 As another instance of such conflict potential within the Life Drive, Freud points to cases where the sublimation of sexual desire towards others into tenderness renders sexual intercourse impossible: "Where they love they do not desire, and where they desire they cannot love" (Freud 1912d, p. 183).
8 I here follow the German translation of the dictionary, since in the English one at my disposal the entry on "Eros" (as distinct from that on "Life Instinct") has been elided.
9 Strachey discusses this in a footnote of his translation.
10 By contrast, when Robert W. Gehl (2012) judges the Facebook interface to be "muted" and "bland," attributing this blandness as intended not to "detract from marketing efforts" (p. 100), this gestures effectively towards the totalitarian aspects of Facebook's erotic mission again, which "reduces users to data sets and cybernetic commodities" (ibid.).

11 See Hans Block and Moritz Riesewieck's documentary film, *The Cleaners* (2018), for an impression of the conditions under which this work is done.
12 See Porter (2018), for a good analysis of the roots of this sentiment: https://www.nytimes.com/2018/04/17/business/economy/facebook-regulation-privacy.html (accessed 08/09/2023).
13 https://about.fb.com/news/2007/11/facebook-unveils-facebook-ads/ (accessed 08/09/2023).
14 *The Seminar of Jacques Lacan: The Four Fundamental Concepts of Psychoanalysis (Book XI).*
15 https://about.fb.com/news/2021/10/facebook-company-is-now-meta/ (accessed 14/04/2023).

Chapter 2

The feeding tube – YouTube, oral cravings, and the question of addiction

The media researcher Zeynep Tufekci dropped the following crushing critique of YouTube into an already heated debate, during a time when the video streaming platform had come under sharp criticism, mostly from investigative news media:

> YouTube has created a restaurant that serves us increasingly sugary, fatty foods, loading up our plates as soon as we are finished with the last meal. Over time, our tastes adjust, and we seek even more sugary, fatty foods, which the restaurant dutifully provides. When confronted about this by the health department and concerned citizens, the restaurant managers reply that they are merely serving us what we want.

(Tufekci 2018)

Along Tufekci's lines, the investigations claimed that YouTube's recommender system, i.e., the algorithm suggesting what video to play next (Zhao et al. 2019; Covington et al. 2016), had seemingly suggested increasingly extreme content to its users in an attempt at keeping them in front of their screens. With YouTube's AutoPlay function left 'on' by default, the service appeared to literally feed users this increasingly unhealthy 'grub on tap.' YouTube, these inquiries held, offered ever stronger admixtures of whatever 'substance' its users craved for as long as users passively nodded their acceptance. As Tufekci (2018) observed: "Videos about vegetarianism led to videos about veganism. Videos about jogging led to videos about running ultramarathons" (n.p.).

While this extremism appeared thus first and foremost to be an *extremism of form* – an *intensification of the affective stimulus* in the suggested videos – the political tensions and polarisations of the late 2010s in the USA, which reached a highpoint with the 2016 election of Donald Trump as president, added a more directly political dimension to this debate from the start. An inquiry by the *Wall Street Journal* had found that YouTube offered either far-right or far-left videos to users who would usually watch "relatively mainstream news sources" (Nicas 2018). This inquiry was related to computer-based experiments that ex-Google engineer Guillaume Chaslot (e.g., Lewis and McCormic 2018) had been conducting with YouTube's recommendation algorithm in which he managed to unearth a bias of

DOI: 10.4324/9781003307044-3

the system towards sensational and extreme contents put in place to keep viewers watching for as long as possible. After all, summarises Tufekci (2018), YouTube is owned by Google and Google is an "advertising broker selling our attention to companies that will pay for it. The longer people stay on YouTube, the more money Google makes" (n.p).

In the wake of these journalistic interventions, significant numbers of academic research studies have been conducted in attempts to test the accusations in more empirical depth (e.g., Chen et al. 2023; Matamoros-Fernández et al. 2021a; Faddoul et al. 2020; Hosseinmardi et al. 2021; Kaiser and Rauchfleisch 2019; Schmitt et al. 2018; Möller et al. 2018; for an overview of the field, see Yesilada and Lewandowski 2022; Snow 2021). While the findings have resulted in an ambiguous picture, YouTube itself has responded to the waves of critique by announcing changes to the ways its recommender system assembles the videos it suggests to the platform's users (e.g., Goodrow 2021; Zhao et al. 2019). While I will *not* devote much space to the question of automated political extremism in this chapter, it is important to emphasise that many studies have framed the problem of the promotion of extremism in relation to YouTube's recommender system as one in which artificial intelligence (AI) produces a marked dearth of diversity of information sources for users (e.g., Matamoros-Fernández et al. 2021b, Rieder et al. 2020) and thus risks to create "filter bubbles" (Pariser 2014) and "echo chambers" (Sunstein 2001; Dahlgren 2020). Yet, more recent findings suggest that, whereas this might have been true to a certain extent, the most important radicalisation dynamic on the platform is based on channels and subscribers, where people who already show extremist leanings seek out and subscribe to channels that reinforce their attitudes, worldviews, and inclinations (e.g., Chen et al. 2023). While they still make use of the possibilities that digital platforms and their algorithmic content-feeding patterns afford, specifically, to create highly customised and cognitively as well as affectively resonant "holding environments" (Winnicott), the recommender system, studies find, does not prove to be the central triggering factor of radicalisation.

Yet again, I wonder whether these findings and the ways in which they are framed do not short-change Tufekci's initial claim of an *extremism of form* built into the recommender system seeking to pacify people and retain them on the platform by offering increasingly 'sugary' contents. People, Tufekci's argument goes, are being radicalised through programmed, audio-visual feeding patterns, and this claim ties into a cultural imaginary that holds a deep, albeit brooding, fascination. Notions of being glued to one's screen, held, commanded, and transfixed by it, paralysed in front of it, without being able to avert one's eyes, indeed, of being sucked into the screen, are central to cultural imaginations, first and foremost of television, but also of other screens in television's wake, veering between outright horror and more dystopian visions of the fate and future of humankind. Furthermore, the colloquial image of the "couch potato" points to the obverse of the horrors alluded to in folklore, with the association with "potato chips" opening out onto images of stuffing oneself, with the couch as a morally dubious resting place between bed and chair, sitting, lying, and slouching, and the potato as a blueprint of the shape of humans suffering from obesity, lack of exercise and motion, lack of incentive, and lack of life energy. In this respect, the "couch potato" and other imaginaries of screen cultures past and present are not merely stereotypes. Already television throughout the second part of the 20th century tried to programme its offerings so as to retain audiences for increasingly longer times (Jardine et al. 2016). Digital recommendations based on collaborative filtering, data analytics, and machine learning promise to take these attempts at retention to new heights.

It is in the context of the oral appeal of visual materials that I find academic debates about "information diversity" and "deliberate democracy" to be dissatisfying and inadequate for determining YouTube's socialising effects on its users. Rather, what I want to move into the chapter's centre – and what triggered my inquiry into YouTube in the first place – is the theme of orality and oral cravings that Tufekci's culinary metaphor invokes. Hence, what I see Tufekci as tapping into by equating YouTube with a fast-food restaurant and the wider connotations of pacifying people with flavour-enhanced visual stimulation is the broader discourse on media addiction, or media dependency.

This notion of addiction and the fantasies it triggers have gained renewed currency over the past ten years in light of the corporate digital platforms' strategies of user acquisition and retention. These strategies have been oriented towards the maximising of user engagement, interaction, and "time on device" (e.g., Seymore 2019, 64), by engineering the withholding and dispensing of small rewards in the form of likes, shares, comments, and other nudges, such as stimulating content, achievements and user journeys, freebies, and invitations. These strategies have received their bearings from behaviouristic research into habit formation – a line of applied research in closest proximity to commercial enterprises, paradigmatically represented by the Centre for Captology at Stanford University (Fogg 2003).

What practically all reward strategies in current digital media have in common – and what academic and journalistic work of the late 2010s focused on (Alter 2017; Wu 2017; Stark 2018; Pilipets 2019; Aagaard 2021) – is that these engineered stimuli tap into human structures of desiring and gratification-seeking. The oldest, most basic, and primitive of these is derived from hunger and the craving for nourishment. Hence, while the debate about whether food can be seen as an object of addiction in line with other substance dependencies – alcohol and street drugs – is ongoing (e.g., Courtwright 2019), Freud's (1905a) identification of orality as a formative stage in the pregenital development of sexuality was an early pointer towards this connection. Lips, tongue, and mouth receive their sexual-excitational significance through a process of "anaclasis," i.e., a process in which (quasi-)sexual pleasures first arise by '*leaning on*' the infant's sucking of the breast as an instinctual response to basic needs. From there on, Freud held, these pleasures become increasingly independent from the exigencies of life and are then desired for their own sake. Especially disturbances in the infant-caregiver relationship and in the nursing situation can lead to fixations on and deadlocks formed around this erotogenic zone. Such deadlocks put people at risk of dependencies in that cravings derived from the oral zone – the *desire for hunger*, as one could formulate paradoxically – must be seen as an irresistible *desire for desire* itself (Lacan) – a desire which neuroscientific research (Fisher 2016 [1992]) has established as the major driver of dependencies per se.

As I will corroborate in this chapter, in its early instantiations, YouTube's recommender system was clearly designed with the aim of being as dependable to each user as possible and thus to maximise each user's feeding/watch time as far as possible, with the risk of creating dependencies and addictions on the users' part. In this respect, Tufekci's metaphor has been very much to the point, even though, from a psychoanalytically informed perspective, the scene is not a restaurant; rather, it is the nursery, with the primary caregiver feeding their child. By offering this image I do not want to imply that people who watch YouTube are children or are being turned into children; furthermore, I do not imply that there is not agency to be derived or pleasure to be gained from watching videos on the platform. Rather, my point is that *the way the recommender system addresses and interpellates users is as though they were children.* In the case of YouTube's algorithm, moreover, the logic is to never stop feeding, never stop offering food, and, hence, to not merely address people as infants, but *fixate* them at this stage. It is this form of offering nourishment that diminishes the value of what is being offered.

In response to criticism from public and academic bodies, the platform has vowed to be a more responsible 'parental figure' and take better care of its users. Hence, in a lengthy post on the YouTube blog, Christos Goodrow (2021), Vice President of Engineering, makes the point that the platform's system is no longer just about "recommendations," but about "*responsible* recommendations," no longer merely about "watchtime," but "*valued* watchtime" (Goodrow 2021, emphasis added), thus making responsibility and values (read: *virtues*) YouTube's new guiding principles and prerogatives. However, as I will argue, upon consulting existing engineering documents, this new responsibility proves grounded in a quasi-magical – fetishist – thinking, in which YouTube is suspended in a fantasy of 'having one's cake and eating it, too.' Specifically, the programming of YouTube's current recommender system, I hold, is based on the belief that it is possible to increase *both* users' time-on-device *and* the quality of their viewing experience. In other words, YouTube's engineers work on the premise that it is possible to capture people for ever-longer stretches on their devices and yet have this capture result in mental recreation, moral enrichment, and revitalisation. In the words of Zhao and colleagues (2019), their algorithmic structure for recommendations "… significantly improves both *engagement* and *satisfaction metrics*" (p. 48; emphasis added).

It is the inherent contradiction in what can be seen as YouTube's nursing practice – the contradiction between promising to prepare people to meet the world and keeping them locked into the platform's care – that I ultimately see as pertaining to the problem of radicalisation and extremism on the platform. No matter how stimulating the nourishment that YouTube has on offer, it always ends up serving it so as to keep people put. This has the potential to turn the most wholesome food into 'junk' – as it is offered as a retainer and not as a facilitator. Particularly, when YouTube responds to accusations of radicalisation in a fashion of tech-solutionism (Morozov 2013), with attempts at tweaking the algorithm and the system so that it makes better – healthier, more wholesome, and socially sustainable – suggestions, this shows how the debate of subject formation, of healthy upbringing, and of a sustainable basis for human thriving and well-being becomes established in the field of software programming, design, and Human-Computer Interaction. Hence, as I argue, whereas orality and an oral character formation are now defined by at least two qualities – that of feeding/being fed and of holding/being held (with stimulating/being stimulated as the effect of the former two) – addiction needs to be conceptualised as disturbances in one or all these three dimensions. In other words, people with dependency problems suffer either from not having been *fed* adequately according to their needs, or from not being *held* and/or *stimulated* adequately, or from a mixture of these, with the effect that both inner and outer directed relatedness become tempestuous.

What is interesting about the extremism debate is that both dimensions are being addressed here creatively and productively. Hence, the relationship of YouTube to extremism as it comes to the fore in my perspective is one that pushes extremism as a fatalistic affirmation of the malnourishment received and an explosive, cataclysmic response to the ways in which the platform has sought to retain users, while purporting to set them free. In other words, extremism on the platform has frequently taken the form of a vengeful dynamic along the lines of: '*If you treat me like dirt, I'll play dirty in return*' (cf. Johanssen and Krüger 2022; Green 2005). In this respect, whereas research indicates that the brunt of radicalisation on the platform happens through channels and subscriptions and has less to do with automatic recommendations, YouTube, I argue, is nevertheless well-advised to overhaul and work on the premises of how it recommends videos. For, in its current form, its developmental function has a double-binding (Bateson et al. 1956; Lorenzer 1978), and hence fixating and suffocating pull that at least some people seem to surrender to with the kind of nihilism and fatalism that has become a central aspect in late-modern forms of extremism (Figlio 2006; Krüger 2021).

In what follows, I will trace the link between corporate digital media, orality, and addiction by focusing on YouTube in relation to the problem of media addiction. I build my argument by way of an extended review of the existing literatures, with research on YouTube, its recommender system, its modes of production and consumption on the one side, and literature on addiction/dependency and the field of media addiction on the other. While there is insightful research on the conditions of content creation on the platform that would further strengthen my argument (see Glatt 2022; Glatt and Banet-Weiser 2021), I approach the platform exclusively from the side of video consumption. My aim in this respect is to navigate and negotiate the addictive potentials emanating from YouTube as a globally operating, post-televisual medium, as well as the discourses that help shape the social realities around these issues.

Following a notion suggested by Bernard Rieder and colleagues (2020), I have divided my findings into the following "argumentative narratives" (n.p.):

– In the context of the corporate digital platform ecosystem, I argue that YouTube – the second most visited website globally (behind Google Search) – is indeed a *feeding tube* and an oral apparatus that "stills" (in the sense of the German "stillen:" to abate as well as to numb) *those* cravings that have developed in the context of other digital media relations.

– In light of the wider sociocultural, political and economic sphere, I suggest that the oral cravings YouTube has been geared to meet should be seen in the context of the demands of a sociocultural climate in which people are expected to be productive, creative, self-responsible, and full of initiative. Hence, assessing YouTube's role and function in an overall psychic economy of digital media usage, the platform seems to offer a place where social media users can withdraw from the sociocultural and socioeconomic pressures that are importantly exerted by and via other platforms. Put differently, while Facebook, Instagram and Twitter (etc.) help form the ways in which people promote themselves by relating to and communicating with others, YouTube – by virtue of its recommender system and when used for consumption only – facilitates *non*-relating and *non*-communicating. As I show, when Caroline Bainbridge (2019) writes about the phenomenon of binge watching generally that it is "symptomatic of the cultural loss of certainties associated with dominant modes […] of ideological power" (p. 71), this captures my argument well.

– In the context of the wider field of digital social media platforms, then, YouTube takes on the function of an "anti-container." Along Wilfred Bion's (1962) lines, the containing function of primary objects consists in a subject projecting feelings that it cannot process by itself into another who is thus given the task to contain these feelings, by translating them into forms that, when returned to the subject, can be processed and worked through. By contrast, the notion of anti-container means a "thought destructive mechanism" (Sweet 2013, 146), by which unprocessed thoughts and feelings are merely stowed elsewhere without being returned and without being made more processable; rather, they are evacuated and, in this way, escaped from. YouTube, I argue, is a service that makes possible such a process of "anti-containing" as one of its main propositions. This highly problematic, dependency-inducing proposition will remain in place for as long as the platform does not seriously address and overhaul its strategy of keeping people in 'holding patterns.'

– I review the recent changes that YouTube has made on its recommender system along the above lines and make further suggestions for changes toward a more adequate –healthy and positively formative – diet of people's viewing habits.

In what follows, I first shed light on the psychoanalytic concept of orality itself, so as to then turn to neuroscientific advances into the nature of dependencies. This is followed by a coordination of these findings with psychoanalytic conceptualisations of addiction. Consecutively, I will turn to the research findings on media addiction, and here particularly those related to television addiction, which must be seen as a forerunner of and blueprint for discussions about YouTube. Importantly, and despite my overall interpretation of YouTube as an addiction machine, it is important to not misread the overall argument of this chapter as a stimulus-response-like claim of all-YouTube-users-are-addicts. Rather, each instance of addiction must be seen as a personal, individual attempt at addressing subjective suffering and/or enjoyment and solving a subjectively relational problem. And yet, there are cultural institutions and constellations – be they legal or illegal – that offer widely available recipes for such acts of problem solving. YouTube's recommender system, I argue, has largely been designed as one of them.

Part I: the question of orality

Considering the low esteem in which psychoanalytic theory has been held within media studies, it is little surprise that a focus on orality is nearly absent from current research on digital media (see Bainbridge 2019 and Kahr 2013 for exceptions). Indeed, not even within psychoanalytic theory-making itself does the category of the oral enjoy much currency. What has driven people working in a psychoanalytic paradigm to distance themselves from the notion of orality and has also kept non-psychoanalytically oriented people away from it are the belittling, pathologising, individualising, and moralising notions associated with it. As Edith Sabshin (1995) states: "The early psychoanalytic formulations often depicted drug addicts as hedonistic pleasure-seekers, bent on self-destruction" (p. 7).

Rooted in the early phases of psychoanalytic theory-making, offering oral understandings of addiction now seems, in the words of psychiatrist, psychoanalyst, and neuroscientist Edward Khantzian (1999), "highly speculative and embarrassingly unuseful" (Johnson 2003, 147, quoting Khantzian 1999, 375). However, while steering clear of paternalistic perspectives and assessments and by returning to Freud's conception of erotogenic zones and stages as anthropological (in the sense of true for all humans), I hold that the notion of the "oral" still has a strong explanatory potential, especially for current digital media culture that is geared towards the industrial production of craving (Courtwright 2019). In this context in particular, the primitive qualities of sucking/sucked, nursing/nursed, feeding/fed, holding/held, caring/cared for, nourishing/nourished, ingesting/ingested, but also biting/bit, devouring/devoured, incorporating/incorporated, introjecting/introjected, identifying/identified, and so on, have much to teach us about the affective forces that orient people and move them in certain social directions.

To offer a YouTube-related example, when Sharif Mowlabocus (2020) interprets the pleasures of the platform's "Unboxing" video genre (in which people take new, untouched objects out of their packaging and haptically demonstrate their sensual qualities) as quasi-sexual ones that, in line with Laura Mark's notion of "haptic visuality," make spectators "more inclined to graze than to gaze" (Marks 2000, in Mowlabocus 2020, 574), the category of the oral can help qualify the sexuality at play. Specifically, I maintain that this grazing, oral desire created in the joyful fetishisation of the wrapping and unwrapping of a product might be decisively *less phallic* than the author's references to hardcore pornography (Williams 1989; van Doorn 2010) suggest. Rather, I argue they might be more productively understood along the lines of what Darian Leader in his study on *Hands* (2016) observes as the original link between hand and mouth in human life. Thumb sucking, Leader writes, can start as early as 18 weeks after an embryo's conception in the womb (p. 15), and, until the dominance of sight intervenes, the mouth-hand interdependency is central to a neonate's relation with its environment. This interdependency, in turn, is particularly perceivable in the feeding situation: "Sucking and gripping correlate here, and [...] the activity of the mouth 'overflows' on to the hand, as the rhythms of sucking and swallowing saturate the hand musculature," Leader writes (2016, 16–7). With reference to Mowlabocus's (2020) interpretation of "unboxing" videos, one can say that this link between mouth and hand, which never vanishes completely, is operative in these videos, only in their cases, the activity of the hands overflows on to the mouth, producing a salivating, craving-inducing effect. And while babies in the first months of their lives bring all objects they touch up to their mouths for inspection, this is what is implied in unboxing videos, too – albeit symbolically.

Oral attachments – towards an expanded conception of orality

The above example's focus on body parts and hand-mouth coordination must not blind readers to the centrality of interpersonal relations in oral phenomena. As Stephen M. Johnson (1994) stated, dynamics that point to oral character structures have long since been approached from the perspective of attachment (Bowlby) and attunement (Stern). In this respect, the drive towards being "stilled," which rests on an anthropological need for food, warmth, and protection, must be seen as falling into (at least) two major phenomena: that of being fed – of being offered and taking in nourishment –and that of being held, calmed, and sheltered. The psychoanalyst Dianne Elise (2019) has given a vivid description of the aesthetic qualities of the nursing situation along the lines of what Julia Kristeva (2014) has coined "maternal eroticism":

> One can easily picture the sensual fascination infants and toddlers have with the mother's bodily presence: the "jewelry" of her face, eyes glistening, surely glass ornaments in their color and shine; teeth gleaming like a string of pearls, sensuous swirls of hair, the aromatic scent of her flesh, her milk. These aspects of color, light, and texture – beauty – must surely stir a pleasure center in the brain and intensify the erotic attachment to the mother, who appears as an aesthetic immanence sparkling like a human mobile over the crib.
>
> (Elise 2019, 6)

This primary scene – "an erotic relation *a deux*," as Elise (p. 5) calls it – literally *forms the mind*, she holds, and she quotes Meltzer and Harris Williams (1988) to drive home this point: "The infant-soul's interaction with the body spaces of the world-mother constitutes the formation of Mind ... the inside emerging outside, the outside sinking in and holding like a dream" (Meltzer and Harris Williams 1988, 189, quoted in Elise 2019, 6).

Such a scenic, interactional conception of subject formation (Lorenzer 2022 [1986]) is importantly connected to and based on the works of Donald W. Winnicott (2005 [1971]), who famously brought Lacan's (2006 [1949]) notion of the mirror stage in touch with the infant being held by the mother – *physically*, in mother's arms, as well as *mentally*, in the sense of mother and child making contact with each other's eyes in mutual love, appreciation, and acknowledgement. On the basis of this double dimension of being fed and held, Elise adds one more decisive aspect to the realm of oral attachment, specifically, that of *inspiration and stimulation*. She writes: "Certainly, providing a calm, secure atmosphere ('holding') and modulating distress ('containing') are crucial parental capacities, but in order to thrive, children also need stimulating engagements" (Elise 2019, 4). Returning to Winnicott, she points to his notions of "play" and "creative living" as coordinates for imagining what these engagements might entail. Furthermore, when Iain MacRury and Candida Yates (2016), in an article on mobile phones as transitional objects, refer to Winnicott's (1958) notion of "the capacity to be alone" as a "subtle specification for creative, independent and engaged living" (p. 47), this captures the aspect of stimulation well.

Yet, this stimulation, I hold, does not merely consist of positive aspects, but necessarily entails a degree of what Heinz Kohut (1971) has called "optimal frustration." Due to its negative connotations, this notion, which Kohut meant to refer to frustrations that are inevitable and unavoidable in human life and thus important challenges for further development and growth, has encountered significant resistance within psychoanalytic and therapeutic circles. Subsequently, it has mostly been replaced by less ambiguous words, such as "responsivity" and "resonance." Contrary to this discursive practice, I find "optimal frustration" an apt notion in the context of the technological envelopment of human needs and desires in that it points to the need to envisage – as well as design and programme – ways for people to exit, grow out of, and leave behind such quasi-parental (maternal) folds.

Ultimately, of central importance to an updated psychoanalytic conception of orality, Didier Anzieu's (1979) work between holding and attachment introduces notions of lack and dynamics of compensation into Elise's vision of ideal dyadic eroticism. Anzieu, too, refers to Winnicott's holding and Bion's containing functions which he connects with a human-being's capacity to think as a foundationally creative act (Anzieu 1979, 23). Presenting materials from one of his analyses, Anzieu speculates about a key moment in his analysand's treatment: "Perhaps the reason [the analysand] comes to these sessions is not so much to be fed by me," he ventures, "but rather to be carried and warmed by me; to be manipulated and, through the exercise, to regain the potential offered by his body and mind" (Anzieu

1979, 24). Based on the reconstruction of the analysand's early memories, Anzieu concludes that "he was adequately fed, but he expected me to provide [...] stimulation of his psyche" (p. 25).

In these negotiations between being fed, being held, and being stimulated, I argue, we find an adequate, relational field for understanding addiction and dependency through a psychoanalytic lens. This field, I argue further, is coextensive with a contemporary definition of orality and oral attachment, and it is in these primary-oral dimensions of feeding, holding, and stimulating that YouTube as a platform and the debate about the platform's recommender system need to be brought into view. In this perspective, as I unpack below, addiction can be defined as a precarious form of stilling – an anti-containing of the feeding, holding, and stimulation functions.

Approaching the 'stilling' zone

Perhaps the most poignant example of how and to what ends orality works in addictive human-machine relations can be found in Natasha Dow Schüll's (e.g., 2005; 2014) ethnographic work on machine gambling in Las Vegas. Here, she focuses, as she writes, "on the design and play of digital gambling platforms to illuminate the distinctive rationalities and libidinal investments of the 'digital age'" (2005, 66). While many media studies scholars have pointed out that Schüll's findings pertain to digital media more generally,[1] what has received less attention is Schüll's detailed analysis of the gambling industry's attempts at recreating the primary oral nursing situation. As she details, gamblers are to be made physically comfortable, with "special seats to 'eliminate hard, sharp edges coming in contact with the main arteries of the legs,'" with "screens that slant at 38 degrees and game controls positioned within easy reach," with "embedded television" and "personal messaging" options, as well as "noise cancellation technology to remove 'destructive interference' coming from the outside world" (Schüll 2005, 68). Along the same lines, Courtwright (2019, 196) remarks that digital gambling machines now usually offer the possibility to click-order customised drinks to one's seat ... and come with YouTube built in as a pre-set channel.

The effect that these amenities are calculated to have is a "dissociated subjective state that gamblers call the 'zone'" (Schüll 2005, 73). This "zone" has the qualities of: "being alone, not being interrupted, speed, choice, tempo" (ibid). As the author emphasises, *being alone* is equivalent to creating the conditions for "getting lost" and for facilitating the flow that players do not want to have interrupted. *Speed* results in an "illusion of control" where a constant string of *choices* has the effect of suspending gamblers in a paradoxical opposite of control, specifically, "a sort of holding pattern" (ibid). As one of the gamblers in Schüll's study explained: "You can play the machines when you're totally numb and exhausted because they require just enough of your attention that you can't really think about anything else" (ibid). The tempo, in turn, is similar to what psychoanalyst Daniel Stern (e.g., 1985) has labelled attunement; Schüll quotes an industry spokesperson who calls the rapport between player and machine "hitting the harmonic" or being "in tune" (p. 74).

Money, as such, disappears: "You're not playing for money; you're playing for credit. Credit so you can sit there longer, which is the goal. It's not about *winning*; it's about *continuing to play*" (Schüll 2005, 75). At its core, this playing thus means a state of fusion with the machine – "human and machine seem to *merge*" (p. 76) – which allows a state of "bodily abandonment" that can last for hours – "the next thing I knew the sun was coming up," a gambler is quoted (ibid).

But what drives this craving for such spells of fusion? In a stunning chapter in her book, Schüll (2014) sheds light on gamblers' life stories, with the central recurring theme in them being an existential lack of control. Abusive and/ or absent parents, dying siblings and children, harsh poverty, and an alarming lack of stability are the problems that are addressed – and 'stilled' – by habitually latching on to gambling machines. Gambling in this perspective is a way of repeating the losses in one's life which one could *not* control and replacing them with losses that one feels one *can* control, even if only in a precarious way. In line with Freud's (1920) notion of the "death drive," Schüll (2014) finds in her gamblers the ultimate goal of returning "to a state of rest, stillness, and peace in which all needs and desires [...] were cancelled out" (p. 223). She suggests that: "addictions can be understood as a pathological intensification of the death drive, in which an individual attempts to bypass the roundabout struggles of life in order to 'attain its life's aim rapidly – by a sort of short-circuit'" (Schüll 2014, 223, quoting Freud 1920, 39).

Elegantly, this captures the way in which I understand addiction in this chapter as well, with a fixation on being fed and being held serving an interminable, inexhaustible longing for being 'anti-stimulated.' Hence, when Alistair D. Sweet (2013) suggests Bion's (1962) term "anti-container" and Green's (2002a) "anti-time" as ways of defining the core of dependency, explaining that "the addict progressively inhabits a liminal space, [...] where inter-personal relationships break down, self-neglect becomes common and the flow of time slows" (p. 144), this once more points to the relevance of a process of "stilling" as presented in this chapter.

Part II: perspectives on dependency and addiction

Desiring desire – neuroscientific works on addiction

Despite its life at the margins, the early 21st century has been an exciting time for psychoanalysis. After all, neuroscience and its project of mapping the brain and understanding basic ways of human functioning continue to corroborate psychoanalytic theories of human relatedness significantly more often than they refute them. Tragicomically, neuroscience frequently does this in a way that ignores the relevance of people's real-world relationships and the patterns of their lives' interwovenness with others so that there now seems plenty of room for psychoanalytic thinking to re-enter the field as a missing link.

This is clearly the case in research on addiction, which has undergone major changes in the era of neuroscience. Whereas early research had established the substance and a person's preference for it as the most significant elements of a dependency, with the activity of 'enjoying something' as the main connector, improved ways of mapping the brain centres entailed in addictive behaviours and experimenting with their responsiveness to varying stimuli brought about a new paradigm for understanding dependency overall: the Brain Disease Model (BDM). While it had already been apparent that drugs and other stimuli can release dopamine which then activates the brain's "reward pathways" (Courtwright 2019, 167), what brain imaging technologies have added in the meantime is that the brain's dopamine receptors become reduced in the course of their repeated activation, which increases both "tolerance to and dependence on the outside stimulus" (ibid). This reduction could be traced to those brain centres responsible for mood-regulation as well as those occupied with judgement and self-control. "Addiction was like a workout in reverse," writes the historian of addiction David T. Courtwright (2019), "Instead of adding self-discipline, it inexorably reduced it, along with the pleasure to be had from the activity" (p. 167).

Building upon these findings, further advances have underlined the robustness of once-established dependencies, showing that human brains not merely release dopamine in a situation in which an activity is performed and rewarded. Rather, in Courtwright's words: "They released the neurotransmitter not just when we engaged in these activities, but when we encountered cues associated with them" (ibid). Put differently: "Desire escalated independently of the pleasure it produced [...]. Wanting was a keener and more persistent feeling than liking" (ibid). As media critic Richard Seymore (2019) sums up these findings poetically, addiction is "not about pleasure, but desire. Addiction is something that is done with wanting, by those who are done with wanting" (p. 67). When Seymore refers in this context to Helen Fisher's neuroscientific work on love and romance, the latter's findings go to show just how flexible dependencies can be in relation to the objects and substances people become dependent on. Together with colleagues, Fisher (2016) made functional magnetic resonance imaging scans of the brains of people who had recently gone through a severe relationship breakup with a beloved person. Prompting these people to think of their ex-partners, the results, she writes, were "stunning":

> Brain activations occurred in several regions of the reward system. Included were regions of the ventral tegmental area (VTA) associated with feelings of intense romantic love; the ventral pallidum, associated with feelings of deep attachment; the insular cortex and the anterior cingulate, associated with physical pain, anxiety, and the distress associated with physical pain; and the nucleus accumbens and orbitofrontal/prefrontal cortex, brain regions associated with assessing one's gains and losses – as well as craving and addiction. Most relevant to our story, activity in several of these brain regions has been correlated with the craving for cocaine and other drugs.
>
> (Fisher 2016, 163)

The circumstance that one human-being can 'check' all the 'neurotransmitting boxes' of a dependency in another is a strong indication for the central role that our relationships with one another play in the cravings to which we succumb. Displacing this hunger for love on a wide palette of objects and (anti)containers, the universal structure of addiction is one of a desire that increases while its possibility of satisfaction/gratification decreases over time. What is interesting from a psychoanalytic perspective is that, in this gradual disappearance of gratification which leaves desire unbound, Lacan's conception of desire as *desire for, or of, desire* (e.g., McGowan 2015, 10) has found a corroboration and neuroscientific proof.

The oral, in turn, appears central in this conception of addiction, as urges and cravings increasingly stray from their contexts of gratification to become urges in and for themselves. Remarkable, too, in this context, is that, as Courtwright (2019) observes, the BDM was not introduced and made popular in relation to drug addiction, but rather in relation to "morbidly obese individuals who could not quit eating" (p. 171). He further points to a Yale international conference on food and addiction held in 2007 as the breakthrough moment that helped introduce the link between hunger and addiction to a wider public. In the wake of this conference, writes Courtwright, food addiction received "good press, and lots of it" (p. 172), and he quotes Oprah Winfrey as a central influence. "My drug of choice is food. [...] I use food for the same reasons an addict uses drugs: to comfort, to soothe, to ease stress," Winfrey confessed (2009, quoted in Courtwright 2019, 172).

Courtwright (2019, 193ff) places his chapter on "Digital Addictions" in direct succession to that on "Food Addictions." And whereas I am not following the author in his strongly generalising approach of pooling all digital social media into the same 'phenotypical pot' of digital dependency, the close ties between digital media design and dependencies of an oral kind, alluded to in his book's organisation, hold true. Yet, whereas neuroscientific research, with its individualising focus on individual brains, tends to emphasise the feeding aspect of orality, especially Fisher's (2016) research on love also points to a quality of holding and the highly addictive effects of becoming barred from such holding. Elise (2019) evokes a similar image of withdrawal suffering when vividly envisioning the experience of the primary dyad: "[W]ho is this fantastic creature we come into the world to meet?" she asks taking on the perspective of the newborn child:

> She belongs to us, or does she? Doubt creeps in, tainting paradise. One thing is clear: we want her, and in the most erotic of ways – body and soul. Our lust is total, all-encompassing. She must be ours. Possession is essential. But she is coy, not always available, making us wait, playing "hard to get." Where does she go? (We don't yet know to wonder – too painful – "Who (else) is she with?") We are each a lover naïve to the possibility of infidelity. She is surely ours; it is a question of waiting—which is hard enough, almost impossible. But she is worth the wait. When she returns, she is lovely, wonderful, the most beautiful, sensual

of creatures on any earth. We are together; this is heaven on earth. What could go wrong? (We have, for the moment, forgotten about the waiting part ...).

(Elise 2019, 5–6)

Translating this vivid rendering of the *Fort Da* game – of the comings and goings of mother – (Freud 1920) into patterns of dependency, the question of "possession" which is entirely bound up with that of "waiting" in addiction points to the related, intersubjective question of being held (or not) that seems to play an equally central role.

Psychoanalytic approaches to dependency

As Edith Sabshin (1995) shows in her historical overview of psychoanalytic approaches to addiction, an advanced understanding of drug use as having strong defensive as well as adaptive relational elements has long been in the making. As of today, a notion of addiction as a precarious solution to relational disturbances and an inability to tolerate closeness and regulate emotions has become a widespread scholarly paradigm within and beyond the borders of psychoanalytic research.

The psychoanalytic study of drugs and addiction proper is frequently seen to begin with Sandor Rado's 1926 article, "The Psychic Effects of Intoxicants, an Attempt to Evolve a Psychoanalytic Theory of Morbid Cravings." Rado's neologism, *psychothymis*, which he added to his work on addiction in 1933, already points to *that* process of the becoming autonomous of craving and desire from the object which neuroscientific research has corroborated much more recently. A first important connection between orality and primary relationality, i.e., of being not merely fed but also held, was drawn by Ernst Simmel in a paper published three years after Rado's, called "Psychoanalytic Treatment in a Sanatorium" (1929). As Sabshin (1995) summarises the sanatorium's central treatment strategy:

> When the patient was completely deprived of the drug he was permitted to stay in bed and assigned a special nurse who encouraged him and looked after his personal welfare. In spite of conscious torments the patient had his deepest longings satisfied, namely, the longing to be a child, to be in bed, to have a kind mother attend to him and feed him, a mother who is always there when he is anxious. Withdrawal from this phase of treatment was understood as a repetition of the weaning period.
>
> (Sabshin 1995, 11, referring to Simmel 1927, 85–6)

In this passage, it becomes perceivable how, from the first, primitive oral cravings are entangled with likewise fundamental modes of holding. As Simmel (1927) himself writes about his sanatorium's treatment-as-weaning strategy: "We create the situation of having the mother once more close at hand" (p. 86).

This idea of a return to the primary dyad is also central in Robert Savitt's 1963 paper "Psychoanalytic Studies on Addiction, Ego Structure and Narcotic

Addiction." Here, Savitt's main point (derived from Fenichel's [1945] work) is that the addict's principal aim is to get rid of pain and "escape from intolerable tension," and this point makes explicit the compensatory viewpoint that henceforth has dominated psychoanalytic theory-making in the field. When Victor Wurmser, in his influential "Psychoanalytic Considerations of the Etiology of Compulsive Drug Use" (1974), emphasised as the motivation for drug use to abate the accusatory voice of the super-ego which attacks the ego for both its carelessness and its dependency, this added another important piece in the mosaic of understanding dependencies psycho-dynamically.

From Wurmser onwards, the development of the field and its entering into dialogue with neuroscience hinges significantly on Edward J. Khantzian. In an article from 2003, Khantzian powerfully sums up his work at the intersections of neurobiology and psychoanalysis in the dictum that "[a]ny theory or explanation of addiction that does not address what it is in the workings of the mind (i.e., the inner psychological terrain) and a person to predispose and cause them to repeatedly relapse to addictive drugs is incomplete" (p. 8). The way in which he addressed this individual predisposition is through a vision of dependency as a "self-regulation disorder" and drugs as specific means of self-medication in response to subjective distress or suffering: "Addictive substances relieve human psychological suffering, and there is a significant degree of psychopharmacologic specificity in the appeal of addictive drugs," he writes (2003, 10).

When psychiatrist and neuroscientist Hedy Kober (2014) corroborates Khantzian's findings of drug use as problem solving and an attempt at emotion regulation (p. 430), this indicates how deeply the psychoanalytic paradigm has sunken into the neuroscientific and cognitive mainstream. At the same time, however, it also suggests how submerged this paradigm and its merits have become by this mainstream in that the psychoanalytic roots of this knowledge are no longer clearly visible. Rather, they are covered over by cognitive-behavioural approaches whose success rates have proven more easily quantifiable in treatment (cf. Kober 2014, 438–9). And while it remains a point of contention whether psychoanalysis is indeed a less adequate treatment form for dependencies (see Dodes 2003, for a critique of this widespread view), there is little in the literature at my disposal that would give reason for hope for a psychoanalytic revival in the field. Rather, psychoanalysis seems to have settled for a second-tier status, where, as Brian Johnson (2003) writes, it may be "essential for those patients who have failed at shorter, less expensive treatments" (p. 153).

Shifting the "addictive focus" – from substance to media

When Lance M. Dodes (1996; 2002) defines all addictive acts as displacements, "in which addictive behaviour is a substitute for taking a direct action to combat the intolerable state of powerlessness" (Dodes 2002, 125), this anticipates once more recent neuroscientific findings of the fluidity of the addict's object of dependency. Hence, Kober and colleagues' (2016) functional Magnetic Resonance

Imaging (fMRI) scan findings that gambling addiction shows strong similarities to substance addictions in terms of the neural processes involved give fresh lease to Dodes's (2002) claim of a "lack of importance of physical addiction" (p. 125), where people might shift their "addictive focus" (p. 126) from one preoccupation to another, for example, from drugs to gambling or 'workaholism.' It is this fluidity and flexibility in relation to one's object dependency that makes the transition from drugs to food, or from food to media, possible and plausible in the first place.

Furthermore, recent work by Ana Estevez and colleagues (2017), who have researched the relationship between emotional regulation and attachment "with substance (alcohol and drug abuse), and non-substance-related addictions (gambling disorder, video game addiction, and problematic Internet use) in adolescents and emerging adults" (p. 534), found that, while emotional regulation was a prevalent issue in all addictive behaviours, attachment issues came more clearly to the fore in non-substance and media-related addictions. While their study shows that all addictive behaviours were used incrementally in order to resolve and counter negative emotional states, non-substance-related addictions were more often correlated to poor relations with and attachments to parents and/or peers. This finding feeds into my claim that YouTube – on the consumers'/viewers' side – might indeed be understood as a tool with which to *still* relational social pressures. Additionally, the study found a gender difference, with female participants turning more to "Internet overuse" to address problems of attachment to their parents and peers, while male participants tended to turn to gambling and gaming in response to similar problems. Arguably, it remains anybody's guess what labels such as "Internet overuse" mean in practice; yet, in broad strokes, these findings gesture towards a partitioning of social scenes in which girls and women seek to abate their relational challenges in social media's containment of acknowledgement in metrics, while boys and men rather seek out the anti-containers of controlled loss.

Especially the male 'drugs of choice,' gambling and gaming, which can be seen as predominantly oral, come close to the context of YouTube as a digital, user-based, and user-generated iteration of the television genre. With respect to the theme of television and addiction, or better: the presumed addictiveness of television as a medium, a review article by Robert McIlwraith and colleagues (1991) offers a very plausible bottom line. Importantly, what they found is that the phenomenon of television addiction was mostly attributable to a "third-person effect," specifically the belief that television was *not* addictive for oneself personally, neither for one's close ones, but rather for *other people, elsewhere* (McIlwraith et al. 1991, 111). Yet, for those who *judged themselves* to be television addicts – which, depending on the respective study, amounted to up to 12% of respondents – findings were very much in line with the oral attachment-style thesis that I am fleshing out in this chapter.

What studies corroborated to relevant degrees is that self-professed TV addicts used television as a form of escape and withdrawal from overstimulation, as well as from negative emotions and life circumstances. They frequently had the television on as a way of dividing their attention while doing other things and thus used television as a mood regulator. Particularly dysphoric, painful, and negative emotions were sought to be abated through watching, and the television was also kept on so as to fill unstructured, unfilled, and empty time. Self-defined TV addicts often watched with, and despite, feelings of guilt and shame, as well as despite being aware that the programmes they watched were of poor quality. The reward that most of them connected with watching TV was that of relaxation. As McIlwraith and colleagues (1991) write: "Not only does television relax people, it does so quickly. Within moments of sitting or lying down and pushing the power button, most viewers will feel more relaxed than they did before" (p. 117). However, in line with other addictions, heavy viewers reported decreasing degrees of relaxation and a need to prolong watching time so as to reach a desired point of relaxation again. "Viewing begets viewing," the authors state, "One must keep watching in order to feel relaxed" (ibid).

To bring the focus back onto YouTube, Bernhard Rieder and colleagues (2020) recently conducted a large-scale, automated mapping exercise in an attempt to map the YouTube platform in its entirety. Based on an aggregation of datapoints from over 36 million channels (those with 1,000 followers or more), what they found is – somewhat anticlimactically – that the platform, once hailed as driving the democratisation of television, has begun to look increasingly like traditional mainstream television. In the authors' words, what their findings suggest is YouTube's overall evolution towards a "saturated mass media outlet, where a small number of high-visibility channels preside over a large mass of channels struggling to join their ranks and achieve economic viability" (n.p.). These high-visibility channels lead the way towards an overall professionalisation of content producers that goes hand-in-hand with a mainstreaming of content so as to make it advertising-friendly, with most of the heavily watched channels being English-speaking and US-based. Simply put, YouTube, by and large, now looks suspiciously like traditional television, with "'softer' topics like Lifestyle, Entertainment, and Music indeed mak[ing] up the vast majority of contents on offer" (Rieder et al. 2020, n.p.). In yet other words, what people seem to be looking for on YouTube is the comforting warmth of a familiar 'safe space.'

Part III: the feeding tube – YouTube's oral recommendations

At this point, I have brought together the most relevant positions from the fields of psychoanalytic, neuroscientific, and media studies research on addiction and orality. In the following, I want to change tack and offer a close reading of YouTube's algorithmic architecture so as to bring the above positions to bear on it. Hence, what I want to show is how the platform's recommender system has become oriented towards the processes of feeding and holding of users along the lines of anti-containment and stilling outlined above. I will do so in four consecutive steps. First, I introduce the major developmental steps that have led up to the kind of recommender system that can currently be found in automated information retrieval systems. Second, I zoom in on the specific architecture of YouTube's system. Here,

I identify the design goals of *entailment* and 'responsibility' as the strategic build-ing blocks at the centre of YouTube's oral orientation. Third, I shed light on the programming changes that have been introduced to the recommender system in recent years in response to the widespread critique levelled against it. In so doing, I aim to show in a fourth and final step how these attempted changes are caught in a quasi-magical, fetishist thinking of "having one's cake and eating it, too."

"People who also..." – early advances in reinforcement learning

As far as the historical development of recommender systems is concerned, Seaver (2019) locates their origins in the mid-1990s, where they were developed "as tools to help users manage increasingly large catalogs of information" (p. 428). The main metric that dominated the system development in the 1990s was the "Root Mean Square Error (RMSE)," which allowed predictions about how users would rate an item by continuously comparing actual ratings with the system's prior predictions (Seaver 2019, 428). While this trial-and-error approach to self-learning, known as reinforcement learning (Williams 1992), has remained a central tool in AI for recommender systems, the importance of ratings has waned. As much as engineers strove to make their systems produce relevant recommendations, there remained a margin of error that could only be lowered with programming complexity and computational resources that went far beyond what is possible and economical for large-scale services such as Netflix[2] or YouTube. From a psychoanalytic perspec-tive, the "magic barrier" that engineers bumped up against might just as well have to do with the human condition itself, that is, with a principal 'un-satisfiability' of desire, with a narcissistic current in humans that resists all-too eager attempts to please them.[3]

While there are trends perceivable in the recent engineering literature that also such human vulnerabilities are being taken into the design of self-learning sys-tems (which I will broach below), the belief in the perfect computation of human wanting remains undeterred. And a major step in this direction was made when, by virtue of the tracking of user engagement data, companies and their engineers obtained access to data sources that proved superior to ratings. Specifically, track-ing users on and across various platforms showed that there is a viable difference between what people *rate* highly (if they submit ratings at all), and what people *actually spend time engaging with*. Hence, what the analysis of "dwell time," i.e., the time users spend engaging with items as a form of "implicit feedback," has made possible is to determine what people *really* do on a platform. In line with the definition of addiction in this chapter, it is mainly features related to "dwell time" that make it possible for YouTube to offer diets to individual users that are customised to be soothing and comforting – sugary and fatty, as Tufekci (2018) put it – and thus compensatory and precarious.

Yet, it is *not* first and foremost at the level of the *individual user* that engage-ment data becomes relevant for automated recommendations. Rather, at a first level of analysis, what the availability of this data makes possible are processes of "collaborative filtering" (Koren, Bell and Volinsky 2009), i.e., the establishment of similarities across larger groups of users, which facilitate the creation of *neighbourhoods* of likeminded people on a platform with reasonably similar tastes. Amazon's "People who bought this product also bought…" is merely one of the better-known examples of such algorithmic user-affiliation processes. In a related context, Weston and colleagues (2010) dub the analytic yield of such aggregate processing "sibling precision" (p. 22).

Entailment and 'responsability' – the oral logic of YouTube recommendations

How recommendation systems move from the preferences of neighbours and siblings to those of individuals is unpacked in a key text on YouTube's algorithmic structure, "Deep Neural Networks for YouTube Recommendations," by Google engineers Covington, Adams, and Sargin (2016). This text holds a central place in the engineering literature, due to the advances it presents in the use of AI. Announcing "Dramatic performance improvements brought by deep learning" at an "industrial" scale (p. 191) also helped this publication's fame well beyond informatics and programming circles. Indeed, part of the public outcry against YouTube has been related to this publication.[4]

The article outlines the general structure and main building blocks of YouTube's recommender system. Along the lines of what is known in the field as a "classic two-stage information retrieval" model (Covington et al. 2016, 191), this system is divided into the tasks of (a) finding videos that fit certain preferences (candidate generation) and (b) the ranking of these candidate videos into a list of recommendations personalised for each user. Both tasks are performed by neural-networked AI, grounded in Google Brain's Tensor Flow project (Abadi et al. 2015).

While candidate generation consists in the system going through the vastness of YouTube's ever-growing video archive, which it then narrows down to a selection of hundreds of videos that it subsequently feeds into the ranking network, this latter's task is to create a hierarchy of the generated items according to a probability of video watches, which is ultimately slimmed down to dozens (Covington et al. 2016, 192). On the side of candidate generation, write the authors, the network "only provides broad personalisation via collaborative filtering," with the similarity of users being "expressed in terms of coarse features such as IDs of video watches, search query tokens and demographics" (ibid). By contrast, on the ranking side, "presenting a few 'best' recommendations in a list requires a fine-level representation to distinguish relative importance among candidates with high recall" (ibid). This is done, write Covington et al. (2016) vaguely, "by assigning a score to each video according to a desired objective function using a rich set of features describing the video and user" (ibid). Harking back to Tufekci's (2018) food metaphor, candidate generation can thus be imagined as a 'canteen' where what is made will be halfway palatable for a large amount of people. At the level of candidate ranking, in turn, each user, at least in theory, gets their own 12-course (and beyond) menu, catered specifically to their 'unique' tastes.

But what are the mysterious "objective function[s]" and "rich set[s] of features" describing videos and users? The "desired objective function" seems easy enough to guess, namely, that the user indeed clicks on and watches the videos offered to them. However, also this function is quickly complicated even by general considerations as for example how to treat videos containing nudity or violence. The "rich set of features," in turn, is still harder to come by. However, there are hints strewn across various texts connecting to Covington et al. (2016). Hence, already the "coarse" collaborative features of the 'canteen phase' entail significant refinements. Spatial information, for example, as to where users are in the world holds nuanced cues about what to offer – e.g., spicy or bland; or prone to like coriander or not. Likewise, information on whether users arrive at their YouTube starting page or click on a video embedded elsewhere (dining out or home delivery), and temporal cues such as when a user logs on (breakfast, lunch, or dinner), how long it has been since they searched for, clicked on, or watched a video last (seldom guest or regular customer), and the sequence of videos watched (starter, main course, or dessert), can offer relevant hints about what might be watched next. This information, paired with knowledge about collaborative watch histories (table for four, please), the kind of device with which a user is accessing YouTube content (TV dinner or grabbing something on the go), their logged-in state, plus simple demographic information as age and gender already make for a reasonably well-rounded impression.

In terms of temporality, a substantial gain in accuracy in recommendations has also been reached through the system's time sensitivity as concerns the content that is constantly published on the platform. While "users prefer fresh content, though not at the expense of relevance […,] Machine learning systems often exhibit an implicit bias towards the past because they are trained to predict future behavior from historical examples," write Covington et al. (2016, 193). For this reason, You-Tube's recommender system has an "example age" feature built into its candidate generator – an "expiry date," so to speak – that improves user clicks and video watches by forecasting "the future peak day of viral videos" (Jiang et al. 2014). Leaning on Bucher's (2020) notion of the "right time," one can say that YouTube recommendations are highly sensitised towards meal or feeding times across the breadth of the platform.

Turning to the ranking procedure, Covington et al. (2016) write that "we have access to many more features describing the video and the user's relationship to the video" (p. 195). However, it is on this point of concrete user relationships that the article becomes markedly vague. This is in line with Google's overall approach. Time and again, Google/Alphabet has asserted that such features are extremely hard to pinpoint and describe to laypeople. Similarly, Facebook keeps referring to the protection of personal data to keep their programming design secret. "Due to the data sensitivity in nature and the company policy, we are not able to reveal the detail on the actual features we use," write Xinran He and colleagues (2014, 7) about Facebook's automatic ad auction model.

Beyond the protection of corporate secrets, however, determining how neural networks actually work in the construction and analysis of features has indeed proven difficult. Accordingly, in a survey of AI-driven recommender systems, Shuai Zhang and colleagues (2018a) emphasise the importance of transparent recommendations with deep learning "to make explainable predictions to users, allowing them to understand the factors behind the network's recommendations" (p. 5:27). At the same time, however, when they bemoan that existing works "do not utilize [the] various forms of side information in a comprehensive manner to take the full advantages of the available data" (p. 5:26), this refers not merely to "contextual information" and its pairing with "implicit feedback" from the users' histories on the platform. Rather, they also suggest to further investigate "users' footprints (e.g., tweets or Facebook posts) from social media and the physical world (e.g., Internet of things)," arguing that "the deep learning method is a desirable and powerful tool for integrating these additional pieces of information" (Zhang 2019, 5:26). In this respect, then, it does not seem overly farfetched for the case of YouTube to expect data from other Alphabet/Google-owned services, for example from Gmail accounts, to be fed into YouTube recommendations, so that people's state of employment, the field of their occupation as well as further interests and hobbies etc., might also weigh in on personal recommendations. In any case, prior studies with a focus on the features guiding recommendations have shown that "historical features" (He et al. 2014), i.e., features that pertain to "long-time accumulated user behavior" (p. 8), are by far the most important ones for predictive uses. Studying the predictability of users clicking on ads on Facebook, Xinran He and colleagues (2014) found that: "The top 10 features ordered by importance are all historical features" (p. 7).

Expanding on this focus on user histories, Covington et al. (2016) see the main challenge in feature engineering "in *representing a temporal sequence of user actions* and how these actions relate to the video impression being scored" (p. 196; emphasis added). Now, this statement might seem relatively unremarkable, even to critical readers who have become reasonably thick-skinned about the intrusiveness of corporate digital platforms. And yet, the exact wording of this quotation is striking. Specifically, what is etched out here as the target result is not so much a series of snapshots of user actions over time. Such a snapshot model would merely be in line with the common knowledge that, in dynamic environments, it is worth "retraining [the system] on a daily basis" (He et al. 2014, 4). By contrast, YouTube's engineering team is not so much concerned with identifying user characteristics *independent* of the videos on offer. Rather, the key to the engineering task as Covington et al. (2016) define it is to find those "forms of interaction" (Lorenzer 2022) that are neither the properties of the users alone, nor those of the videos to be ranked, but of both these together.

For the field of psychosocial studies, psychoanalyst and sociologist Alfred Lorenzer defines specific "forms of interactions" as the relay stations between a socialised subject and this subject's object world, explaining that: "The scenic unity of the sensorimotor experiential patterns can be illustrated through a banal analogy: Just as the sound of the mouse *entails* the cat's turn of the head, so the stimulus always finds its reaction" (Lorenzer 2022, 59, emphasis added). It is this conception of entailment, I argue, that has been the aim of designing YouTube's recommender system. Hence, when Covington et al. (2016) observe that "continuous features describing past user actions on related items are particularly powerful because they generalize well across disparate items," this demonstrates the platform's interest in creating such entailment relations through what Covington and colleagues call "responsive recommendation." Going beyond a naïve conception of user and video features and aiming to identify those interlocking forms of interaction between user and platform that can no longer be located merely on the user's or the platform's side; rather, what the recommender system aims at is the form of rhythmic attunement that already Schüll (2014) found in the statements of engineers of gambling machines and industry representatives. On this basis, what Covington et al. (2016) want their system to reach is a level of responsiveness that makes it possible to "model expected watch time" (p. 197) for each of its users. This is a remarkably realistic approach: not all forms of interaction can lead to the exploitation of the same potential for maximising results, and the recommender system that the authors design is geared to reflect that. Rather, each relationship – although embedded in homophilic neighbourhoods – is being negotiated individually so as to arrive at *that* individual rhythmic pattern of interaction between user and platform which can be maximally exploited. The system, in other words, is engineered to find the optimal point of "respons-*a*bility" with each user. Along Lorenzerian lines, one could say that the infant's cry entails the onset of milk in mother's breast.

All watched over by machines of loving grace – YouTube in search of a parental role

In the years after the publication of Covington et al.'s (2016) article, this idea of "respons*a*bility" has been pursued further. Shuai Zhang et al. (2018b), for example, emphasise the advantage of a "sequence-aware recommendation model," stating that modelling "item-item relationships within a user's context history [...is] crucial to understand fine-grained relationships between individual item pairs" (p. 1). Yongfeng Zhang et al. (2017), in turn, introduce a design feature that makes it possible "to obtain the joint representations for users and items" (p. 1449). However, as much as engineering efforts flow into this idea of "respons*a*bility," it is clear that this is decisively different from "responsibility." Touching upon notions of accountability and liability, the meaning of responsibility can easily be elevated to a "moral obligation to behave correctly towards or in respect of a person or thing" (OED 2022). In this respect, one can argue that the "respons*a*bility" of the literature on recommender systems is failing this moral obligation exactly because of its incessant accounting work. This fantasy of optimal respons*a*bility (what Cheney-Lippold [2011] has described as "modulation") might still be a long way from functioning convincingly; and Tufekci's (2018) observation of an extremism of form might well have been a symptom of the gap between aspiration and reality in the sophistication of the system at that point in its development. But the orientation of this vision, specifically to create holding patterns for individual users and 'still' them for maximal amounts of time, is clear.

It is against the mounting critique of this strategy that YouTube started to act, at least rhetorically. In 2021, Cristos Goodrow, Vice President of Engineering, effectively stepped into the role of the caring parent who, in an effort at calming other parents, announced that YouTube had made "delivering responsible recommendations our top priority." Indeed, in a tech-solutionist move (Morozov 2013) characteristic of Silicon Valley entrepreneurialism, Goodrow goes as far as to make recommendations the most important warrant of the platform's responsibility itself: "That's why recommendations play such an important role in how we maintain a responsible platform. They connect viewers to high-quality information and minimize the chances they'll see problematic content" (Goodrow 2021, n.p.). In an effort to show that this parental, mentoring role had been a priority all along, Goodrow's article, published on the YouTube blog, comes with a timeline where the most virtuous modifications of the system are logged: 2011 saw racy and violent content being demoted, 2015 "sensationalistic tabloid content"; and while the text claims that already in 2017 authoritative voices had been raised, in 2019 "borderline content," i.e. political content at the verge of breaching community guidelines, was deprioritised. When Covington et al. (2016) refer to the system's "rich set of features," those identifying and weighing the above content categories can be seen as part and parcel of this.

Beyond the political dimension, a central aspect of YouTube's newly defined responsibility is to shift recommendations away from a preoccupation with increasing people's "watch time" (which is synonymous with the more general "dwell time"; Goodrow 2021; see above) and in the direction of recommendations that increase people's "*valued* watch time" (ibid, emphasis added). It is here that Kohut's (1971) concept of "optimal frustration" (see above) and Winnicott's "value of […] disillusionment" (Abram 2007, 242) can be turned productive for an understanding of YouTube's responsibility. What both concepts point to is the formative importance of *moments of weaning* at the very core of the oral complex of holding and feeding. Indeed, it is the moments of frustration and disillusionment that make the unfolding of stimulation possible. For the case of YouTube one can say that *that* which has the potential to turn *watch time* into *quality watch time* would be the very failures in the acts of holding and feeding, predicting, and recommending.

Along these lines, Abram (2007) points towards the formative importance of the caregiver's necessary failures in giving care reliably and exactingly. She quotes Winnicott (1968) who writes about the emerging communication between mother and baby that:

The baby does not know about the communication except from the effects of *failure* of reliability. This is where the difference comes in between mechanical

perfection and human love. Human beings fail and fail: and in the course of ordinary care a mother is all the time mending her failures. These relative failures
with immediate remedy undoubtedly add up eventually to a communication, so
that the baby comes to know about success.

(Winnicott 1968, 98; in Abram 2007, 243)

In my assessment of the engineering literature on recommender systems, there is
hardly a passage anywhere that might be more important than the above one by
Winnicott. To paraphrase, what Winnicott sees as a decisive moment for healthy
development and a central responsibility of an infant's caregiver is to *fail at being
perfect*.

Now, such a preoccupation with failure is not entirely new for the field of AI,
either. Matteo Pasquinelli opens the introduction to his anthology, *Alleys of Your
Mind* (2015), on the theme of augmented intelligence and trauma, predicting that:
"One day, it will not be arbitrary to reframe twentieth century thought and its intelligent machines as a quest for the positive definition of error" (p. 7). He refers to
research on "war trauma and brain plasticity from the First World War" (p. 7), to
Deleuze and Guattari's (1983) well-known statement that desiring machines "in
fact run only when they are not functioning properly" (p. 8) and David Bates's
(2014) observation that early "cyberneticists were intensely interested in pathological break-downs" (p. 33). And yet, such sophistication withers in the competitive sphere of the engineering literature, where the focus has inevitably been on
reducing the margins of errors between the various prediction trials. Nevertheless,
I want to argue that there are now traces becoming perceivable in the literature on
recommender systems that suggest that human imperfectability might indeed become a preoccupation and an aim of the engineering task. As far as I can see, this
preoccupation is currently fleshed out under the labels of "fairness" (e.g., Beutel
et al. 2019), "attention" (e.g., Tay 2018; Zhang 2018), "policy correction" (e.g.,
Chen et al. 2019; Yi et al. 2019), "exploration" (e.g., Schnabel et al. 2018; Chen
et al. 2019), and "selection bias" (e.g., Zhao et al 2019).

Have your cake and feed it forward, too – magical thinking in YouTube's responsible recommendations

The necessity and productivity of a 'failure to fit' already show in a common
problem of machine learning that Covington et al. (2016) broach: "Somewhat
counter-intuitively," the authors write about the set of materials with which the
system is trained, "great care must be taken to withhold information from the classifier in order to prevent the model from exploiting the structure of the site and
overfitting the surrogate problem" (p. 193). Overfitting, i.e., the problem that oc-
curs when a self-learning system has become so familiar with its training materials that it is no longer open for the analysis of new ones, shows how failure and
learning go together – not merely for people, but for the recommender system, too.
In the words of philosopher Odo Marquard (1982), experience is the opposite of

expectation; similarly, a deep-learning system in which everything is exactly as expected tends to lose its capacity for new predictions.

With respect to Goodrow's (2021) promise of "valued watch time," the problem of overfitting already suggests that *both* people and machines need to be adequately stimulated to grow. In this respect, when Zhe Zhao and colleagues (2019) refer to the familiar problem that "a user might have clicked and watched a video simply because it was being ranked high, not because it was the one that the user liked the most" (p. 43), this problematisation of "a feedback loop effect" (ibid) or "ranking selection bias" (p. 44) points to the ambiguity that opens up in the field between engineering tasks and notions of responsibility. After all, the "artificial idiocy" (e.g., Bratton 2015b) of feeding users the same recommendations over and over again has little chance of improving either the quality of these users' experience or their watch time metrics. To alleviate these problems, Zhao et al. (2019) propose to substitute a more traditional ranking model (a Rectified Linear Unit [ReLU] model) with one that has proven better at taking into account multiple objectives (a Mixture of Experts [MoE] model; p. 47). Testing the system with the new MoE model, write the authors, significantly alleviated the "misalignment between user implicit feedback and true user utility" (p. 45).

However, when Zhao et al. (2019) then move to flesh out how they measure "true user utility" and the "significant improvements of our proposed system" (p. 43), Goodrow's (2021) promises of "responsibility" and "value" fly out of the window. "Our ranking system learns from two types of user feedback: 1) engagement behaviors, such as clicks and watches; 2) satisfaction behaviors, such as likes and dismissals," the authors write (p. 46), so as to then announce that the introduction of their new model "significantly improves *both* engagement and satisfaction metrics" (ibid; emphasis added). Following Winnicott's insights into "good-enough" parenting (1968), it is just as implausible to increase *both* the length of people's "engagement" as well as the mental quality of people's satisfaction, as it is to proverbially eat one's cake and have it, too. This is not to say that something can only be 'good' if it is scarce and finite; yet, announcing improvements in "user utility" while at the same time advertising to "improve performance on *all* objectives" (p. 44) cannot be convincingly kept in line with notions of responsibility. Formulated along the lines of orality, it is just not credible to keep people in increasingly longer feeding and holding patterns and still expect them to come out the qualitatively better stimulated for it.

This quasi-magical mode of thinking of 'having one's cake and feeding it forward, too,' I argue, is a constant feature of the engineering literature, which time and again gives the lie to YouTube's newfound cloak of responsibility. In this respect, Minmin Chen and colleagues' (2019) study of "Top-*k* off-policy correction for a Reinforce recommender system" offers another productive example, since it makes perceivable how YouTube is indeed trying to negotiate between their public responsibilities and commercial interests. (And whereas these two need not always be at odds, in the case of recommendations they have proven thus.) Chen et al. (2019) ask how far users can and should be enabled to explore different video types through a nuanced weighing and correcting of how recommendations are generated and ranked (Chen et al. 2019, 2). The article thus goes right to the heart of how a responsible parental role might be engineered into a recommender system. Unfortunately, though, it inevitably returns to the narrowly oral horizon of "user satisfaction metrics, e.g., indicated by clicks or watch time" (ibid).

Chen et al. (2019) depart from roughly the same point as Zhao et al. (2019) – specifically, "Learning from the logged [implicit] feedback" of users. This feedback is, as the authors write, "subject to biases caused by only observing feedback on recommendations selected by the previous versions of the recommender" (p. 1). In line with Zhao et al.'s (2019) formulation, there is an unfortunate "feedback loop effect" caused by the circumstance that user engagement, which the system analyses to drive further recommendations, is already based on recommendations of prior versions of the system. The term "off-policy correction" from the article's title thus refers to the challenge of creating a 'policy' for recommendations[5] that is free of prior recommender feedback and corrects this bias in further recommendations.[6] "Top-k," in the most basic sense, refers to the circumstance that, on YouTube, such a corrected recommendation policy needs to suggest "multiple items at a time" (p. 1).[7] What the article is ultimately interested in is to showcase "the value of exploration" (ibid), with exploration here meaning to develop a policy that weighs the costs and rewards of "actions rarely taken by the existing system" (p. 6). Drawing on neuroscientific findings on human proclivities towards "exploration versus [the] exploitation" of existing options (Daw et al. 2006), Chen et al. (2019) present an algorithmic structure that balances recommendations so as to "get the benefit of exploratory data without negatively impacting user experience" (p. 6).

With this aim, Chen et al. (2019) again follow the quasi-magical logic that equates user satisfaction with the quantity of time users spend watching. Comparing YouTube's prior system with a novel version "more likely to observe the outcomes of some rarer state," they observe "a statistically significant increase in View Time by 0.07% in the test population" (p. 7). This improvement is by no means large, the authors admit; yet, the category of "exploration," which accounts for how much people are stimulated and challenged, is thus made vitally dependent on the quantity of their engagement again. In other words, people are only invited to explore different tastes as long as this does not hurt – and ideally helps – the overall amount of food they eat on the platform. Again, it is the oral craving of the platform itself that comes in the way of the value and responsibility it promises.

(Instead of a) conclusion: towards genuine public responsibility

At this point I can hear myself protesting and objecting to the general arch of the chapter's argument, specifically, whether all this is not to be expected from a company that earns money by distributing videos that some people make so that others watch them. As Nir Eyal put it in a speech in 2017, "Just as we wouldn't blame the baker for making such delicious treats, we can't blame tech makers for making their products so good we want to use them" (Eyal 2017). From the perspective of the present study, the apt response to Eyal's equation is that, once this bakery literally feeds whole nations in ways that it qualifies as "valuable," then, yes, responsibility for the well-being of its costumers needs to be claimed. Translated to the case of tech companies: once they are being used as public utilities (Basu, Caspi and Hockett 2021), they need to be held publicly accountable as such.

Beyond this accountability, however, lies the question of *how* YouTube might realistically develop and create the conditions for it to take, and make good on, its responsibility. More concretely put, how to programme and design the recommender system further so that it might balance the oral dimensions of *feeding, holding,* and *stimulating* in a way that does not set up the former two against the latter, using stimulation merely as a bait to maximise feeding volume and holding time. In this respect, a promising path is shown by Seaver (2021) and his concept of "decorrelative ethics." Along Seaver's lines, I argue that an ethical approach to revising YouTube's recommender system would have to start with bringing the tight correlation between quality and quantity, valued watch time and overall watch time, in the engineering literature to awareness in the first place. If one were to place "value" and "watch time" on two separate (x and y) axes in a two-dimensional vector model, as Seaver observes for the notions of "care" and "scale" in his article, what would come to the fore would not be the gains in quantity and quality that the industry tries to engineer into existence. Rather, one would receive a roughly stochastic equation, with the "value" of watching YouTube first increasing over the length of a session, but then reaching a peak past which it would swiftly decrease again. In other words, and on the basis of psychoanalytic research on dependency, we would see how "valued watch time" would initially 'scale,' but then reach a point of saturation before going into decline. It is in the current system's push for people to watch on in this phase of decline that addiction becomes structurally embedded in it.

Teasing this speculation about features and correlations a little further still, the main path for YouTube to orient its service towards genuinely "responsible recommendations" thus needs to lead via this decorrelation of "value" and "watch time." As unpacked above, Goodrow (2021) presenting these two values *as already decorrelated and independent of each other* is proven wrong by YouTube's engineering papers themselves. Indeed, if YouTube wants to take its public relations (PR) talk of prioritising "responsible recommendations" seriously, it will need to modify its system in a way that enables, *even assists,* people to wind down a viewing session and exit the platform's holding pattern in an easier way. Merely offering a time-tracking function, as the platform did in 2018 (YouTube Blog, 27/08/2018), so that people can 'take charge' of their own viewing habits amounts to a typically neoliberal responsibilisation of consumers so that the platform itself need not take more substantial action.

Instead of such façade work, a vast range of plausible changes to the overall recommender policy are conceivable that would help people "[r]emind [themselves] to take a break" and "set a limit," as the 2018 blog post has it. For example, it would be possible to make expanded use of rating data again, which have been vastly deprioritised to the advantage of engagement data. And while this preference for the latter is based on the – all-too human – difference between what people *claim* they value and what they *actually consume*, the policy of feeding increasingly more videos based on people's prior *ratings* into their recommendations might serve the double function of giving them more of what they might consciously *need* and less of what they unconsciously *want*, while making it easier for them to stop a viewing session altogether. Indeed, it would be a meaningful exercise to compare the differences between people's *ratings* and their actual *engagements*. My hunch is that what people rate highly will be considerably less oral (in the sense of anti-containing) than what they engage with.

A similar strategy could lead via the function of "exploration." In this case, a path towards "optimal frustration" (Kohut 1971) could be developed by gradually increasing the degree of exploration across the length of a session and beyond the point at which it leaves watch time untroubled. Rather, by integrating higher levels of exploration while making sure that these explorative choices are not extreme(ist), the user would gradually be taken into video genres that might either be so challenging that they would have an experiential (as opposed to an expected/'expectational') effect, or they would become so unfamiliar that users would be enabled to disengage.

Somewhat cruder ways of designing optimally frustrating recommendations might lead via suspending the "autoplay" function (in case it is "on") after a certain amount of time, offering increasingly *less* engaging thumbnail images, or upping the number of videos in the recommendations that are *lacking* exactly those attention markers that have proven to perform strongly with a user.

In any way, the current correlation of stimulating users while continuing to hold them tight follows a psychosocially unsustainable logic. This comes further to the fore in recent discourse analytical work on the construction of media addictions in public news features. Vanden Abeele and Mohr (2021) have compared news discourses about television addiction from the 1960s through the 1990s with more current news features on smartphone addiction. What the news on television addiction in the late 20th century emphasised was a loss of morals and traditional values with respect to religion and family life. By contrast, the current features on smartphone addiction stress the "importance of productive time and the individual's responsibility for managing their smartphone use accordingly" (Vanden Abeele and Mohr 2021, 1549). This latter focus on productivity becomes echoed in Courtwright's (2019) account on digital addictions, where he pinpoints the "constant distraction from personal conversation, sleep, driving, study, reflection, practice, and work, which translates into difficulty achieving or maintaining intimacy, health, safety, knowledge, creativity, expertise, and socially constructive flow states" as these addictions' "primary dangers" (p. 209).

Whereas Vanden Abeele and Mohr (2021) offer these discursive positions to point to the social construction of the cultural imaginaries of addiction, showing how "conceptualizations of media addiction reflect hidden social norms and structures" (p. 1539), such social construction will all but stop people from physically and mentally suffering from their addictions. This is not to say that one should not be aware of the risks of pathologising certain modes of media consumption in an attempt at finding addictions where there might be none (ibid). However, it is likewise important not to fall into the trap of using constructivist arguments to strip phenomena of their subjective reality of suffering.

This leads to the final point of this chapter, which returns me to the question of the political dimension in the extremism of form that Tufekci (2018) found in the functioning of YouTube's recommender system. As regards such subjective suffering from socio(technological) reality, it seems relevant that there are now widespread online subcultures that paradoxically resist the neoliberal dogma of productivity and achievement by casting themselves in the stereotype of the (predominantly male) gamer nerd who exists outside of, and in opposition to, "socially constructive flow states" (Courtwright 2019, 209). This subcultural type is non-achieving and non-productive, even *anti*-productive, as he (sic) seeks to stop, derail, or hijack socially constructive flows. Having his origins in the anti-social media spaces of 4chan, Something Awful and Urban Dictionary (Ging 2020), this type does not so much *negate* current hegemonic ideologies as to dialectically perform their underside, proudly claiming labels such as "shitlord" or "the asshole of the internet" to indicate how the 'freshly bathed and clean-shaven' corporate internet of Web 2.0 is to be counterposed, soiled, and drawn into the gutter.

When cultural analysts observe how these subcultural currents have been vulnerable to indoctrination into right-extremist ideologies exactly by virtue of their anaesthetic and anti-productive stance, this casts a curious light onto YouTube's contradictory functioning of seeking to stimulate people as well as possible, while at the same time wanting to keep a hold of them for as long as possible. This paradoxical combination seems to approximate exactly *that* scenario and mental state which particularly Incel (Involuntary celibate) subcultures have stylised into an identity pattern. Whereas research might have confirmed that it is less YouTube's recommender system and rather channel subscriptions that drive the spread of extremist content on the platform, Tufekci (2018) still has a strong point when she suggests that this system drives an *extremism of form*. It does so by mimicking and facilitating a form of viewing that is extreme and has in recent years been funnelled into extremist affiliations.

Notes

1 The gambling industry has sought to merge with computer gaming to polish its image, while the gaming industry has been suffusing their products with gambling-like rewards (e.g., the infamous "loot boxes") to increase profits.
2 Netflix had even awarded a price of 1 million dollars to a team of researchers that reduced the service's RMSE by 10% (Seaver 2019, 428).
3 On YouTube, the relevance of active user feedback seems to have diminished to such a degree that a study found that pushing the "not interested" or "dislike" button had little to no effect on the recommendations (Mozilla 2021).

4 Lewis (2018), for example, in his critique of YouTube, refers – and links – directly to the paper.

5 While I am using this term in a non-technical way here, it is important to point out that "policy" has another meaning layer in that there are two major paradigms for candidate generation, "value" and "policy" based approaches. For a good explanation, see Ma et al. (2020).

6 At the same time, "off-policy" means that a dataset that has been created for a specific purpose is re-analysed for another (Ma et al. 2020).

7 "Top-k", furthermore, is a programming solution to the problem of how to reduce processing power in query and recommender tasks; for alternatives, see Hazimeh et al. (2021), who suggest a "DSelect-k" model as a smoother solution for this same "sparse gate" task.

Chapter 3

Anxious narcissism – Instagram, self-image practices, and the persistent question of narcissism

When founders Kevin Systrom and Mike Krieger launched the image-sharing app Instagram in 2010, it was enthusiastically greeted, both for its photo filters and its seamless sharing functions. The early iPhone models for which it was designed came with cameras that were still significantly worse than the analogue ones or standalone digital cameras on the market at the time. And Facebook as the most popular social networking site was still struggling to translate its desktop application to mobile phones and move visual communication into the centre of interaction on its site. In this context, creating an online social network designed exclusively for mobile phones and with a focus on images that could easily be uploaded from the phones to the network might not have been the most disruptive idea to come out of Silicon Valley, but it proved to be immensely well-attuned to the technocultural Zeitgeist and elevated the app-cum-social-networking-platform to a global "cultural powerhouse" (Victor 2018). As Systrom himself stated, the idea of photo filters, paired with social distribution, turned out to be "the magical combination" (in Jarvey 2016).

Especially the photo filters Instagram introduced and the one-size-fits-all square shape it initially offered as a standard picture format – an easy and effective way to improve the look of snapshots and turn them into idealised pieces of instant nostalgia – became tokens of this Zeitgeist. They paired processes of augmentation and beautification with those of playful limitation and standardisation that proved to be highly alluring. "A filter on Instagram was like if Twitter had a button to make you more clever," technology journalist Sarah Frier (2020, 45) writes in her inside story of the platform. The names of those early filters, Clarendon, Valencia, or Amaro, derived from random associations the designers took from their surroundings: cocktail bars, parks, and places in their San Francisco neighbourhoods (Jarvey, 2016). These names underline the playful dreaminess they were intended to induce. Filters endowed the app with notions of everyday artistry and the direct upload function made a wildly democratised image-making creativity accessible to rapidly growing user numbers around the globe.

With smartphone cameras improving significantly throughout the 2010s, the original filters were soon no longer needed to improve on, or gloss over, the quality of the photos a smartphone could take. What followed was a 'no-filter' trend in

DOI: 10.4324/9781003307044-4

which people demonstrated pride in their artistry through the marked avoidance of embellishing effects. Yet, photo filters would soon have their revival, as the idea of touching up one's images was given a new lease with the introduction of the *Face-Tune* app in 2013 – an app whose functionality would become synonymous with self-image practices on Instagram. As Leaver, Highfield, and Abidin (2020) write in their book-length study on the platform: "Instagram filters helped to normalise notions of editing and touching up content before posting, and reduced the amount of artistic and technical ability required to make images appear that way" (p. 52). Instagram thus became the application that "mainstreamed (at least in the Western context) the idea that editing is, or should be, a default action prior to posting an image to social media," observes Tiidenberg accordingly (2018, 56). Hence, filtering practices, which started on Instagram, have now established a general acceptance that "simply taking a photograph is not the end of the process" (ibid). The FaceTune app was the most popular paid app on the Apple store in 2017, with over 10 million downloads (Frier 2020, 243). The app-economy analyst Sensor Tower found in 2018 that only the Minecraft game had spent more days on the App store's number-one spot for paid iPhone apps worldwide. While downloads have declined throughout the past years, the app's free version is still downloaded almost 5 million times every quarter year.[1]

While "selfies" – i.e., images taken of oneself, without the presence or help of others, with one's smartphone camera and shared on digital social media (cf. Tiidenberg 2018) – are by no means the most often posted image genre on Insta-gram (Caliandro and Graham 2020; Tifentale and Manovitch 2014), they have never-theless become paradigmatic of the platform as a whole in the cultural imagination. As Sofia Caldeira and colleagues (2020) put it, "the idea of self-representation and selfie-taking occupies a central place in popular culture imagery on Instagram" (p. 2). In this respect, particularly the practices of filtering and touching up self-images have emerged as a cultural norm. It is this norm that is at the core of this chapter's analysis. Practices of self-editing poignantly capture the very mundane-ness of people's preoccupation with themselves that, driven by social media, has incessantly been decried as pathologically narcissistic in public – and parts of aca-demic – discourses. Social media users engaged in such practices have been widely criticised for being egotistical, self-absorbed, and prone to illusions of self-grandeur. While, in this chapter, I side unambiguously with scholars of digital culture who have sought to counter and disperse this myth of the social media narcissist (e.g., Rettberg 2014, Tiidenberg 2018, Caldeira et al. 2020; see Goldberg, 2017, for an analysis of this myth), I nevertheless suggest that there is merit in continuing to engage with the notion of narcissism, *as long*, that is, *as we resist the simplistic and reductively individualising definitions of the label* that are in circulation.

The 110-or-so years of psychoanalytic work on narcissism, starting with Freud's publication of "On Narcissism" (1914), can help in this effort, since at the heart of this ongoing debate sit exactly those questions that also go to the core of the Instagram selfie debate. Specifically, in how far is self-love a necessary ingredi-ent of self-constitution? And if it proves so, when does such a formative process become hindered by its own means and dynamics? How must one interpret the forms of individuation and, at times, isolation that the selfie appears to bring about? And how detached from others are those immersed in self-image practices really? Drawing on the wealth of psychoanalytic theorisations as well as psycho*social* efforts to mediate these theorisations with social and cultural dynamics, I seek to develop and unfold weighed answers to these questions – answers that do justice to the unsolvable tensions present in both the psychoanalytic theory of narcissism and the by-now highly normalised cultural practices of online self-image making.

Ultimately, what I develop out of these ruminations is the notion of *anxious narcissism* as a psychosocial figuration (Elias) of our time. As a tense, conspicuous double of relatively inconspicuous practices of self-constitution, this figuration homes in on the contradictory and conflicted aspects of subject formation on corporate online platforms and brings to the fore a conception of narcissism that functions as a defensive formation in response to an instable and volatile notion of one's (social) worth in late-modern societies. According to Foucault (2008) and thinkers following in his tradition (e.g., Bröckling 2019), the standards with which to measure one's social worth have become increasingly grounded in the competition between individuals in open markets, which become in this way contingent and dependent on the shifting demands of these markets. Instagram has, since its foundation, been continuously implementing measures to boost its market orientation and has thus increasingly exposed its users to this volatility. Its core propositions of *instant image editing* and *instant image publishing* mimic and double down on this volatility. Originally intended to *ease pressure* on the users (Frier 2020, 45), filters have become the ultimate pressure cooker in processes of self-evaluation. In this respect, beyond the formative necessities of *beholding of oneself as another* and, vice versa, *finding oneself in the image of others*, the drive towards self-idealisation, which has so widely been criticised as narcissistic, must be understood in elongation of this basic self-constitutional function and against the current societal backdrop. Specifically, it consists in the continuous attempt at creating the best possible conditions for obtaining positive answers to the anxious question of: *Am I ok? Am I good enough?* In this respect, *anxious narcissism* is the symptomatic expression, not merely of a narcissistic wound (Kohut), but of an *existential* one,[2] with the immaculate displays of an optimal self (King et al. 2019) pointing to a fundamental insecurity as to one's self-worth in a context in which one does not seem to have 'much of a say' when it comes to such assessments.[3]

In what follows, I first delve deeper into the self-editing culture that has arisen around Instagram to subsequently take readers on a brief tour through the increasing commercialisation of Instagram over its existence so far. I will then cast light on the public mental health discussion that has arisen as a reaction to the self-image practices the platform facilitates. After addressing the problematic standing of "narcissism" in this discussion in particular and as a concept in digital media studies in general, I turn to the presentation of key psychoanalytic, psychosocial, and cultural-studies positions on narcissism which I then use as a springboard for the assessment of the self-image culture to which Instagram has so firmly been tied since its launch. Overall, I argue that anxious narcissism is paradigmatically driven by Instagram through its paradoxical intentions for filters to lower the pressure on user posts while at the same time constantly raising the bar on these posts' quality. As Frier (2020) observes:

> Systrom, who sought out well-crafted things and experiences in his own life, did want images on Instagram to meet a higher bar. But, he'd say, the pressure wasn't on the users, it was on Instagram – to deliver a quality boost automatically with its filters.
>
> (Frier 2020, 81)

Filters were thus intended to 'democratise' beautification. However, success, influence, and control were to be granted only a lucky few, creating an enervating situation in which many would be given the means for success but not a realistic chance of achieving it.

Part I: the building blocks of anxious narcissism

Self-editing between conscious practice and defensive reflex

Image-manipulation tools along the lines of FaceTune were first introduced to a mainstream social media usership on the Snapchat app – a serious competitor of and threat to Instagram (Frier 2020, 179ff) – in 2015. However, while these were frequently oriented towards humorous effects of *masquerade* (comp. Abidin 2016, 6), creating convex mirror effects or overlaying a user's face with, for example, elephant ears and a trunk, FaceTune aimed at the opposite, specifically, impenetrably and perfectly beautiful surfaces and ever new instantiations of the hegemonic female beauty ideal (big almond eyes, small nose, high cheekbones, fair and smooth skin), and it is this orientation that has been characterising the Instagram platform and its cultural importance (Butkowski et al. 2020, Marwick 2015, Abidin 2018). In FaceTune, users are not merely enabled to tweak the lighting, colour, and contrast of their own likenesses and bodies in photographs; much rather the app affords them to modify skin tone, airbrush visible pores, remove pimples, lines, wrinkles, and other blemishes, modulate the shape of faces and bodies, correct jawlines, or the position, shape, and size of the eyes, etc. More recently, the Chinese-owned TikTok, Instagram's biggest rival, has further automated these virtual cosmetic correction tools with the introduction of its "enhance filter," which at the press of a button performs "skin smoothing, contouring and highlighting, teeth whitening, facial reducing, lip amplifying, and eyeshadow application" (Hu 2023, n.p.).[4]

Even though a "body-positive" trend purports to promote and push more realistic, imperfect bodies and faces into wider circulation, thus attempting to challenge and gradually change cultural norms (e.g., Simon and Hurst 2021), the actualisations of this alternative ideal often prove to be mere variations on the hegemonic ideal.

Frequently, the models presenting themselves to the camera might have slightly rounder faces and might be wider than the thin and tanned variations that have been representing the norm for decades; however, they mostly display very similar hourglass proportions and surface perfections than the former. After all, also the "body-positivity" movement has FaceTune at its disposal (cf. Gibson 2023).

While bodies play a massively important role in this drive towards optimisation, it is still first and foremost the face, as the defining marker of one's self-identity, which holds the main cultural significance. The existence of a gap, or disconnect, between the face and the body has been thematised by Deleuze and Guattari (1987), who state that:

> The face is produced only when the head ceases to be a part of the body, when it ceases to be coded by the body, when it ceases to have a multidimensional polyvocal corporeal code – when the body, head included, has been decoded and has to be overcoded by something we shall call the Face.
>
> (Deleuze and Guattari 1987, 170)

This general observation offers an evocative way of thinking about how the face becomes the main token of a process of individuation on the platform that feeds people into a market of attention which works along the lines of the logic of quantified popularity (Van Dijck and Poell 2013).

In this respect, whereas much research on self-image practices has rightly pointed to the self-empowering effects of users being able to edit their self-images before publishing them, thus remaining in control of the self they are making public (Caldeira et al. 2020, Tiidenberg 2018, Rettberg 2014), this kind of agency still needs to be seen in the context of techno-cultural forcefields that reign it in significantly. These forcefields surge to the fore, for example, in the doubling up of screen-based filtering practices in well-established plastic-surgery procedures. In an article for *The New Yorker* (2019), Jia Tolentino points to a process of gradual convergence between female beauty ideals (female, because, as of yet, the majority of consumers of both plastic surgery and image manipulation tools are still women)[5] as they emerge from Face-Tuning practices on Instagram and the various forms of face-lifting and cosmetic surgery that people can undertake so as to make their faces meet the filtered screen fantasy (see Miller and McIntyre 2022; Maes and de Lenne 2022). As one of Tolentino's interviewees, a celebrity make-up artist, explains:

> My job used to be to make people look like that [i.e. beautiful according to dominant norms], but now people come to me already looking like that, because they are surgically enhanced. It's great. We used to have to contour you to give you those cheeks, but now you just went out and got them.
>
> (in Tolentino, 2019, n.p.)

Referring to "Celeb Face," an Instagram account specialised in spotting and pointing out celebrities' use of image manipulation tools, Tolentino qualifies this gravitation towards strikingly similar ideas of female beauty as "both mundane and pathological. You get the feeling that these women, or their assistants, alter photos out of a simple defensive reflex" (Tolentino 2019). Now, this notion of a "defensive reflex" stands in stark contrast to, for example, Jill Walker Rettberg's (2014, 33ff) account of a, mostly conscious, "curatorial agency" on the part of selfie creators (Caldeira et al. 2020, 5). Without wanting to discard the existence of this agency, advanced automation has vastly reduced the time and effort that it takes to bring about this kind of curation and has rendered the activity more intuitive and reflex-like. Moreover, what most academic contributions readily acknowledge is that this agency functions in a context in which the metrics of likes, shares, comments, and followers, which constitute the commercial setup of the platform, always also turn this agency into a defensive formation.

The billion-dollar start-up – Instagram's market orientation

Before Instagram, the app's co-founder, Kevin Systrom, had developed another app, Burbn, which, as a variation on the relatively successful Foursquare, invited people to showcase to others which places and establishments they frequented – preferably those serving bourbon – awarding users points for making their hanging out with friends public on the platform (Frier 2020, 10ff). While the app eventually proved unsuccessful, an analysis of user activity on it showed that what people *did* use was the photography and photo-sharing functions. Together with Mike Krieger, who had been hired to improve Burbn, Systrom decided to shed all excess baggage and focus exclusively on these two functions:

> They began by studying all of the popular photography apps, and they quickly homed in on two main competitors. Hipstamatic was cool and had great filters, but it was hard to share your photos. Facebook was the king of social networking, but its iPhone app didn't have a great photo-sharing feature. Mike and Kevin saw an opportunity to slip in between Hipstamatic and Facebook, by developing an easy-to-use app that made social photo-sharing simple.
>
> (Sawyer 2013, quoted in Garber 2014)

While Systrom had already received venture capital for Burbn – amongst others from Twitter co-founder Jack Dorsey – the quick rise in user numbers after the app's relaunch as Instagram, which saw it acquire 1 million users within the first two months after its launch, already brought the next round of capitalisation, this time with 7 million dollars, in February 2011, four months into its existence. A year later, in early April 2012, Instagram raised another 50 million dollars funding in venture capital, only to be bought up by Facebook a few days on for an estimated 1 billion dollars, roughly double the amount of its market evaluation. By then, however, it was already close to growing past the 50-million-user mark – a number that it would double again within the coming ten months.

While Leaver et al. (2020) state, surprisingly, that "the platform did not start out with commercial intentions" (p. 100), I see Instagram's commercial market orientation as having already been built into Burbn's core proposition of people showing themselves in desirable contexts of consumption: in their favourite bars, cafés, shops, restaurants, pop-up stores, and art galleries. Instagram would now leave it up to its users where and for what reasons they took photos, but the combined foci on embellishment/editing and publicity conserved Burbn's original emphasis on desirable objects, which, due to the rise of the selfie,[6] soon intuitively entailed the photographer themselves. This photographing subject would henceforth become increasingly objectified. From 2013 onwards, Systrom with the help Charles Porch, who had managed Facebook's relationships with celebrities and then changed to Instagram, sought – and obtained – close ties to the rich, beautiful, and famous, towards whose representational needs Instagram would henceforth pay specific attention. Furthermore, soon after its acquisition by Facebook, new terms and conditions were introduced that made it legally possible for Facebook to sell the image rights of photos posted to Instagram to third parties without informing users prior to, or recompensating them after, a deal. On the vast masses of everyday users, this move must have had an ambivalent effect: while disenfranchising them on the one hand, on the other hand the sale of a user's image is also a potentially flattering crowning of their artistry and ties in with the proverbial 'internship mentality' of the job market. In what Brooke Erin Duffy (2017) calls "aspirational work," people are infinitely enrolled in building their CVs and portfolios, in the cruelly optimistic (Berlant) hope of these investments paying off sometime in the future.

Notions of CV and portfolio building were further expanded in spring 2013, through the introduction of photo tagging by way of which users could now find all photos in circulation on the platform in which they were shown. Later the same year, Instagram started introducing the function of sponsored posts, followed by the creation of a new position at the helm of the platform: "Global Head of Business and Brand Development." From 2014 on, advertising functionalities have been continuously strengthened and business tools, including user analytics and direct links to web shops, developed and launched at pace. Hence, apart from the steady introduction of new formats and functions with which to aggressively move into the terrain of its competition, the one dominant characteristic in the evolution of Instagram has been the careful commercialisation and commodification of the platform. Whoever has joined Instagram after 2013 knows – be it implicitly or explicitly – that they are entering a field in which they will operate as a commodity alongside other such commodities and as such they need to advertise and promote themselves in order to create demand for themselves. As the Instagram joke has it: "An Instagram user walks into a #bar #pub #brewery #happyhour #bigplace #beer #night #party #fun #photography #conceptual #art #drink #peperoni #olives #lights #table #chair #followme".[7] As Frier (2020) observes, while the most successful users of the platform, first and foremost the Kardashian-Jenner family, managed to heavily influence the platform's design and optimise it for their marketing needs, all other users have been breathing the air of this atmosphere. "An Instagram user's path to success was obvious," she writes, "based on benchmarking against others" (p. 233). This perhaps is the "unthought known" (Bollas) of Instagram: its inevitable status as a place for assessing and being assessed, consuming and being consumed.[8] Quoting Jean Baudrillard, Aurélien Daudi (2022) calls the body on Instagram "the finest consumer object" (p. 50).

"How do influencers weigh themselves? In Instagrams!" – *the platform as culprit*

As a societal symptom of this widespread shopping-mall atmosphere, there has been a heated public debate on the toll that social media, and particularly Instagram, have had on mental health. Numerous opinion pieces in mainstream news and lifestyle media have been decrying the damaging effects of using the platform. "You Won't Find Your Self-Worth on Instagram", warned *The New York Times* (Marikar 2019); "How Instagram Is Ruining Our Self Esteem", bemoaned Cosmopolitan (Fleming 2017); "Why Instagram Is the Worst Social Media for Mental Health", asked *Time* magazine (MacMillan 2017). Articles with headlines such as the above accompanied, but by no means perturbed, Instagram's steady ascend beyond the 1-billion user mark.[9]

Empirical research findings on the relationship between Instagram use and an unhealthy internalisation of beauty ideals, such as the widely debated report by UK's Royal Society for Public Health (2017),[10] tend to corroborate the pointed and headline-grabbing mode of debating public mental health on part of the legacy media. Important as their findings are, by narrowing the research down to a few isolated variables – e.g., Instagram use and body image – they tend to imply that these phenomena indeed can be isolated from other societal and political-economic factors. Jasmine Fardouly and colleagues (2018), for example, in a study of women between the ages of 18 and 25 in the USA and Australia, find that "greater overall Instagram use was associated with greater self-objectification" (Fardouly, Willburger & Vartanian 2018, 1380). The more these women showed an acceptance of the beauty ideals on display on the platform, the more they strove to objectify themselves. Complementarily, Marika Tiggemann and Mia Zaccardo (2018) find in their content analysis of 600 images taken from the Instagram "Fitspiration" hashtag (a combination of "fitness" and "inspiration") that "the majority of images of women contained only one body type: thin and toned" (p. 1003). Like Fardouly et al., they conclude that, together with the objectifying elements contained in the images, the promotion of this body type is "likely to have negative effects on the viewer's body image" (2018, 1003). As a last example, Joshua Hendrickse and colleagues (2017) found that "Instagram photo-based activities positively predicted both drive for thinness and body dissatisfaction through the mediating variable of appearance-related comparisons" (p. 92).

Instagram was neither the first social media platform to be suspected of being involved in the production of feelings of self-deficiency, nor has it been the last. As the result of a generational shift, this structure of feeling (Williams) migrated mostly from Facebook to Instagram throughout the 2010s (see e.g., Fardouly 2018, 1382) and is now resurfacing in modified form on Chinese/Bytedance-owned Tik-Tok (cf. Frier 2020, 278). While Facebook, which carries the preoccupation with the face and appearance in its name, had been pushing the importance of idealised self-presentations since its launch in 2004, Instagram, with its emphasis on imagery and artistry, entered the social media market at a point at which this market had significantly matured and unfolded its commercial potential. And whereas TikTok is now a serious contender for the position of main facilitator of teenage angst, Instagram's continuous attempts at developing new functions with which to emulate and venture into the territories of its competitors – short video formats, ephemeral picture-story functions, slideshow mode – are signs that it will not concede defeat easily.

In this respect, while academic research inquiring into the connections between mental health issues and social media is well advised to widen its perspective and include social structures and dynamics in which these media are embedded, the particular ways in which online platforms mediate, modulate, and take part in producing what is being discussed as a public health crisis in western countries are still key to a deeper understanding of the entire sociocultural complex. Instagram culture has become such a widespread phenomenon, one might argue, exactly because of the platform's emphasis on and seamless facilitation of negotiations of norms of beauty that each user is continuously engaged in by comparing their own likeness with those of others – close friends, loose acquaintances, mid-range influencers, as well as far-away celebrities. From this perspective, Instagram's core propositions of instant image editing and instant image publishing must be seen as practices that have managed to capture a much more general cultural logic. As mentioned above and unfolded further below, this logic, in turn, needs to be seen as both an anthropological, developmental need in each human being *and*, more culturally specific, as part and parcel of the commodification of the self, or what Foucault (2008) has called the making of the "entrepreneurial self" (cf. Bröckling 2019). In this way, Instagram's success lies in the convergence and entanglement of an anthropological need with current political-economic maxims.

Narcissism in digital media studies

Before saying more about this anthropological need and market-oriented conception of the self from a psychoanalytic perspective, I want to broach the notion of narcissism in the context of digital culture. As regards this relation, the scenarios discussed in the journalistic and academic work highlighted above might *not* immediately suggest a close connection to narcissism. To the contrary, the current version of the International Classification of Diseases (ICD 10), for example, seems to rule it out, defining "narcissistic personality disorder" as a "disorder characterized by an enduring pattern of grandiose beliefs and arrogant behavior together with an overwhelming need for admiration and a lack of empathy for (and even exploitation of) others," as well as "excessive self-love, egocentrism, grandiosity, exhibitionism, excessive needs for attention, and sensitivity to criticism."[11] However, while most elements in this definition point to the exact opposite of the findings of low self-esteem and negative body images above, it is this very contrast that dialectically connects the negative findings to the clinical definition. Both converge on the concept of self-objectification. Understood as the act of "view[ing] one's body as an object to be gazed upon" (Fardouly et al. 2018, 1381), self-objectification points to the idea of a self-love that runs the risk of consuming the self, which is also at the heart of many psychoanalytic conceptions of narcissism.

And yet, in the cultural studies literature on social media, narcissism is hardly ever mentioned, let alone seriously grappled with (see Daudi 2022; Özdoyran 2019; Goldberg 2017 for productive exceptions). This relative absence becomes all the more curious when one beholds of its omnipresence in other, closely neighbouring fields. Shifting the focus just slightly towards quantitative studies on the psychology of character types and social media usage, for example, one finds a deluge of articles and reports homing in on narcissism as a factor in media use patterns (cf. Campbell and McCain 2018; Lowe-Calverley and Grieve 2018). Yet, in these publications, narcissism is frequently applied in a way that tends to render the concept essentialist. Santokh Singh and colleagues (2018), for example, in their study on the relation of selfie taking and narcissism, define the latter straightforwardly as "a personality construct marked by grandiose sense of self-importance, low communion with others, and feelings of entitlement" (p. 308). These traits are not traced back any further into individual or cultural histories but tested for their affinity to certain types of online social networking behaviour. Overall, what transpires from the findings of studies along these lines is that narcissists, due to their personally derived will to self-aggrandisement, are prone to spend more time on social media than the average user, amass more followers and post more status updates and selfies (see Campbell & McCain, 2018, for an overview of the field). *Being who they are, they do what they do*, might be a shorthand way of summing up these approaches. What is largely absent from them are attempts at understanding narcissism as more than the personal characteristic of an individual and their will to power and to instead embed it in the societal figurations that drive the formation of narcissistic traits, as well as in the functions that narcissism fulfils in people' lives and in the cultural dynamics that support its manifestations on social networks and beyond.

It is the absence of such a psychosocial interest in, and empathetic attitude to, the issue of narcissism – the absence of an understanding that would allow for narcissism to appear as a *relational style* with a *relational rationality* – that seems to have turned research on social media use cultures off the concept. As Katrin Tiidenberg (2018) observes rightly, the judgement of narcissism, as it is meted out by and against different stakeholders in contemporary digital culture, must rather be seen as a power tool with which social and cultural capital is distributed. It "relies on the assumption that other people, social norms and institutions have the right to decide if you are worthy of looking at" (2018, p. 81; see also Paasonen et al., 2020, for a similar argument). By contrast, what a turn to psychoanalytic conceptions of narcissism can unfold in this context is how this distribution of power comes about and how we, the users of Instagram and other platforms, inevitably become complicit in it. Particularly, what psychoanalysis can offer here is a perspective that homes in on the paradoxical utopias and 'secondary gains' that lie in the various vulnerabilities which emerge from what a given cultural constellation facilitates as normal. In this respect, the recourse to psychoanalytic, psychosocial, and critical-theoretical literature can also help address the question that current research into digital media and mental health often shies away from, specifically, how it is that so many people engage in – and enjoy – practices that research has found to cause them suffering and gravely damaging effects.

Psychoanalytic and critical-theoretical approaches to narcissism

Preparing the ground for the assessment of narcissism on Instagram, here is a short run-through of the relevant theoretical sources, starting with Freud. In Freud's oeuvre, narcissism holds a complex, transitory place in the development from his first psychodynamic theory to his later metapsychology. Central to the present study, Freud (1914) differentiated between primary and secondary narcissism, the former being constitutive of the creation of a self-object in infant development. Famously, he referred to the infant as His/Her "majesty the baby" (1914, 91) and ascribed a "primitive feeling of omnipotence" (p. 98) as the primary narcissistic origin of all notions of self-regard. As such, narcissism as a developmental stage became the foundation for other, more mature object choices – as well as the default position to which people would regress in cases of frustration and deprivation. This regressive position was what Freud called "secondary," or pathological narcissism. To only love oneself, to withdraw one's attachments as if in mourning, and to shy away from extending one's affection to anybody but oneself makes for a lonely, isolated, and worrisome existence, indeed. While Freud's drive-theoretical groundings as well as his clear demarcations between normal and pathological narcissism have been critiqued (cf. Honneth and Whitebook 2016), I still find them useful as structuring devices that can then be deconstructed in further discussions.

Departing from "On Narcissism" (1914), Freud fleshed out his notion of "ego ideal" as a mature formation of narcissistic self-love and, from there, the super-ego would gradually enter his writing and emerge as a separate entity, receiving the role of "the vehicle of the ego ideal by which the ego measures itself" (Freud 1933a [1932], 64–65). That both the ego-ideal and super-ego are shaped by one's relationships with others, parental figures as well as peers, brings notions of incorporation (Abraham), introjection (Ferenczi), and identification, which I discuss further in the text, into play and thus gestures towards the complexity of intersubjective dynamics that later theorisations (especially Winnicott) would see as feeding into the formation of ego and self.[12]

Following in Freud's footsteps, Karl Abraham's (1994 [1924]) concept of "negative narcissism," which is directly related to the underestimation of oneself and self-hate, is particularly evocative for the theme of online self-objectification. André Green (2002b) uses the same differentiation of "positive" and "negative narcissism," which he also calls "life" and "death narcissism":

> *Life narcissism* is a way of living—sometimes parasitically, sometimes self-sufficiently—with an impoverished ego that is limited to illusory relationships that support the self, but without any involvement with objects. Here I refer to living objects, not those that are essentially idealized. *Death narcissism* is a culture of void, emptiness, self-contempt, destructive withdrawal, and permanent self-depreciation with a predominant masochistic quality: tears, tears, tears.
>
> (Green 2002b, 645)

Green emphasises the consolidating functions of both narcissism types, whereby even "death narcissism," despite its utterly masochistic negativity, makes a paradoxically constructive contribution to subject formation in that it provides a firm place for the subject beyond any doubts and ambiguities. This place might be imagined as at the very bottom of every conceivable social hierarchy, but it is a place, nonetheless. By contrast, the anxious narcissism that I want to unfold here misses this firmness. Rather, and somewhat closer to Green's "life narcissism," it brings into view the instability of the subject's position and its constant strive to create visions of itself that allow it to remain worthy of social contacts. "Self-doubt and neediness are presented as toxic states," Rosalind Gill (2017, 619) observes about the psychic life of postfeminism (see also Gill and Orgad 2022). In this respect, anxious narcissism delineates the struggle against destructive withdrawal and repeated disavowal of the reality of frustration, disappointment, and, ultimately, dependency.

As refers to this production of acceptable visions, psychoanalytic theorisations of practices of mirroring, which again are closely aligned with the theme of narcissism, become central to this chapter's interest. Jacques Lacan's (1949) famous introduction of the mirror stage, erecting an inescapable *ideal ego* that haunts – but also spurs on – its subjects throughout their lives, has become paradigmatic of critical approaches to media representations, first and foremost Laura Mulvey's (1975) theorisation of the male gaze in narrative Hollywood cinema. Aurélien Daudi (2022), Rambatan and Johanssen (2022), and Güven Özdoyran (2019) have discussed Lacan's theory in relation to social media; their work has informed this chapter. Similarly, in the field of Internet studies, Marc Flisfeder (2021) emphasises the renewed importance of the Other in social media users' thought and action:

> In the context of social media, we see how we perform, not necessarily for our own sense of self – we curate our identities, not to satisfy our own desire, but to satisfy the desire of the Other in the form of likes, shares, comments, follows, and so forth. It is this ambiguity that provides the pretense for our activity, and

social media is the platform through which, today, in popular culture, the big Other continues to be operative.

(Flisfeder 2021, 67)

The opening out of the subject's experience of itself into the social context (of the 'big Other'), which Flisfeder articulates through a Lacanian, Žižekian idiom, has found a decisive counterpoint in Donald Winnicott's (1971) depiction of the mirroring function in which the infant mirrors itself in, and finds itself recognised by, the mother/caregiver's look. Being "not yet separated off" from the caregiver (Winnicott, 1971, 130), the child finds in their look the first clues to its separateness and uniqueness while still mostly existing in a state of fusion with them. This contribution to practices of mirroring and self-constitution has been of central importance for the relational turn in psychoanalysis (Beebe and Lachmann 2003), not least since it has offered a more optimistic understanding of self-constitution, compared to Lacan's emphasis on the principle feeling of lack and on metonymic desire resulting from this process. In the field of internet studies, Aaron Balick (2014) has based his account of online social networking on a Winnicottian and (Jessica) Benjaminian (1988) interplay of holding and being held in the mind of the other. While my theoretical position of anxious narcissism is significantly informed by Balick's contribution, I side with his own reassessment (Balick 2023) as well as Greg Singh (2016) who, in a detailed discussion of Balick's text, cautions against a too optimistic view of social media users' possibilities to express their identity, writing that: "Not only is there a danger that users will identify with the presentation on social media as the whole thing, but social media itself, through its algorithms and filtering mechanisms, *identifies the profiled user as the whole thing*" (Singh 2016, 181; emphasis in the original).

Winnicott's contributions to early processes of self-constitution have also been key in wider debates in recent critical theory. Infant research after Winnicott has largely corroborated Winnicott's theses on the interactional dynamic of self-and-other constitution, and this emphasis on interaction has led to a strong focus on relationality also in social philosophy. However, while this focus has clearly been productive, it has at the same time risked rendering the notion of human subjectivity overly sociable, mutualistic, and reality oriented (Whitebook in Honneth and Whitebook 2019). In this way, it has tended to side-line the more troubling, sombre, and extreme – i.e., anti- and/or excessively relational – aspects of human existence that are captured in the notion of narcissism.

In a recent paper, Axel Honneth and Joel Whitebook (2016) have discussed what relevance central aspects of narcissism – particularly the primitive feeling of omnipotence (Freud 1914) and the related experience of fusion with the primary caregiver – should have in a post-Winnicottian conception of the subject. With both agreeing that phantasmatic experiences of, on the one side, complete independence from the other (omnipotence) and, on the other side, complete protection by the other (fusion) should be central elements in an adequate conception of the subject, Honneth gives more relevance to the relational experience of fusion, while

Whitebook insists on the importance of the more aggressive and separating notion of omnipotence. The way they coordinate their divergent perspectives serves to unfold the dynamics of anxious narcissism. Drawing on work by Fred Pine (1994), Honneth describes moments of fusion as "the original experience to be so fully loved that the other is resistless and not independent, so that all your wishes, ambitions, intentions, are experienced somewhat automatically, in a kind of fusional process, fulfilled" (Honneth and Whitebook 2016, 178). Adding a thanatotic touch to Honneth's argument, however, Whitebook responds by reintroducing Freud's idea of omnipotence, which in the context of Honneth's description turns into a primitive defence against the fear of this state of fusion breaking down: "[W]hen that begins to break down, when the child experiences anxiety, privation, deprivation, and so on, […] the primitive anxiety that that creates mobilizes attempts to deny, disavow the independence of the object, through different omnipotent defenses" (Honneth and Whitebook 2016, 178). Along these lines, anxious narcissism, I argue, arises as *the enactment of complete independence as a defence against the danger of being left alone* – against insufficient protection and the anxieties this entails.

This position, in turn, comes very close to what Earl Gammon (2017) and Alessandro Ferarra (2019) have unpacked in their readings of the self-psychology of Heinz Kohut (2014 [1977]). In a remarkable article, Gammon (2017) coordinates Kohut's understanding of narcissism as "defensive, covering over of self-defects" and attempting "to maintain self-unity against incessant threats of dissolution presented by reality" (p. 515), with the neoliberal requirement of becoming an entrepreneur of oneself (Foucault 2008, 226). In the context of corporate social media platforms, the circumstance that empathic mirroring and states of fusion always seem to be in reach but are never granted turns users into constant seekers for shelter, protection, and care within their own skin. In this way, narcissistic displays of omnipotence on online platforms become the symptomatic response to a digitally mediatised other we simply cannot depend on – an other who's very mediatedness makes them systematically unreliable.

Finally, a word on Christopher Lasch's monumental *The Culture of Narcissism* (1991 [1979]). Those familiar with Lasch's work will see that the present argument shares points with his critique of culture. When Lasch (1991 [1979]), by drawing on Otto Kernberg (2004 [1975]), offers "the incorporation of grandiose object images as a defense against anxiety and guilt" (p. 36) by way of a clinical definition that would capture what he saw as a trend of cultural decline in the USA, this again has parallels with the present project. However, when Lasch reinforces a categorical differentiation between normal and pathological narcissism so as to pass general judgement on "The Narcissistic Personality of our Time" (Lasch 1991, 31ff), characterological and essentialist tendencies slip into the study that diminish its value. While also the present work, true to its psychoanalytic orientation, is tilted towards the subjective and cultural losses of techno-social and socio-economic development, it nonetheless seeks to steer clear of characterological descriptions by homing in on the ambivalences and ambiguities of the formative interplays between people, media, culture, and society. In this respect, it is closely aligned with Lynne Layton's (2014) observations about the links between neoliberalism and grandiosity, which Layton conceives as firmly rooted in the social-systemic: "Neoliberalism," she writes, "has led to split states of, on the one hand, immense insecurity, and, on the other, grandiose denials of the dependency that signifies *poor*" (p. 464; Layton's emphasis). As I hope has become clear, this link between insecurity and the denial of dependency is at the heart of my conception of anxious narcissism.

Part II: anxious narcissism and self-image practices

Let's take a brief pause and a deep breath, since, at this point, I have gathered all the main components needed to delve deeper into the discussion of the formative functions of online self-image practices. And I will do so in two interrelated steps. Firstly, I want to sound out the more general, anthropological dimension that is entailed in the selfie as what might be called an auto-communication – an image practice intended to be *of*, as well as *for*, oneself. A practice, however, in which the self is always oscillating between subject and object, self and other positions. On this anthropological basis, I, secondly, venture into more problematic terrain, represented by the affordances of instant filtering and editing. It is these affordances that turn the continuous work of self-identification into the ever-cascading aspirational labour (Duffy 2017) of self-idealisation along anxiously narcissistic lines (see Johanssen and Krüger 2022, 85ff).

Selfies as self-creation

A meme of a painting of Narcissus, attributed to Caravaggio,[13] made the rounds online in the mid-2010s. In this meme, Narcissus does not glance down into the pond and his reflection on the water, but into the screen of a mobile phone instead. This is an admittedly blunt comment on social media culture. And yet, the idea of going back to the Narcissus myth itself as a way to negotiate the anthropological dimension of self-love and self-constitution is by no means misguided. Robert Graves (2011 [1960]), still the authority on Greek mythology, gives a nuanced summary of the relevant part of the Narcissus story:

> [A]s he cast himself down, exhausted, on the grassy verge to slake his thirst, he fell in love with his reflection. At first he tried to embrace and kiss the beautiful boy who confronted him, but presently recognised himself, and lay gazing enraptured into the pool, hour after hour. How could he endure both to possess and yet not to possess? Grief was destroying him, yet he rejoiced in his torments; knowing at least that his other self would remain true to him, whatever happened.
>
> (Graves 2011, 520)

Two moments are decisive here: first one of misrecognition during which Narcissus reaches out and tries to get a hold of whom he recognises as another. The second moment contradicts the first in the realisation that, *No, this is really I myself there* (see also Goldberg 2017, 7). However, Narcissus becomes so enraptured in his realisation that this moment of recognition becomes suspended and never fully realised. As Graves writes, Narcissus becomes caught up in the mire of *possession and non-possession* of himself and, in this respect, the question of who Narcissus beholds remains open to a degree. The pleasurable torment and tormented pleasure (*jouissance*) that is imputed to the experience resides in this suspense and openness.

As Julie Walsh (2015) writes, the oscillation and unsolvable tension between possession and non-possession, as well as the pleasurable suffering entailed in it, is "the critical moment of any interpretation of narcissism" (p. 34). Lacan's (1949) well-known introduction of the mirror stage shows clear affinities to its central aspects. Remaining loyal to Freud's theoretical proposition, Lacan conceived of the mirror stage as an anthropological constant. While the validity of this claim has been debated (Billig 2006) and Lacan himself revised it in later works, its basic idea of an alienating and haunting vision of a better, more desirable shadow of oneself – the "ideal ego" – holds. It is this ideal that seems to be intimately tied to what studies into the psychological effects of social media use have identified as the diminishment of self-esteem (Daudi 2022). Indeed, in a Žižekian turn, one could take the whole complex of self-image practices on Instagram and their reported negative effects as proof of the efficacy of Lacan's construction of the ideal ego and its principal unobtainability. This extends to Lacan's conception of enjoyment, too. Contrary to the platform's promises of an untaintedly positive, purely pleasurable, and gratifying user experience, Lacan's concept of *jouissance* needs to be understood as in opposition to such tame pleasure in that it always shoots over the mark and entails an unruly, uncanny, excessive dimension and an ambiguous, ambivalent mix of emotions. Graves's (2011) description of Narcissus rejoicing in his torments is a case in point. When Instagram's (as of April 2023) "About" page claims to enable "you" to "create content that's distinctly yours" (about.instagram.com/), a Lacanian understanding would expect this distinctiveness to be systemically disturbed by the human condition itself, the experience always suffused with a certain suffering from their principle unobtainability. In light of the many Instagram users whose engagement with the platform invariably comes with a hint of masochism, this strikes me as fundamentally true. Therefore, if there is one main take-away from Lacanian theory for the understanding of online self-image practices, it is to rule out once and for all the possibility of pain-free and frictionless enjoyment in focusing on one's unique and distinctive self-image.

Lacan does not indicate at all that the adequacy of his mirror-stage theory might indeed depend on social structure, but his text has nevertheless served scholars as a heuristic tool for understanding the role of the social in subject formation (e.g., Copjec 2015 [1994]). And whereas social structures are central in my assessment as well, it is important to remain a little longer with the anthropological scope of the theory. In this respect, Lacan's account of narcissism converges with Freud's on the point of self-creation. The ego needs to be created in a process in which the subject treats itself *as though it were another*, an intensely beloved object. At a point where cognitive categories of self and other are not yet established, the taking of oneself as a love object – of 'investing in' and 'betting on' oneself – founds and triggers the process of the differentiation of 'inside' and 'outside,' Freud held. Loving oneself, subjectivity comes to inhere in the act of giving and receiving love and in becoming both the one who loves and the one who is loved.

In *Narcissism and Its Discontents*, Julie Walsh (2015, 38ff) refers to Juliet Mitchell's classic study on *Psychoanalysis and Feminism* (1974) to emphasise this point. Based on Mitchell's reading of Lacan, it is fundamental for us human beings to behold of ourselves through extensions of ourselves. And while Winnicott (2005 [1971]) has made clear that the most central of these 'extensions' are our primary caregivers, who, by showing us love, show us how to love ourselves, a service such as Instagram, too, can insert itself into and facilitate a formative dynamic that has the potential to remain effective throughout life. Hence, before all preoccupations with the specifics of its sociocultural and political-economic outlook, Instagram needs to be understood as an 'incubator' of general human development.

Self-constitution in the social field

It is this formative function that drives home the absolute mundaneness – the anthropological necessity – that self-image practices on Instagram perform. Each selfie, be it on Instagram or other platforms, is an instance of self-creation, which can never be secured once and for all, but must be repeated and varied over time to vouchsafe continuity in the changes we go through. The media scholar Claire Raymond (2021) writes that, for her students, "the selfie was not a representation of the self, it was the self" (p. 1), and it is in the metonymically formative context established here that this holds true.

When digital media scholars emphasise the positive, self-empowering gains that selfie practices often have, this is vastly in line with the anthropo*logic* of self-creation entailed in developmental conceptions of narcissism. For example, in a study of female content creators on the blogging platform Tumblr, Katrin Tiidenberg, and Edgar Gomez-Cruz (2015) quote a blogger explaining her publishing of sexually charged Not-Safe-For-Work selfies as follows:

It's for me. It's not something I do just to put myself on display. I'm reintroducing myself to a piece of me that has been buried under 20 years of marriage, 4 children, and the mantles of 'wife', 'mother', 'neighbor', 'coworker', and every other role I fill in my daily life.

(Tiidenberg and Gomez-Cruz 2015, 90)

In their article, the authors place this statement in the context of Foucault's late theory of the *Technologies of the Self* (1988). In a similar vein, a Lacanian take brings forth the self-creational drive residing in the attempts at capturing oneself through likenesses. Furthermore, when the interviewee points to the various social roles she needed to peel back – wife, mother, neighbour, coworker – this highlights even more emphatically the relevance of the psychoanalytic emphasis on a desire that cannot be exhausted and dissolved in the social.

Yet, the above blogger's preoccupation with her social roles can also serve as a cue to introduce this sociocultural dimension into the present analysis. In so doing, what can be brought to the fore is how the commodifying and reifying dimensions of the Instagram platform, as well as the self-entrepreneurial culture which it helped create, weigh in on the process of self-creation. Along Lacanian lines, a preoccupation with oneself in relation to other people, objects, and broader social realities (the [big] Other) announces itself from the early moments of self-recognition by virtue of these objects inserting themselves into the gaps that open between the subject and its mirror ideal. Throughout one's life, the distance between ideal and reality remains, and this creates inroads for the production of fantasies of what the Other might expect me to be. In line with the above example, this can be captured in the question of 'What kind of wife, mother, etc. does my husband, do my kids, etc. want me to be?' (cf. Gill 2017).

When strategically building close relationships with celebrities so as to give them an ideal place for self-promotion, Instagram, too, started emphasising and concretely weighing in on the responses people would give to this anxious question. Hence, intuitive ideas of sociocultural expectations have been passed on 'top-down' on the platform and often articulated along gender-stereotypical lines. They have manifested themselves in the body pressures that particularly female users, but increasingly male users as well (Sumter, Cingel and Hollander 2022) report to feel both in relation to their own Instagram posts and others. These pressures can be traced into the conventions that have evolved within the selfie genre across the past decade. The "Model Pout," the "Duck Face," the "Kissy Face," the "Sparrow Face," the "I'm Bored," the "Fish Gape," etc.[14] While these are all in intimate dialogue with basic human registers of emotions, they have also long crystallised into intuitively recognisable codes of, mostly heteronormative, flirtation. They can easily be taken to function as set templates and blueprints for people to aspire to and inscribe themselves into existing cultural ideals and set patterns of self-constitutional interaction. Such set patterns, it seems, become increasingly attractive under the radically flexible and insecure conditions that neoliberal and digital forms of work have brought about (O'Meara 2019; Butkowski et al. 2020). And while it is impossible to grasp the many layers of personal meanings that go into people's self-image production, it seems plausible that the more they feel the need to fend for themselves, the more they might be prone to look for shelter under well-established – approved and approbated – poses.

Seen from the point of Freudian theory, it is here, in the orientation towards established conventions, that the conscience function – the super-ego – emerges; in

Lacanian theory, this is the big Other (Flisfeder 2021). Existing ideals exert pressures to adapt, but also award pleasure and excitation in achieving such adaption. In the context of online self-image practices, a sociocultural task in this respect is for users to fill the existing relational moulds with their likeness. The pleasure accompanying the social pressure to adapt partly comes about through the incredulous moments in which, for a short while, I indeed have approximated a position of cultural iconicity – e.g., when I have 'really pulled off a Selena Gomez, a Kylie/Kendall Jenner, or a Kim Kardashian' (per April 2023, four of the most successful personalities on the platform) and thus recreated a structure of desire put in place by institutionalised dynamics of interpellation. I learn how to desire by regarding the desire of others.[15]

Je est un autre (Rimbaud) – filter-mania and the return of the mask

At this point, Instagram's core affordance of *image editing/filtering* comes into the picture again, by offering very concrete guidance on how to approximate the established cultural positions of ideal otherness. The user-friendliness of FaceTune, for example, promises to make the process of idealising one's likeness effortless, intuitive, and swift, with the process of idealisation coming to mean that I, by being turned into another-like-myself, will secure the adoration of others – i.e., I can prompt a form of acceptance in others that knows no doubt or ambivalence. When Systrom claims that filters are meant to take the pressure off users (in Frier 2020, 45), this implicitly refers to the anxious dimension of the 'desire of the other.' Filters make it easier to post images, goes Instagram's core proposition, because through filters one can warrant and secure acceptance for one's images without much risk and effort.

At the same time, as effort- and riskless as this process seems, the attempt at idealisation through filters inevitably introduces a mitigating step that sets this attempt up for failure. "Just swipe for perfect skin," "Get precisely the results you want," and "Effortlessly, natural results", it reads on FaceTune's App Store profile,[16] but such phantasmatic wish-fulfilment is hardly ever being granted us, not even in dreams; rather, such a swipe usually wakes us up. Purporting to solve and abate the strive for perfection, self-editing tools have the effect of further suspending, complicating, displacing, alienating, and fixating our egos at a distance from their ideals, adding a layer of work in the resulting gap. This displacement tends to lead to further and more radical attempts. Even the women in Tolentino's New Yorker article (2019), who physically enhance their appearances, will be tempted to perfect their likenesses just a little more with the help of filtering tools. Hence, by invariably adding more moments of otherness to the process of self-formation, this impossible process becomes further blocked and sabotaged through the very effortlessness of self-editing technology. In this way, one can indeed say that Instagram, by virtue of having normalised "notions of editing and touching up content before posting" (Leaver et al. 2020, 52), shows a marked overall tendency to fixate people at an anxiously narcissistic stage. Offering a plethora of affordances and cultural strategies that suspend and loop the subject's constitutive negotiations with itself and others, it runs the risk of perpetuating the struggle of people who are already struggling with themselves.

The destructiveness inherent in this dynamic is confirmed by recent studies into the psychological effects of online self-image editing. Javornik and colleagues (2021), for example, find that "AR [augmented reality] make-up […] changes individuals' ideal-actual gap and can decrease their tolerance of perceived appearance flaws" (p. 5). Tiggemann et al. (2020) find that taking and editing a selfie "resulted in an increased negative mood and facial dissatisfaction," and conclude that "[i]nvesting heavily in and editing one's self-presentation on social media is a detrimental activity for young women" (p. 175). Lonergan et al. (2019) find that "photo manipulation and investment were associated with greater body dissatisfaction for both genders" (p. 39). And Lee and Lee (2021) find that the "level of appearance-related photo activity on social media is associated with increased internalization and appearance comparison, which in turn can reduce body satisfaction" (n.p.). "[T]he more one indulges one's narcissistic tendencies and self-objectifies in this way," writes Daudi (2022), "the more at risk of further fragmenting and alienating oneself one becomes" (p. 53).

Drawing on Jiayang Fan (2017), Tiidenberg (2018) observes that, in China, the use of self-editing image technologies has become commonplace to a degree where the practice seems to have shaken off its disallowing spell: "It is considered ignorant to post an image of yourself without beautifying it," Tiidenberg explains (p. 116). Indeed, editing as a convention seems to have been naturalised to such a degree that smartphones in China come with a camera that "automatically beautifies and filters selfies when you take them" (ibid). By the same token, tech journalists discovered that TikTok "changed the shape of some people's faces without asking" (Ohlheiser 2021). And yet, also this promise of anaesthesia-as-default becomes almost instantly relativised by another layer of filtering. As Tiidenberg (2018) points out: "even those pre-filtered images are then edited using additional apps that smoothen skin, change the shape of the face, enlarge eyes and the like" (p. 116). Likewise, in the case of TikTok, even when users switch the "reset" button in the effects menu, the "smooth" function will remain set at a default 30% (Hu 2023). When media scholars Mark Tuters and Daniel de Zeeuw (2020) observe a fault line running through online cultures, between corporate digital platforms that are characterised by the display of "real faces" and subcultural spaces characterised by the donning of masks, this differentiation might approach a dialectical switch point in the 'filter-mania' outlined here. Digital platform users who seek for ever more ideal (facial) expressions of their individuality might indeed end up putting on masks again, bringing about an uncanny switch from a socio-technologically driven, fetishised individuality to the masked anonymity of ideal sameness.

Introjection, identification, incorporation – mourning and (instant) melancholia

The concepts of introjection, identification, and incorporation offer opportunities to delve further into the psychodynamics of such 'face-work' (Goffman 1967) on Instagram. By way of a short definition, introjection sees people taking on the characteristics of others. These characteristics, however, are not so much integrated into a person's personality – they are not fully identified with – but 'swallowed whole,' so to speak, and erected as the other's imago within oneself. Identification, in turn, continues the process of introjection by more thoroughly integrating the introjected objects into a person's own being. While introjects remain alien and often announce their presence as distinct voices within us, identifications become digested and adapted as parts of ourselves. Remarkably, Freud (1917) gained an understanding of these processes through his work on mourning, writing that:

> It may be that this identification is the sole condition under which the id can give up its objects. […] When the ego assumes the features of the object, it is forcing itself, so to speak, upon the id as a love object and is trying to make good the id's loss by saying: 'Look, you can love me too – I am so like the object.'
>
> (Freud 1917, 29–30)

This link between loss and identification – that, in order to bring about an iden- tification, one has to first introject the object so as to gradually dissolve it into oneself – is highly instructive. It implies that, once we have brought about an iden- tification, this part of another that is identified with has been 'deadened' in the sense that it no longer holds a spell over us but can be used by us for our own purposes.

As a third building block, the concept of "incorporation," first introduced by Karl Abraham (1994 [1924]), has been elaborated by Nicolas Abraham and Maria Torok (2005 [1987]). They redefine it as a worrisome double of introjection. While introjection ultimately serves the work of mourning, the mere intake of objects into oneself, incorporation, as Judith Butler (1990) explains, "belongs more properly to melancholia, the state of disallowed or suspended grief in which the object is magi- cally sustained 'in the body'" (p. 92). What the addition of incorporation brings to the fore is that, paradoxically, identification can only be achieved once a person can let go of their ideals, let go of their introjects. It can only be brought about by a process of mourning – of assimilating a loss – that offers identification as a sort of recompense for that which needs to be lost. Incorporation, by contrast, is what happens when we try to 'hop over' and foreclose on the necessity of mourning and assimilation.

Returning to the theme of online self-image practices, it becomes possible to link the melancholic process of incorporation (cf. Cross 2015) to the work that filters do. In this respect, an anecdote related by Frier (2020) is instructive. As she observes, a Belgian influencer couple, Camille Demyttenaere and Jean Hocke, with a following of about 300,000 people on Instagram, earn about $1,000 per 100,000 followers for each sponsored post on their "#backpackdiariez" account.

Most of their income, however, derives from their pre-set Lightroom filters which they sell via a link on their account and with which they make "upward of $300,000 per month" (Frier 2020, 241). While each of the couple's shots is meticulously planned, prepared, executed, and touched up in postproduction, the lure of the filter is to tacitly suggest that such meticulousness can be attained on a more casual basis. And whereas the audience seems to enjoy the couple's spectacularly angled and colour-saturated images, the massive filter sales indicate that it does so not in the way one would enjoy a photo in a magazine or art catalogue. Rather, what a large part of the audience appears to seek in these images are recipes they can copy. Hence, by suggesting to us that we can indeed make the leap across the divide between ego and ideal, filters offer the illusion that there need not be any sacrifices, that we do not have to bid farewell to our illusions of perfection or give up on our icons in our attempts at moving to a position of identification. In this respect, the whole of the 'filtered face net' that Instagram has helped to create appears to be befallen by a melancholia derived from a thoroughgoing denial of loss (Balick 2014). Identifying with others, we must lose parts of them as well as parts of ourselves. On Instagram, we tend to deny the reality of this loss.

Influencing and the labour of identification

When Butler (1990) observes that, in suspended grief, "incorporation *literalizes* the loss *on* or *in* the body and so appears as the facticity of the body" (p. 93, Butler's emphases), this points in the direction of the effects of the Instant Melancholia described above and how it ties in with digital work and its mental toll. In a widely discussed confessional piece, fashion blogger Tavi Gevinson (2019) frames her Instagram-induced breakdown as follows:

> If I received conflicting views of my worth or, looking at other people's accounts, disparate ideas about how to live, the influx of information could lead to a kind of panic spiral. I would keep scrolling as though the cure for how I felt was at the bottom of my feed.
>
> (Gevinson 2019, n.p.)

So many 'introjects' asking to be identified with but ultimately ending up as troubling incorporations. Each new image in the feed asking for another attempt at assimilating an object that, in its representation as ideal, risks blocking the digestive dynamic at the heart of the psychic mechanism.

It is significant that not only Gevinson's well-being hinged on the continuous task of identification on the platform but her livelihood as well, with the collapse of both into one single existential crisis being a typical phenomenon of digital work (Johanssen and Krüger 2022, 110ff). Not merely fashion bloggers but everybody with 'something to lose online' risks becoming overpopulated with unassimilable introjects – still-born, other-self foetuses, all signifying a phantasmatic demand to be adhered to. To drown in a flood of identifications dead on delivery – this, in any case, is how I imagine what Gevinson (2019) describes as the "panic spiral" in her use of Instagram. And this is also what I conceive of as the flipside of an anxious narcissism that continuously seeks to craft displays of sovereignty from a condition of radical dependence.

The negative articulation of anxious narcissism in the piling up of failing identifications offers a viable path, too, towards an understanding of the form of digital work for which Instagram has become most famous, specifically, that of the influencer. As media scholar Victoria O'Meara (2019) defines the notion, the influencer is a "digital content creator who has cultivated an online following and earns an income on a contract basis from advertisers who pay them to promote commodities to their audience" (p. 3). As becomes apparent against the conceptual tools of introjection, identification, and incorporation, however, the influencer's promotional activity follows a specific psycho*logic*. While brands and their commodities are intended to have carefully curated identities, the work of the influencer amounts to the task of enacting an identification with these objects which can be experienced as convincing and authentic (Banet-Weiser 2012). Hence, when Wendy Chun (2021) defines authenticity as "dramatic performances that ring true" (p. 248), in the case of the influencer, the drama resides in acts of make-believe that seek to convince others that it is indeed possible to identify with – to digest, master, and make into one's own – an ideal object. Simply put, authenticity on Instagram means for an influencer to persuasively claim and take the place of an ideal.

That these enactments must ultimately fail is encapsuled in the notion of "performance" in Chun's definition, with the most obvious failure being the one in Gevinson's self-report, where a deluge of identificatory demands leads to a fundamental decentring of being. Yet, also the most successful of influencers must ultimately fail in their performances of authenticity. This usually happens behind closed doors, with a supporting team of professionals – managers and therapists, media coaches, and public relations experts – whose core function is to contain the anxiety at the heart of all ideal enactments. The more influencers are tasked to embody unfettered idealisations, the more they will rely on trusted others to repair the damages that these embodiments inevitably do. "I had to hire help," Paige Hathaway admits, whose account, based on her gym workouts, "skyrocketed into the millions" after Instagram had added the function of uploading videos: "I hired a management team, I had people helping me with clients online, I had people helping me with endorsements. It was beyond my own self to manage everything" (in Frier 2020, 145).

Echoes through the holding environment – the other as entourage

What is thus rendered invisible in the articulations of narcissism, writes Walsh (2015) in accordance with the above, is the narcissist's thoroughgoing dependence on their environment:

[T]he point at which the ego-as-object and the ego-as-subject become integrated – signals a simultaneous turning away from, or overwriting of, his environment of care. At its most acute, the narcissistic paradox demonstrates the simultaneity of knowledge and ignorance in the same breast: Narcissus apprehends his image as his own (knows himself) *and* remains blind to the environment that supports him (does not know his others).

(Walsh 2015, 40)

Apprehending one's image and remaining blind to one's others – this is the formula that also Reality-TV has been following in its display of the existential vulnerabilities of (internet) celebrities in their everyday lives (cf. Prokop, Friese and Stach 2009; Noerr 2006). Here, the heavy dependence on others becomes staged for the camera – and is made meaningful for the audience – as the symptom of a form of being 'pampered' that an abundance of financial means has allowed to unfold. Nevertheless, what rings true in these displays is that the most morally dubious behaviours in them do not so much seem to hail from an unfettered self-love but might better be understood as the *chiffres* of a persistent failure to master and embody the ideals in demand. Paradoxically, the world around those whose job it is to love themselves tends to fade from view exactly because they are anxiously seeking to remain at its centre.

It is this blindness to the environment that has become democratised on Instagram, too. As an effect of the platform's affordances, the social world indeed risks becoming reduced to echoes. The function of "liking" – which from the first was designed as rendering comments such as "Great!" or "Awesome!" more economical (Gerlitz and Helmond 2013) – does little more than echoing Narcissus's words in the tense questions put forth by each selfie: '*Am I ok?*' – '*Ok – ok – ok – ok.*' The function of "Sharing," to which Instagram succumbed at a late point in its development, lets this echo tumble through ever wider ranges of the network. And in most cases, "commenting" amounts to little more than an echo, either: '*Am I ok?*' – '*Sooo ok!*' Directly negative feedback is strongly discouraged on the platform, which creates another parallel between Instagram and advertising rhetoric. The metric, quantitative expressions of these functions either turn the volume and length of the echo up or down.

Furthermore, while the quality of the holding environment in the metrical and measurable forms of 'likes' thus becomes echo-like, there seems to be something in the quantitative form of appreciation itself that tends to shift the aesthetic of self-image making towards the normative. Chelsea Butkowski and colleagues (2020) found in a quantitative assessment of Instagram selfies that, while there is a widespread tendency for these images to replicate "normative feminine cues," the exaggeration and degree of stereotype in these displays was clearly correlated to the quantities of positive feedback that the posts received (p. 817). Simply put: the more obviously and stereotypically the question of '*Is this ok?*' was put forth, the stronger the '*Ok!*' came echoing back. As one of the interviewees in Caldeira et al.'s (2020) study put it, "the pressure to be a naked lady of Instagram is very real" (p. 10). Indeed, metric expressions of support and holding seem to inevitably push self-image creators towards a 'green zone,' not merely of approbated, established tastes, but towards more intimate, privately held tastes. Even though one's name is attached to the "like," the potential for shame always remains with the "naked lady" whose choices one has echoed. It is in this respect that one must see Tolentino's (2019) defensive reflex. In the final analysis, Instagram aesthetics seem to drive a dynamic of people seeking shelter in an ideal average – in a zone where the ideal turns into something bland and common-sensical. Whereas caricatures seek to exaggerate the characteristic, protruding, and ugly features of our faces (Kris 1936), idealisation tends to disappear into the nondescript stereotype of the smiley.

Conclusion – how to thrive with one's sub-ideal self

As shown in this chapter, Instagram inserts itself into a formative, self-constitutive process that can be seen as an anthropological constant. In so doing, the platform endows the anthropological with the sociocultural and political-economic. To be 'self-employed' takes on a specific kind of meaning in the platform's economy in that users literally need to work for and with the maintenance of their countenance. By inserting the logic of instantaneity into the inevitable failings of self-identification, the illusions of obtainability and availability dialectically keep the ideal self at its projected distance *and* fill the gap between ideal and reality with increasingly more work. Along the lines of technological solutionism (Morozov 2013), as soon as this work is being automated under the aegis of comfort and convenience, further steps are being introduced, which, while again promoted by a certain effortlessness, require additional layers of elaboration in one's self-assessment. Hence the risk that the self-ideal, which should spur us on, paralyses us, because it is getting ever more cascaded, toilsome, and frustrating for us to try.

Folded into this logic and dynamic is also the profession of influencing, which is based on inserting ideas of products and brands into this gap between ideal and reality and tasking influencers with enacting its closure (Soloaga and Guerrero 2016). While the more successful influencers can afford to pay for the professional containment of their necessary failure at this task (in the form of assistants and entourages), the cultural ailment that Instagram has been instrumental in bringing about is the melancholy of incorporation – of being unable to digest the objects one has taken into oneself and of a constant feeling of loss that the shadows of these objects cast upon everything. By offering filters to 'democratise beauty,' but at the same time making underhand efforts to retain influence and brand control in the hands of a few victors, Instagram has created a version of self-entrepreneurialism that becomes *structurally befallen by anxious narcissism* where people are constantly haunted by the question *why they are not ok, even though they should be.* As research has corroborated, whereas boys might overall suffer most from what the Internet offers, it is girls in their early teenage years who have proven most vulnerable to suffering from online self-image making (e.g., Orben et al. 2022).

In the face of this inherent dynamic, in which the metaphorical slippery slope of entrepreneurialism (Rosa 2008) becomes ever steeper, and nothing is ever good enough, Instagram's core business of suspended self-objectification has been threatening to eat itself. As Leaver et al. (2020) remark, Snapchat's invention of

Stories – a format in which a slideshow of ephemeral images is made available for others to see for 24 hours before disappearing – ultimately served Instagram to stop its self-cannibalising trend. Copying the format and launching it on its own platform in 2016, Instagram managed to counter a downward trend inherent in its own principal orientation. As the authors observe:

> Before Stories launched, users were spending less and less time on Instagram; the more polished main Instagram feed meant many people were carefully choosing images, but posting rarely, and thus checking Instagram less often. Instagram Stories immediately turned this trend around.
>
> (Leaver et al. 2020, 27)

More recently, Instagram has tried the same with the introduction of "Reels," with which it attempts to curb and absorb TikTok's success. However, since for the aesthetics of both Snapchat and TikTok a moment of rejecting Instagram's artifice and polish is key (Bayer et al. 2015; Kennedy 2020), the incorporation of these by Instagram is only achieved at the price of watering down and betraying its core idea of embellishment and idealisation.

Turning to the fate of the others in our field of vision, when Green (2002b), in his work on life and death narcissism, urges his readers to consider the existence of a "lethal kind of narcissism" – a narcissism that also resides in the neutralising quality that it entertains in relation to others – this describes a danger inherent in the rendering of others into affirmative echoes of one's own faltering self-formation. By suggesting ever more convenient ways for us to get anxiously involved in defending our own goodness and independence, we might indeed become so preoccupied with this task that others will gradually lose their contours as fully-fledged persons. As such, they are at risk to recede into the benignantly neutral ambience that we tend to take for granted when going about 'investing in ourselves.' At this point, then, we might indeed be vindicated in those self-performances that suggest we are the only ones who can be truly empathic towards and take care of ourselves.

Bo Burnham to the rescue

But what is the remedy for these socio-technological malaises? How to counter their socialising pull? In the persistent absence of more wholehearted attempts at restructuring platform capitalism, we need to think in degrees of modification that, despite their modesty, might still have a palpably positive effect on subject formation. When it comes to the question of how to abate the stalemate effects that so frequently result from us trying to get it right online, ideas have been scarce and underwhelming. Jasmine Fardouly and colleagues (2018), for example, encourage users "to follow more Instagram accounts that post nonappearance-related images (e.g., images of landscapes or animals that do not include people) to reduce the appearance focus of their Instagram newsfeed" (p. 1392). As this chapter has shown, this advice, apparently offered as a quick afterthought in an otherwise sound article, is misguided. Oriented towards a kind of 'rehab-logic' – '*Just think of something else until the urge disappears!*' – what it offers is the escape into a state of disengagement with sociocultural reality: collapsed into a garden chair, tucked into a wool blanket, overlooking the Alps.

The 'remedies of degree' that are already practiced in an abundance of cases are those in which the platform's affordances are misapplied in a mild and benign way: frequently, the comment function is used for more philosophical reasonings about the pros and cons of self-promotion; selfies are often made in ways that bring 'other others' – best friends, schoolmates, parents, grandparents, pets, social causes, etc. – into the picture, or acknowledge their importance in other ways. The entire genre of 'Finstagram' (a composite of "fake" and "Instagram") accounts on the platform can be seen as a paradigmatic case in point. "Finstas" are alternative, secondary, and, as Leaver et al. (2020) write, "almost always private accounts, with very low numbers of (trusted) followers, featuring content that was often disruptive, ironic or at odds with the main Instagram aesthetic" (p. 16). These Finstas, one can argue, serve those mirroring needs that the increasing *other orientation* (cf. Flisfeder 2021) of social media made impossible for users to put on display on their official pages (cf. Ross 2019): being goofy, funny, normal, awkward, ugly as acknowledgements of the earth-bound dimensions of our existences.

As Caldeira et al. (2020) put it: "Everybody needs to post a selfie every once in a while" (p. 1). The art, however, would be to make visible in them the ways in which one needs to be held by others for one's performance of independence to come about in the first place. Similarly, when the filtering and self-editing is overdone and exaggerated, the resulting monstrous creations can move into the mainstream, where the borders between 'Rinstas' (real Instagram accounts) and 'Finstas' are rendered fluid. Ultimately, the measure of efficacy in such performances lies in their potential of bringing out and making visible the other that is always within us. And yet, what needs to be factored in and tolerated in all these measures is that, in working around, softening and calming the platform's rigid effects on self-formation, they all implicitly affirm, reproduce, and thus naturalise Instagram and similar platforms as major socialisation agencies in our lives. As a case in point, Melanie Kennedy (2020), in her study on TikTok, revisits McRobbie and Garber's classic (2006 [1975]) feminist study on teenage girls' "bedroom culture." While also these bedrooms, in which TikTok users now often film their amateur dance performances, are a clear rejection of the beautifying backdrops of Instagram posts, Kennedy observes that also these formerly safe spaces have turned spectacular exactly because of their very mundaneness. She quotes *The Sunday Times* (2020) to drive home this point: "Where Instagram is glossy and filtered, TikTok is goofy and relatable" (in Kennedy 2020, 1072), noting that it is this goofiness that is currently being stylised and commodified again.

In the face of this continuous de- and reterritorialisation of processes of commodification, the most empathetic, viable solution – *dissolution*, really – to the ideal-self dilemma has in my opinion been offered by Bo Burnham in his feature film *Eighth Grade* (2018). The film follows a teenage girl, Kayla Day (Elsie

Fisher), transitioning from middle to high school. While she runs a lifestyle Vlog on YouTube to express what is challenging in her life, she also suffers from the anxiously narcissistic imperative to perform that comes with the medium. Yet, what the film takes its viewers to experience through the prism of its teenage protagonist – and what makes the film so valuable – is that, while we will never manage to be good enough for the gaze of the platform, we will only be able to break out of this fixation once we steer the desire that has been absorbed by worrying about ourselves to other objects. Kayla befriends an older girl who is far less concerned with her image; she finds that, despite herself, she is drawn to a dorky boy her age; and she realises that her father, whom she has been pushing away, has weathered these rejections, and remained there for her, discretely and lovingly, all along. In short, what the film takes us to understand is that, for us to get on with our lives, we need to get over ourselves.

Notes

1 https://www.statista.com/statistics/1351687/downloads-of-facetune-by-region/ (accessed 31/03/2023).
2 Relatedly, Žižek (2006) writes of a "constitutive anxiety" which arises in the "confrontation with object petit a as constituted in its very loss" (p. 61; in Dean 2015, 97).
3 This argument comes close to Greg Goldberg (2017), who holds that the "political unconscious" in the discourse of narcissism amounts to the accusation of such narcissists failing to take responsibility for themselves. However, when Goldberg, by drawing on Leo Bersani (2015), suggests that the narcissist's "refusal to desire another" (p. 5) and their preference for the similar "ultimately work to undo the same/different binary so fundamental to social relations and their endemic violence" (p. 7), I cannot follow him. There seems to be an immense risk of further "endemic violence" in the "model for intimacies devoid of intimacy" (p. 8) that he thus suggests.
4 I thank my Master student Zhiyuan Hu for allowing me to quote from his work-in-progress.
5 https://www.plasticsurgery.org/documents/News/Statistics/2020/plastic-surgery-statistics-full-report-2020.pdf (last accessed 20/03/2022); 92% of all plastic surgeries are performed on women (p. 6).
6 Oxford dictionary elected "selfie" as word of the year 2013.
7 https://upjoke.com/instagram-jokes (accessed 19/04/2021).
8 This ties in, too, with the argument I am developing in the chapter on Google and repressive desublimation.
9 Numbers for 2022 estimate 1.28 billion active users: https://www.statista.com/statistics/183585/instagram-number-of-global-users/ (accessed 20/06/2022).
10 https://www.rsph.org.uk/static/uploaded/d125b27c-0b62-41c5-a2c0155a8887cd01.pdf (accessed 03/04/2023).
11 https://www.icd10data.com/ICD10CM/Codes/F01-F99/F60-F69/F60-/F60.81(accessed 21/04/2021)
12 The circumstance that both Karl Abraham and Freud took up the question of narcissism because of problems they experienced with their patients' resistance against their interpretations in particular and psychoanalytic treatment in general puts on display the ambivalences in the relationships of power in which narcissism was intended to intervene from its inception.
13 https://en.wikipedia.org/wiki/Narcissus_(Caravaggio)#/media/File:Narcissus-Caravaggio_(1594-96)_edited.jpg (accessed 20/06/2022).

14 https://www.seventeen.com/beauty/a36410/types-of-selfie-faces-on-instagram/ (accessed 26/05/2021).
15 Lena Lindgren, in her study *Ekko* (2021), works out the influence that the French philosopher Rene Girard and his concept of "mimetic desire" have had on Silicon Valley app development.
16 https://apps.apple.com/us/app/facetune/id606310581 (accessed 25/05/2021).

Chapter 4

Compromised formations – Google, obsession, and the desublimation of knowledge

Let me run through four scenes, dispersed across the history of Google and its search function. Though relatively unrelated to each other, these scenes mark important, formative moments in the development of the platform, its service and the kind of "collective consciousness" it has produced (Vaidhyannathan 2011, 54). Moreover, they are indicative of Google's staggering dominance of internet searches across the past 25 years. All scenes share an obsessive, compulsive moment at their core that, I argue, is characteristic of Google and its impact on the world in the early 21st century.

Scene 1: "I had one of those dreams," remembers Lawrence (Larry) Page, co-founder of Google with Sergey Brin, about the origin myth of Google Search, "[w]hen I suddenly woke up, I was thinking, *What if we could download the whole web, and just keep the links and ... surf the web backward!*" (Page quoted in Fisher 2018, 270, emphasis in the original).

Scene 2: "Pressure for profit mounted sharply, despite the fact that Google was widely considered the best of all search engines," writes Shoshana Zuboff (2019) about the precarious state of Google in the year 2000 – the year the Dotcom Bubble burst. "Page and Brin were seen to be moving too slowly, and their top venture capitalists [...] were frustrated" (p. 72). Zuboff further quotes from Steven Levy's (2011) chronicle of Google's early years, writing that: "The VCs [Venture Capitalists - S.K.] were screaming bloody murder. Tech's salad days were over, and it wasn't certain that Google would avoid becoming another crushed radish" (Levy 2011, 83; Zuboff 2019, 73). Levy (2011) continues that, "Every week or so, Brin or Page, sometimes both," would drop by the ad development section, "to toss ideas around and ask why the system wasn't done yet" (p. 86).

Scene 3: "Jacqueline Laurent-Auger was disappointed when her contract with the private boys' school where she taught drama for fifteen years was not renewed," Meg Leta Jones reports in her study on the EU law of *The Right to be Forgotten* (2016), a law requiring internet search engines to take down information about people that would show them in a false light. Fifty years earlier, Laurent-Auger had played in soft-pornographic films, and now the school was

DOI: 10.4324/9781003307044-5

concerned about her judgment, explaining that: "The availability on the Internet of erotic films in which she acted created an entirely new context that was not ideal for our students. After discussion and reflection, we concluded that adult films must remain just that, a product for adults" (in Jones 2016, 4).

Scene 4: When in January 2023, the US Department of Justice announced that it would once more sue Google for the monopolising practices regarding its ad system, AdWords and AdSense, the scholar and tech critic Scott Galloway exclaimed: "… this feels like ground… It's not even Groundhog *Day*, it's Groundhog *Decade*."[1]

In the first scene, and clad in the genre of an artist's myth (e.g., Kris and Kurz 1979 [1934]), what comes to Larry Page in his dream is an idea – to download the whole web – which is as genial as it is megalomaniac – as well as showing signs of obsession (albeit a socially productive one). This obsessive quality of downloading "the whole web," which went into the very founding of Google, can again be found in the company's mission statement, namely, "to organize *the world's information* and make it universally accessible and useful" (emphasis added).[2] Here it is no less than the information of the entire world that is organised and made useful, and the obsessiveness of this assembling and ordering task has evoked legions of references to the writings of Jorge Louis Borges (1999 [1944]), the specialist of the collapse of logics into psycho-logics into psychotics. In Borges's writings maps become coextensive with the terrain they are to represent; an inability to forget is shown as the epitome of stupidity; and a library of every possible text becomes the obverse of meaning (e.g., Vaidhyannathan 2011, 177, 199; Peters 2015, 347ff).

While Scene 1 offers a positive, socially productive kind of obsession, one based on the play of dreams and fantasies of grandeur and the "healthy disregard of the impossible," as Page liked to put it (Vise and Malseed 2006, 11), Scene 2 brings into view another, more brooding and anxious kind of compulsion, which Zuboff (2019) discusses under the umbrella of Google's "declared state of exception" (p. 75). In the midst of the financial bust of the technology sector, and in a climate of rapidly mounting financial and economic pressures, ideals of a search service untainted by advertising were not so much thrown overboard but, as I will show, obsessively refashioned, resisted, and defended in a long sequence of programming advances and innovations that, despite their ingenuity, have taken on the character of a *compromise(d) formation* typical of an obsessive neurosis.

A question that arises against this background, as well as against the widespread uptake and acceptance of Google Search, is how people's use of the service and the common sense programmed into it take part in shaping human subjectivity and sociality – individuals and societies – over time. Scene 3 offers an – admittedly shrill – example of the psychosocial shaping powers of the service, which are tied to its general capacity to modulate consciousness via the automation of language modelling. Again, obsessiveness becomes relevant in that the findability and retrievability of people's pasts "ushered the 'erotic portion of Laurent-Auger's career into the present,'" as Meg Leta Jones (2016, 4) quotes from the school's official statement. Is there something in Google's ordering of the world's information that makes people unable to let the past rest? Is there a link between Google's lust for storing and retaining information and a widespread tendency towards treating people as objects and commodities to trade and assess on a swift and superficial basis?

Finally, against an(other) attempt at reigning in Google's singular powers in the online ad market, Scene 4 and Galloway's exclamation that it is "groundhog decade" gesture towards the fixating and fixated qualities that have characterised the company in its response to national and supranational governmental bodies repeatedly requesting that it open its tight grip on a field of business, trading, and financial exchange that Google has been presiding over by virtue of an ad system that practically amounts to a system of taxation (Galloway, see endnote 1).

What all scenes share is that they bring to the fore the central relevance that obsessive phenomena and dynamics have been playing in the foundation, structuring, and programming of the service as well as its impact upon users' subjectivities and their modes of socialisation. From the childishly – although admirably intelligently – unbounded ideas of pocketing the internet like putting a genie in a bottle, to the compulsive defence against online ads, via users' displays of obsessively controlling and possessive behaviours, to the company's stubborn refusal to surrender any of its amassed power to the market: obsession seems as much a fundamental driver of development as it is at the root of the company's dead-ends and deadlocks. Reassessing Siva Vaidhyannathan's (2011) decade-old warning about the *Googlization of Everything* and asking what overall direction this 'googlisation' might have been taking and what relational styles it has been transmitting, there are plausible grounds for basing one's answer on the hovering interplay of obsessional dynamics. It is this play with and on obsession that I will trace in this chapter, arguing that a reassessment of Google from this perspective, in an era that has seen the internet gradually seep into every fibre of social life, serves to shed a novel – constructively critical – light on a conflicted approach to order by a company that has steadily strived to be good but at the same time attempted to become all powerful.

From here on out, the chapter roughly falls into five parts. I first introduce the psychoanalytic theory of compulsion, obsession, and obsessive neurosis to establish a theoretical blueprint upon which to base the ensuing analysis of Google Search. This is followed by a detailed reconstruction of the early history of Google and its founders – from the playful and idealist-maniacal beginnings to the introduction of the ad system. In turn, I take a closer look at some aspects of the programming of Search, from the calculation of PageRank to the introduction of a comprehensive system of language modelling, so as to trace in detail how and in how far Google's compromise formation between the 'purity of search' and the 'impurity of ads' led to a veritable obsession with the notions of usefulness and relevance. If ads were to break into the sanctity of search, one can summarise the platform's logic, these ads needed to be even "more useful than search results," as a Google engineer put it (in Levy 2011, 86). On this basis, I then turn to Google's effects on the people using it and society at large. Following the trajectory set by the theory of obsession, what emerges is an overall 'Googlised' form of interaction that approximates what the Frankfurt School critical theorist Herbert Marcuse (1986 [1964]) called "repressive desublimation": a flattening and de-differentiation in people's attitudes and relationships to other people and objects in the world. The chapter ends with a brief analysis of the ways in which Google is seeking to consolidate its monopoly power-structure, which again follows an obsessive pattern. With current antitrust litigations rendering the platform's old company motto of "Don't be evil" doubtful at the very least, the company holds on to its power apparently through a conviction that, when compared with the alternatives, it remains *the lesser evil*.

This chapter has been written in the midst of the current 'AI revolution,' as announced in the consecutive launches of Open AI's ChatGPT (versions 3, then 3.5 and 4), as well as its integration into Microsoft's search engine, Bing, which is hailed to bring about a paradigm change in Internet search, from short keyword-based searches, to more coherent, conversation-based inquiries coordinated between human and machine. And yet, even if search now seems set to transition towards "Large Language Models" (LLMs), the *small* language modelling efforts that I describe in this chapter for the case of early Google Search are by no means overcome, just massively multiplied and their multiplications coordinated.

More importantly, the major lesson entailed in this chapter is that the slippery slope from the "drive to knowledge" to the "drive to wield power," which I work out as a central formative danger of Google Search, will by no means be overcome in this paradigm change, but most likely become more pronounced and important to reflect upon as humans have increasingly more of their knowledge processed and handled by computers. As I will unfold, the compromise formation at Google's core has been about defending its search engine against advertising while at the same time seeking ways to integrate advertising into it. And while, in Google's case, the solution has been to morally purify advertising by boosting its usefulness, one of the central questions currently being asked in relation to Microsoft Bing's AI-chatbot extension is how and where in its design advertising will find its place. In this respect, it looks very much as though the compromise/d formations this chapter unpacks will be with us for a long time to come.

The psychoanalytic theory of obsession and the founding of modern psychiatry

"[W]hat does someone who cries all day in thought of her dead father have in common with a person who cannot leave the house without verifying twenty-seven times whether the gas and the taps are turned off?" asks the French psychoanalyst Marc Strauss (2014). His answer: while both suffer from what is now called an "obsessional compulsive disorder," there is no single symptom that would "characterise one structure or clinical type" (n.p.). Rather, people suffering from obsessional phenomena share a coherent structural trait, namely, the way in which they try to arrange "an impossibility," specifically, the impossibility of an embodied being needing to endure its physical existence and at the same time harbour lofty ideals about itself and its world. In the case of obsessional neurotics, their ideals must be spotless and hold together "without any hole, for one single hole can ruin the whole edifice" (Strauss 2014, n.p.).

Strauss's (2014) formulations circumscribe the contours and dynamics of obsessive-neurotic thinking, where tabooed impulses – e.g., to rid oneself of one's authority figures or blow up and shatter what sustains oneself – push onto and force themselves into consciousness, trigger anxiety, and are subsequently defended against in rituals of purification, e.g., in forms of undoing/reversal and isolation. They then become consolidated in compromise formations with intricate psychic-economic balances. While already the thoughts and images that force themselves upon the subject have a distinctly compulsive character (in that one cannot *not* think them), the defences that one musters up against them and the compromises into which one binds them again take on an obsessive quality.

Such compromises frequently articulate themselves as something massive and vast, absolute, and totalising – e.g., to *always* stay vigilant and awake *forever*, to *never* blink or let go of the reigns, to be on guard *at all times*, to pray *each day*, to write "I shall not..." *a thousand times*... Freud remarks that it is by no means easy to differentiate between the obsession itself and the defences against it, since the defence must of necessity be as compulsive as the obsession itself, with the former bleeding into the latter and vice versa.

Marc Hayat (2005), in turn, points out that Freud, "by giving obsession its status as a symptom, something that is both a compromise and has an economic function, enabled dynamic psychiatry to become thoroughly modern" (p. 1178). He writes: "The description of obsessional neurosis served as a model for all psychoanalytic theory" (ibid). Something excessively intimate makes its presence felt, is found to be painfully intolerable to one's sense of self, and needs to be sanctioned. This sanctioning takes on the form of an ongoing process which takes its toll on the subject, with this subject's character structure becoming changed as an effect of the continued obsessive work of the defensive operation. In broad outlines, this is how Freud conceptualised the unconscious to arise and the mind to take on a life of its own.

In an obsessional neurosis, the unrelenting quality of both the forced thoughts and the defence usually have their roots in a correcting, exacting, and sadistically punishing conscience function, the super-ego, which turns against the obsessive subject's ego itself. In this way, with the symptom being a main driver of character formation, obsessive phenomena cannot invariably and inevitably be deemed pathological. Rather, with the obsessional as blueprint for mental functioning per se, one can easily find cultural contexts and social situations in which compulsive states are conducive of and bring forth habits that are highly valued. Positive notions of dedication, single-mindedness, unerringness, endurance, and stolidity of vision are all informed by a substantial injection of obsessiveness and mental rigidity – as well as inspired by a substantially strict way of handling this obsessiveness – at their core.

Along similar lines, Hayat (2005) observes that compulsive phenomena are present in some of the most highly developed forms of mental functioning, such as focus and concentration on tasks, where the challenge also often lies in keeping derailing and self-sabotaging thoughts at bay. This again echoes Freud's (1913) suggestion that, while obsessive phenomena should be seen as a regression to or fixation at the more primitive level of anal sadism, their refinement and sublimation would be represented by the "drive to knowledge" (*Wißtrieb*). Hence, there is a proximity and family relationship between this drive to know (or thirst for knowledge) and the "drive to gain power" over objects (*Bemächtigungstrieb*, see White 2010), which Freud (1913) also mentions. The former is a refinement of the latter, with the latter falling somewhere between the psychosexual impulses typical of this stage and the defence against them, specifically, to control, secure, store, retain, police, survey, gift, barter, exchange, etc.

In this way, obsessive phenomena appear characteristic for all intellectual endeavours where they inevitably mean an aggressive expansion of one's controlled territory and a subsequent – as well as 'après-coup' – setting up of moral laws with which to protect the territory, as it were, against one's own advances into it. When Hans Loewald (1951) defines Eros, the Love/Life Drive, as arising along formative lines, as "an urge towards re-establishing the original unity" which emerges through the infant separating out of the caregiver-child unit (Loewald, 1951), the anxious attempts to exert control and gain power over the resulting field of communication must be seen as Eros dialectically switching into an obsessive mode of 'holding fast,' amounting to a thanatotic double of this erotic process. Ultimately, when Strauss (2014) writes that a final, inevitable dimension of obsessional neurosis is that *it must fail*, one can say with the author that:

> We already know that obsessional neurosis does not consist only of control but also of symptoms that signal the failure of control. It is a fiasco that makes a more or less big spot on the immaculate tissue of well-controlled world; a spot for which we know that it is shit.
>
> (Strauss 2014, n.p.)

The result of these various strivings (and failings) of gaining control and controlling one's gains are driving a continuous construction of obsessive advances and defences – an intricate network of rules of conduct that are intended to weigh up and compromise for, repay, delimit, translate and trope, displace, or remunerate one's forays into the world. Hence, when I suggest in this chapter to use the concepts of compulsion and obsessional neurosis as productive blueprints for thinking about Google and its search function (as the core of the platform's many operations), then I do so along the lines of the continuum of intellectual capacities and their dialectical shadows in regressions and sublimations – between the drive to power, compulsive compromise, and the thirst for knowledge. Google, I argue, is a product of both an admirably virtuous sublimation of obsessive traits and a fixation on a regressive rigidity.

In this respect, this present chapter gravitates towards the neurotic as well, not merely because its author has clear tendencies in this direction, but also because there is a precarious compromise and a delicate balance, which all too easily is tipped in the direction of a regression from the drive towards knowledge to that of wielding power, that is at the heart of Google's operation itself. When Siva Vaid-hyannathan (2011) remarks that "Google figured out how to manage abundance while every other media company in the world was trying to manufacture scarcity, and for that we should be grateful" (p. 11), this ties in well with the thinking around obsession that this chapter sets out to inquire into. And yet, importantly, this claim does not stand without the qualification that the management of abundance only became viable once the company managed to gain something that was scarce again, specifically, people's attention, or, as Hayat (2005) put it, people's focus and concentration.

"The world wide web of feces" – psychobiography of a tech company

What kind of company and endeavour is Google? What has been most character-istic of it? A good way to ease into answering these questions is via a comparison between Google's general organisational outlook and that of the second behemoth to arise from Silicon Valley, specifically, Facebook. As shallow and impressionistic as such a comparison might be, some of the fundamental phenotypical peculiarities come to light immediately. Hence, while Facebook, in direct counter-distinction to Google's engineering culture, has long basked in the glory of being a place for hard-partying, hard-drinking, yet also high-octane and ingenious hacker culture, Google, despite its "alarmingly relaxed dress code" (Vaidhyannathan 2011, 187), was somewhat frowned upon from the start for being a strait-laced place for em-ployees who wanted normal 9-to-5 jobs (Frier 2020, 8). In an interview with Play-boy (2004), Page is introduced as "Google's clean-cut geek in chief" and Brin as "a quieter, nerdier Steve Jobs" (n.p.).

While Facebook's inofficial motto, "Move fast and break things," highlighted youthful irreverence and disrespect for established conventions and laws, Goog-le's motto, "Don't be evil," and its mission to order the world's information have been combining childlike, pre-oedipal inoffensiveness with the parental demand for their kids to tidy away their toys. Where Facebook founder Zuckerberg would invariably be seen wearing hoodie and flipflops, a nonconformist look that, at least among programmers, earned him a certain 'street cred,' Larry Page would be so ordinary and unobtrusive, he would hardly be visible during student meetings at Stanford University (Vise and Malseed 2006, 24), where both Page and Sergey Brin were pursuing PhDs from the mid-1990s. Brin, in turn, was described as brash, driven, and intense, bursting into professors' offices without knocking. But again, this brashness always came wrapped in such geekiness that also he would appear a far cry from cool. There are pictures and videos online that show him on his signa-ture inline rollerblades, skating through the Stanford University's computer science building. Other hobbies included sailing and swimming, the trapeze, and yoga (Malseed 2007). Whereas Zuckerberg invented his infamous Hot-or-Not online game, inviting Harvard students to rate and rank the attractiveness of their female co-students in repeated rounds of photo duels, Brin worked on an idea "for generating personalized movie ratings. 'You rate the movies you have seen,' he explained. 'Then the system finds other users with similar tastes to extrapolate how much you will like some other movies'" (Vise and Malseed 2006, 20). A similar idea for rating books "would soon become popular on Amazon.com," Google-chroniclers David Vise and Mark Malseed remarked admiringly (2006, 20), and the benignity and polite cleanliness of these ideas do not merely stand in stark contrast to Zuckerberg's bad-boy image but also indicate from how different a mindset Google was born.

When talking about the ambition behind founding Google, Page liked to quote a phrase he had learned in college, which advises a "healthy disregard for the impossible" (Vise and Malseed 2006, 11; see above); yet, this disregard and its implications of raising bars, pushing limits, and shifting boundaries were firmly directed at notions of introducing order and taming unwieldy terrains – "managing abundance," as Vaidhyannathan (2011, 11) called it. "In the mid-1990s, the Web was a virtual Wild West – unregulated, uninhibited and unruly," write Vise and Malseed (2006, 24), but instead of indulging and engulfing themselves in this unwieldiness and building off of it, the impulse that seems to have come most naturally to Page and Brin was to pack it up, back it up, clean it up, and bring it into a legible order. And while this gravitational pull towards owning, ordering, and controlling clearly displays an obsessional trait, this should not be understood as a stigma. As stated above, the borders between normalcy and pathology, regression and progression, crudeness and refinement, and vice and virtuosity are fluid in obsessive phenomena and sometimes non-differentiable. This comes nicely to the fore when Biz Stone, co-founder of Twitter, who, between 2003 and 2005, held a senior adviser position at Google, remembers walking around the Googleplex:

> … like the kid in *Willy Wonka* going around the chocolate factory. […] Like one day I walk into a room and there was just a whole bunch of people dazed out on these automated contraptions with lights and foot pedals and books. And I was like "What are you guys doing?" They said, "We are scanning every book published in the world." And I was like, "Okay. Carry on." […] And then I distinctly remember going into what I thought was a closet, and there was this Indian dude on the ground with no shoes on and he had a screwdriver and he was taking apart all these DVRs. He looked like he had been up all night or something. And I said, "What are you working on in here?" And he said, "I'm recording all broadcast TV." And I was like, "Okay. Carry on."
>
> (Stone in Fisher 2018, 345–6)

As these deadpan-anecdotal memories imply, a significant number of Google's many 'moon shots,' as those seemingly impossible projects are called, was based on a logic of accumulation, retention, digesting, controlling, ordering, and apportioning. Freud sees compulsive symptoms as making people gravitate towards the anal stage of psychosexuality, where the withholding and expulsion of excrements become linked with quasi-sexually charged pleasures of sadistically dominating others or masochistically subjecting to the power of others. And while this might appear as a bad-taste psychoanalytic cliché, I insist on the heuristic value of tracing these relations and their power dynamics to early toilet training, where, from the age of around two years, toddlers and their parents enter into often strained negotiations with each other about conflict-laden questions of cleanliness, control, domination, and surrender. With astonishingly wry humour, Brin's father, Michael Brin, gestured towards the overall gravitation of Google Search in the direction of these themes in a poem he wrote for the occasion of Sergey's birthday in the late 1990s. Here, amongst disarmingly laboured rhymes such as, "You are tough, you mine data/You surf first and think later," one can read: "You work hard to squeeze a thesis/From the world wide web of feces" (quoted in Vise and Malseed 2006, 19). And indeed, when cultural analyst Dominique Laporte writes in his seminal *History of Shit* (2000 [1978]) that, "No doubt beautiful language has more than a little to do with shit, and style itself grows more precious the more exquisitely motivated by waste" (p. 10), we are returned to the extraordinary 'sublimability' of anal orientations and the fecundity of balancing and calculating the retention and expulsion of waste. When in the early 2000s, Google would announce that it would use the "data exhaust" of the many searches on its site – i.e., the metadata of users' searches – to refine its systems, this follows Laporte's analysis 'to a T.'

'The hormones that boys have' – safe search and repressed sexuality

Along similar lines, Vise and Malseed (2006) recollect a Q&A between Brin and Page and students at a High School in Israel which casts another spotlight on the psychosexual economy and organisation of Google as rooted in the upbringing of their founders. Upon being asked what they thought about pornography and about people using Google to find it, Sergey's longwinded and pained answer evokes a feeling of harsh inhibition which again harks back to themes of compulsion:

> "I want to tell you about something else Larry and I share in common. Both of us at a very early age went to something called a Montessori school. The theory of Montessori is you let kids do a lot of what they want when they are six, seven, eight, nine, ten, eleven, twelve. But after that, because of the hormones that boys have, you actually need to send them to do hard labor in their teens. Otherwise, their mind gets distracted." Brin seemed to be subtly answering the pornography question after all. "In this case, there are many ways to apply yourself. You don't have to do hard labor on the farm—but it is important to maintain focus, even through these difficult years."

> (Brin in Vise and Malseed 2006, 15)

Without mincing words, Brin's official line on online porn thus appeared to be that, instead of masturbating, hormone-shot boys should get a grip of another, more sophisticated phallus, namely, that of hard work and focused dedication. This part-defensive, part-sublimating attitude to sex can be reencountered in Google's programming and design, where the "safe search" function is switched on by default and buried in the settings. Again, I agree with Vaidhyannathan (2011), who emphasises that Google "has ensured that the Web is a calmer, friendlier, less controversial and frightening medium" (p. 14). Yet, while Google's ad business received a significant amount of its early revenue from Ad-Word auctions related to porn searches (see Fisher 2018, 341–2), porn-related search results are usually well suppressed underneath a layer of 'less frightening' results. And whereas Facebook attracted early users through its open flirt with sexual allusions, such as the "poke" (see Losse 2012, 10; see Facebook chapter), in the case of Google, the label "*Safe Search*" intimates a more anxious, pietistic, and parental attitude, with the safe/unsafe option tying into fears of contamination and infection which, in the late 1990s, were still vividly tied to the HIV crisis. In other words, whereas Facebook, along the lines of fraternity college culture, suggested for people to 'poke around' to their heart's desire, Google has been telling its users to either allow it to help them focus or accept the risks that come with 'barebacking the internet.'

Technology, religion, and exacting standards

But not only are Page and Brin both ex Montessori students, they are also both from Jewish families, Page American-Jewish and Brin Russian-Jewish. Brin's parents migrated with Sergey to the USA at the end of the 1970s, when Brin was six years old. In a portrait on Brin, Mark Malseed (2007) has Brin's father talk about the overpowering institutional antisemitism in Russia, which barred him from an academic position as a mathematician and forced him to accept a job as a state economist instead. In this way, he can be seen as a representative case of both the Jewish stereotype of the 'economically minded' and, more importantly, of the way this stereotype has been produced and reproduced by societal and institutional pressures. It was only upon the family's arrival in the USA that Michael was offered a professorship in mathematics at the University of Maryland, and Sergey's mother, Eugenia, eventually became a scientist at NASA's Goddard Space Flight Center.

Larry Page was born into a family with likewise strong academic acumen. His father, Carl Victor Page, was one of the first to graduate in Computer Science at the University of Michigan in the 1960s, the field in which he would go on to acquire his PhD. He "spent most of his career teaching at Michigan State University," where Larry's mother, Gloria Page, who also held an MA in Computer Science, was teaching, too (Vise and Malseed 2006, 16–7). The divorce of Larry's parents when he was eight created absences of his father in Larry's life that seemed to have strengthened his admiration for and idealising of this "fun-loving, gregarious dad, who among other things took him to a Grateful Dead concert" (Vise and Malseed 2006, 17). Hence, when Carl died of pneumonia at the age of 58, this loss will have been a further significant push for Larry into an idealisation and, eventually, identification which entailed pursuing Carl's wish for him to become an academic himself (ibid). When Page claims that the idea for Google Search came to him in a dream (see above), this corresponds well with what Vise and Malseed (2006) write about the family's spiritual leanings: "While Larry's mother is Jewish, his father's religion was technology" (p. 17).

Hence, while both Google founders grew up in secular Jewish households filled with mathematicians and computer scientists, in Page's case, the divorce and early death of the father strongly points to the idealisation and strive for identification with this father's leanings. By contrast, Sergey's father remained a very strong presence and super-egoic influence on Brin. This influence could be humorous – a consoling and protecting voice of conscience – as Freud outlines it in his late essay "On Humour" (1927). Yet, this voice could also take on a more persecutory tone. At the same Q&A that saw Brin struggle with questions of pornography, he offered the following anecdote about his whereabouts:

"I have standard Russian-Jewish parents. My dad is a math professor. They have a certain attitude about studies. And I think I can relate that here, because I was told that your school recently got seven out of the top ten places in a math competition throughout all Israel." The students, unaware of what was coming next, applauded their seven-out-of-ten achievement and the recognition from Sergey. "What I have to say," Sergey continued, "is in the words of my father: 'What about the other three?'"

(Brin in Vise and Malseed 2006, 13)

This joke points both in the direction of the exacting pressures that Brin's father must have applied to his son's education and how Sergey managed to navigate them. Students of Brin's father described him as "engaging but intimidating." "Attending his classes was like experiencing the drill sergeant in Full Metal Jacket," Vise and Malseed (2006, 20) quote one such student saying. "He would often hand graded tests back to his math students with a simple, 'My sincere condolences,' or amuse himself by making fun of wrong answers, saying, 'That's perfectly incorrect'" (ibid). And whereas it is unclear how much Sergey was the target of such sardonic remarks, he is remembered at Stanford as the wiz kid who passed all ten of the qualifying entrance exams on his first attempt (in Fisher 2018, 269).

Back-rubbing the internet – the making of search

In the goldrush climate of the late 1990s, it must have been extremely difficult to retain scholarly and academic loyalties. While Vise and Malseed (2006), who paint an idealistic picture of the Google founders, assure readers that both "were focused on pursuing their Ph.D.s, not on getting rich" (p. 21), the sheer amount of these assurances renders them dubious. Famously, Page and Brin did realise their "vision of how things ought to be" (p. 32) while they did not actively avoid "getting rich" from it, either. Most search engines at that time worked unsatisfactorily, shoring up results based on the number of mentions of the search terms on a website. Page and Brin's idea, by contrast, would produce search results based on the links that would point to a website. Originally called "BackRub," because the programme traversed websites backwards by retracing the links that pointed to them, Google Search would produce results based on the counting and ranking of those links. This has remained the core paradigm of well-working web searches to this day: the more links point to a website and the more prominent those links are, the higher does this website rank in the search results. Eventually, they called the algorithm PageRank, not only to avoid the sexual innuendos of "BackRub," but because it had been Page's idea and the algorithm literally facilitated the ranking of online pages amongst one another (Halavais 2017).

Regarding this algorithm, what seems very much in keeping with the characteristic outlooks of Brin and Page, and what has come to define Google as a company, is the orientation towards storing and accumulating that is then made to ambiguate between the gaining of power over this material and the gaining of knowledge of and from it. In Google's paradigm, the main dimensions of search engines are those of (a) crawling the web (where pages and their metadata are being downloaded and stowed in Google's ever growing net of computers); (b) indexing it (where pages and their hyperlinks are registered, their relations mapped, and their value relative to each other calculated); and (c) the processing of user queries (where the search request is broken down into anchors/keywords and phrases which are then matched with relevant items from the index, with those matches then being reranked and filtered according to the user's query as well as additional variables. These latter variables would grow significantly in numbers over time – location and time of search, search history, user demographic, and other information). The fourth dimension, which is (d) the system matching ads to user queries, would be added at a later point and is discussed below.

Evocatively, Bernhard Rieder (2020) points to the epistemological effect of PageRank ordering of the web when he writes that:

> Attributing an 'importance score' to every document 'independent of the page content' fundamentally means giving up the idea of a 'flat corpus' of documents where relevance is only determined in relation to a query. […] As an unsupervised machine learning technique that tries to find an optimal description for specific aspects of a dataset, PageRank establishes a global 'pecking order' for the web.
>
> (Rieder 2020, 286)

PageRank is geared towards finding the web equivalents of the joke's top-ten math competition finalists – i.e., those hubs, agencies, firms, institutions, etc. with the most official merit – thus mapping a "universal network of 'authority'" (Rieder 2020, 286). Vaidhyannathan (2011) points to a similar notion of authority by referring to Walter Kirn's (2009) neologism "aptocracy," a specific understanding of meritocratic achievement measured by focusing on "standardized, predictable tasks" which can be quantitatively assessed through "test scores, diplomas, and certifications" (p. 69). Vaidhyannathan writes:

> Google may be the perfect realization of Aptocracy. Google hires the best of the best from America's top university technological programs. Even those who work in marketing and sales must demonstrate aptitude via tests and gamelike interview questions. [...] In Web Search, a link ends up high on the first page of search results if it has qualified in a mathematically demonstrable way. It must satisfy a number of tests of viability and quality.
>
> (Vaidhyannathan 2011, 69)

To the dismay of more left-leaning critics, Vaidhyannathan holds a cautiously positive view of aptocracy, writing that "it has transformed America largely for the better over the past forty years" (ibid). And indeed, assessing qualifications mathematically and making decisions and selections based on such calculations seems fair compared to the dependencies on class, social status, race, gender, and ability that have permeated decision making for centuries. Yet, when Rieder, in his study of PageRank and its historical forerunners (2020), finds clear traces of a market thinking having seeped into PageRank's "conceptual horizon" (p. 279), this points towards an underside of what, at first sight, looks like meritocratic fairness. For example, in his discussion of Pinski And Narin's (1976) work on the infamous "impact factor" in academic publishing – a direct forerunner of PageRank – Rieder finds a subtle process of commodification that takes root in algorithmic-aptocratic modes of assessment, "in particular," he writes, "if we take into account that Pinski and Narin's metric was intended for a 'funding agency with its need to allocate scarce resources'" (Rider 2020, 278–9, quoting Pinski and Narin 1976, 312). Once the question of allocating resources comes into the picture, an allegedly neutral assessment system such as PageRank runs the risk of re-erecting the old fault lines of class, gender, and ethnicity, as if by law of nature and without explicitly referring to such categories (Chun 2021; Rieder 2020).

'Divide and control' – the discomforts of venture capital

As far as the commodification of academic merit is concerned, this had already been established at Stanford University and would now give birth to Google. What Brin and Page seemed to sense, however, was that accepting money from investors posed the risk of ceding control. They were markedly hesitant when, after having decided to create their own company, they received their first angel investment. Andy Bechtolsheim, a co-founder of Sun Microsystems, famously signed a cheque over 100,000 dollars – "a nice, round number" – to Google Inc. Yet, this cheque remained unused, stowed away in a drawer in Page's room, for several weeks (Levy 2011, 32; Vise and Malseed 2006, 31). Chroniclers attribute this slowness in cashing the cheque to the circumstance that Google had not been formally created as a company (Levy 2011, 32; Vise and Malseed 2006, 31), and they interpret this as the founders' dedication and disregard for 'earthly goods.' This disregard, however, can also be read from within the theory of compulsion. When Freud (1926) emphasises the defence mechanisms of "undoing" and "isolation" as the two most common ones in obsessive symptoms, the Google founders' heroic disregard for money becomes complemented with a more compensatory reluctance in granting this money – together with the accompanying notions of impurity, indebtedness, and a partial loss of control and ownership – the value of reality. Cashing in the cheque meant partly ceding control of their product.

Indeed, when Page and Brin in a later funding round insisted on both Kleiner Perkins and Sequoia Capital, two heavy-weight investment firms, to step in with equal investments, this advance was not only a sign of their self-confidence, but a 'divide-and-conquer' strategy intended to keep the influence of each single investor at bay (cf. Vise and Malseed 2006, 39). When the DotCom Bubble then burst in mid-2000, it might have been this strategy which bought Google leverage and time in the face of what Zuboff (2019) calls the "impatient money" of the Venture Capitalists (p. 71), who "were screaming bloody murder" (Levy 2011, 83) and, in the grips of widespread panic, began to urgently demand returns on their investments. Even if Google was in a more comfortable situation than most other Silicon Valley start-ups, which were mostly cannibalised, by 2001 also Google's funds were getting so low that Eric Schmidt, by then Google's CEO, "instituted a tight-pocketbook policy" (Levy 2011, 83). CFO Patrick Pichette compared the situation with "having a gun to your head every quarter on financial matters" (in Levy 2011, 120).

An obsessional-neurotic state of exception

In this situation, in which the Venture Capitalists swiftly mounted their pressure on the company "to make some real money" (Levy 2011, 86), Zuboff (2019) sees Google to increasingly slide into a "state of exception" (p. 71), which made them throw overboard their academic ideals and introduce profit-making strategies. This state, I argue, pushed the company into an overall mode of operations strikingly similar to how psychoanalysis defines a full-flung obsessional neurosis. In an early research paper on their search algorithm, Brin and Page had added an appendix in which they stated that "we believe the issue of advertising causes enough mixed incentives that it is crucial to have a competitive search engine that is transparent and in the academic realm" (Page and Brin 2012 [1998], 3832). Clearly, this insistence on the academic realm was a bow to their parental voices of conscience, external and introjected. Even in the summer of 2005, when "each of the founders had a net worth in excess of $10 billion," Brin's mother still "wanted him to return to Stanford, write his thesis, and finish his Ph.D." (Vise and Malseed 2006, 157). However, only two years on from the publication of the above article, Google's operations were firmly located outside the university, steeped in secrecy and non-transparency and, while highly competitive, still in dire straits.

When investors now demanded that Google be monetised by aggressively developing its ad business, this cannot but have represented a major endangerment of this purity of vision. Instead, Google's chroniclers describe how nightmares of noisily coloured, irritatingly blinking, clunky and click-baity ad banners forced themselves into the thoughts of founders and staff (Vise and Malseed 2006, 51) – or even worse: the option of accepting payment for placing websites higher in the search results, as Page and Brin had derided others for doing (2012 [1998], 3832). Under immense pressure, Google came up with a solution that had all the qualities of a compromise formation with a specific psycho-economical balance.

'Highly focused ads'

Hayat (2005) writes about obsessional neurosis:

> In the same way that the obsessional patient enacts the taboo against touching [...], the isolation of an impression or an activity, by means of a break in the chain of thoughts, symbolically indicates that he [sic] does not want to allow thoughts relating to it to 'contaminate' other thoughts.
>
> (Hayat 2005, 1180)

Applied to Google, this fear of contamination translated into a string of defensive and repetition-compulsive actions and rituals that made sure search results and ads did not formally touch either. With Google searches frequently proving to be interested in relatively 'marginal' topics and formulated in "esoteric keywords" (Levy 2011, 85), engineers grappling to find viable compromises to the ad problem saw that:

> there was a possibility to sell ads for categories that otherwise never would have justified placement. [...] If you made the system 'self-service,' they found, you could handle thousands of small advertisers, and the overhead would be so low that customers could buy ads very cheaply.
>
> (Levy 2011, 85)

Google's ad system would come in the form of micro-auctions (an idea first developed by Overture, resulting in a bitter patent battle), in which ad clients bid against each other for specific word searches.

Here, then, was one way to make up and recompensate for the damages that Google risked inflicting on its service during its "state of exception" (Zuboff 2019, 71). If the company managed to allocate very specified ads with the very specific searches that it kept processing and managed to sell these ads at prices that would make the placing of ads very accessible to smaller businesses, this 'democratisation of ads' might be a redeeming factor. In what can be read as a direct continuation of the notions of "focus" and "hard labor" that Brin had offered in response to the question of pornography (see above), he now proudly announced that Google would not be selling *normal* ads; rather, the answer to their purity problem was: "*highly focused ads*" (Brin in Vise and Malseed 2006, 51). Such focused ads would not just be placed anywhere; Google's start page, for example, was not to be touched. No noisy banner ads would sully the company's minimalist cleanliness and playdoh-coloured innocence. Rather, text-only ads would appear on the search results pages, but only with a very strict and clear differentiation between ads on the right side and with what henceforth came to be called "organic" search results on the other, left side of the page. Google made sure, writes Levy (2011), "to label the ads 'sponsored links' *to further distinguish them from the purity of its organic search results*" (p. 85, emphasis added).

But the purification of ads did not end there. Rather, if Google was doing ads at all, it wanted them to be better than any kinds of ads existing before them, and as Levy (2011) writes enthusiastically, click-throughs became the "first stab" at raising that bar (p. 86). Instead of charging advertisers for the number of people to which an ad was shown, Google would charge their – often small-to-mid-size – ad clients only for those showings that resulted in a person clicking on the ad and being brought to the client's landing page. Hence, the magic potion driving Brin's vision of "highly focused ads" was that of *relevance and usefulness*. Ads would be shown only if they were relevant to a person's search query; and if they indeed proved so, then they would function like the ads in the Yellow Pages, "in which businesses paid a premium to place their ads in the relevant category" (p. 87). Moreover, "a well-placed search ad could be more useful than a search result," a Google engineer is quoted saying in Levy's study (p. 86). Levy celebrates this compromise formation so uncritically that he reproduces Google's reverie of "a virtuous triangle with three happy parties: Google, the advertiser, and especially the user" (p. 86), without any reservation or qualification. "From the start," he writes (p. 92), "Page and Brin had an idealistic view that Google would run ads only if users deemed them as a useful feature." The resulting ad system, he writes, had realised "that fantastic aspiration" (ibid).

When Hayat (2005) emphasises that obsessions "temporarily deprive the individual of freedom of thought and action" (p. 1179), this morbid enthrallment shows in Google's double preoccupation with integrating advertising into its service *and* keeping the service untouched by advertising at the same time. Sheryl Sandberg, who had worked in the Clinton administration and would go on to develop ads for Facebook, is closely connected with this endeavour and particularly with another defining push towards the purification of ads. Under the label of "AdWords Select," she introduced the idea of adding "financial incentives for *better* ads. It lowered the price for effective ads and meted out monetary punishment and even an online ad version of the death penalty for bad ads" (Levy 2011, 91). In other words, if an ad proved too irrelevant, it would literally be *undone*, because, as businesses around the world would soon notice, if you were not findable on Google – be it as an ad or an organic result – you were virtually non-existent. Interestingly, this purity requirement was not only applied to ads, but to the whole of the World Wide Web. Just as Google would mete out low quality scores for ads that were "irrelevant, misleading, or even spamlike" (Levy 2011, 92), it would make webpages in breach of its aesthetic sense of cleanliness disappear into the oblivious long tail of its search pages.

This policing of webpages themselves was to go hand in hand with Google's ad business, which was soon expanded to these webpages themselves. Whereas Ad-Words is the auction-based system that shows relevant ads on Google's own search result pages, AdSense was added to export a similar system to the vast number of websites that internet users would then visit, mostly via a Google search. Regardless of where one would land in the vast expanse of the WWW, depending on what this website was about, one might receive an ad based on exactly *that* logic which had already matched ads with search words on Google's search pages. One might receive such an ad, that is, if a visited website had joined Google's AdSense programme *and* if Google had deemed this website worthy of ad placements.

As Vaidhyannathan (2011) writes: "If a firm's site does not say what it means and mean what it says, or if it installs malicious code onto users' computers, or if it is just ugly and complicated, Google will not reward that site with revenue, no matter how high the bid" (p. 28). From there on, Google's – more or less healthily – rigid relational style has had significant and very concrete effects on the character of the World Wide Web as we know it, with several of the operational updates to the ways it indexes and valuates websites during the past years risking harshly punitive outcomes for these sites. In 2011, for example, Google rolled out an update to their search algorithm called "Panda," which boosted the assignment of quality ratings to websites. The year after, in 2012, Google added "Penguin," to detect spam and artificial links and to ensure the relevance of a page. In 2016, "RankBrain," the AI augmentation of the search algorithm, was introduced to facilitate more seamless reinforcement learning for the searches of each Google user.

These updates are not so much continuous refinements of an ever-improving system, but rather moments in a continuous cat-and-mouse game between Google and a vast industry of Search-Engine Optimisers (SEOs). However, while Google's updates generally *did* lead to improvements – or at least repairments – in the quality of search results, their purifying drive also continually risked penalising trustworthy pages. Louis Chevant (N.D.) from the SEO Smart Key Words, for example, sought to calm the nerves of aggrieved business owners when writing about Google's Penguin update: "To know if a drop in traffic is due to a Penguin penalty, you should find out which pages are affected, and then analyze their backlinks" (n.p.). If your website claims to sell shoes, goes Chevan's example, and you have a lot of pages about "pumps," it might be "the Penguin has been there" (ibid).

A massive economy of tiny gifts

In December of 2000, *BusinessWeek* ran a story under the befitting headline of "Will Google's Purity Pay Off?" (in Vise and Malseed 2006, 53). For the past two decades, the answer has been, yes, very much so! What started as an idea with clear obsessive traits, and what had always oscillated between knowledge and power acquisition, generous sharing and rigid hoarding, eventually found its compromise in a complex defensive apparatus with which to integrate and at the same time resist advertising – to integrate it only in the most purified and cleansed form. While people in the world were invited to share in the knowledge that Google had amassed, they were now asked to leave tiny morsels as gifts in return. "[A]gainst all odds," Levy (2011) writes enthusiastically, Google "was making [...] profit without surrendering its ideals" (p. 94).

Malseed (2007) remembers about his interview with Brin's father that the latter would regularly skip out of the bagel shop, "keeping close tabs on the parking meters, his and mine, and tak[ing] care when the time runs out to drop in more quarters" (n.p.). What Sergey seemed to have learned at home was that also the smallest sums could be of utmost importance – that 'many a little makes a mickle.' Now, Google had eagerly started to build small 'parking metres' and would place them all across the Internet. People would 'donate' a bit of their interest in the world to advertisers and, in exchange, advertisers would put their 'spare change' into Google's metres. Intentionally, the name "AdSense" not only evoked the human "senses," but "cents," too. This economy was thus one of grand generosity and, at the same time, utter control and penny-pinching. The obvious associations with toilet training find their high point when, on 1 April 2004, Google, as a requirement of becoming a publicly traded company, had to share their financial information with the bankers who would handle the IPO. George Reyes, Google's financial officer gathered the bankers in a room and put up slides with figures:

> The slides indicated that Google was indeed making pretty good profits. Not earthshaking but more than respectable. [...] Then Reyes told the bankers he was sorry, but he'd mistakenly put up the wrong slide. Could he display the real numbers? A balance sheet appeared with more than double the revenues and profits on the previous slide. It exceeded even the wildest expectations. April fool!
>
> (Levy 2011, 69)

An interpretation focusing on the anal characteristics of the above anecdote might state that the "Google guys" (Playboy 2004) were indeed showing their superiors (i.e., their investors) how 'very big and grown-up' they were by making them some 'big presents.'

'To know everything' – the obsession with user data

Delving deeper into the programming and design of Google Search, what seems striking, particularly from a perspective focused on compulsion, is how free from such symptoms the service has been running. While "engineering obsessions" (Levy 2011, 100) of an amassing kind have steadily been at the roots of Google's ventures – *All of the Web! All the world's books! All television!* – Google has just as steadily managed to relax this obsessive drive, once a service was up and running, and it is this ability to relax that been key to its high functionality and success. Durham Peters (2015), for example, writes that:

> Google treats its search algorithm not like a logical positivist, searching for the purity of a rigorous definition that would eliminate the semantic penumbra, but like a happy-go-lucky pragmatist willing to crawl the snail trails of associations wherever they lead. (p. 331)

Just as Facebook managed to sublimate raw, phallic libido into playfully subdued flirtation, Google's PageRank algorithm has been geared to make pragmatic priorities based on practical approximations (see also Vaidhyannathan 2011, 61–2). Indeed, there seem to be key aspects in the programming of PageRank that are relaxed to such a degree that they border on the careless. For example, as Rieder (2020) points out, included in the PageRank algorithm is a "damping factor that limits the extent to which a document's rank can be inherited by children documents" (Page 2004, 7). This so-called "alpha value," Rieder (2020) explains, is instrumental for determining "how far through the network authority should propagate" (p. 288). Despite the obvious importance of this value, however, Alpha has been determined on an "intuitive" basis, as Page and Brin (2012 [1998], 3827) admit. And Rieder (2020) rightly critiques this as "the exchange of robust theoretical involvement for little more than commonsense reasoning" (p. 289), even evoking Lacanian vocabulary to gesture towards the ephemeral, insubstantial nature of this value by calling it "Objet petit Alpha" (p. 288).

Nevertheless, the more relevant shaping powers of Google Search are informed by a continuation of its obsessive traits and their expansion into other territories. And, once the smooth functioning of search was firmly warranted, the company's gravitation towards the obsessional saw this latter being displaced onto the amassment and accumulation of user data. "To keep making consistently accurate predictions on click-through rates and conversions, Google needed to know everything," Levy writes dryly (2011, 120), and indeed, Zuboff's (2019) exemplary reading of one of Google's patent applications, "Generating User Information for Use in Targeted Advertising" from 2003 (see p. 77ff), suggests as much. When she finds here a logic implemented that serves to perform an "instant translation from query to ad" (p. 78), already this notion of translation flies in the face of Google's principle of purity. Accordingly, the patent etches out major inroads into the mining of user profile information (UPI) by means of inference, presumption, and deduction (p. 79), either in relation to individual users or user groups, or reliant on third parties and/or automated modelling techniques (ibid). Zuboff (2019) argues that what is being produced through this all-penetrating mining strategy is a "behavioural surplus," and this surplus she wants to be understood *literally*. She writes:

> Behavioural data, whose value had previously been 'used up' on improving the quality of Search for users, now became a pivotal – and exclusive to Google – raw material for the construction of a dynamic online advertising

marketplace. *Google would now secure more behavioural data than it needed to serve its users.*

(Zuboff 2019, 81; emphasis added)

Overlooking the Google patents dealing with advertising of the early 2000s, one cannot but agree with Zuboff, and what she, in political economic terms, calls "behavioural surplus," in the perspective of the present study is understood as a symptomatic marker for the displacement and return in a different guise of those obsessive structures which have been characterising the company from the start. According to Zuboff, this displacement marks a radical turn from the 'virtue of Search' to the 'vice of Ads' – from the forces of light to those of darkness. The ad system's hunger for user data, she writes, transformed Google from a "youthful Dr. Jekyll into a ruthless, muscular Mr. Hyde" (ibid).

I agree that this obsession with user data has played a central part in the formation of "social relations of surveillance based on asymmetries of knowledge and power" (p. 81), and I will look deeper into how these asymmetries play out in social interactions below. However, the compromise formation that made the ad system morally permissible in the first place also suggests ambivalences and ambiguities, conflicts and contradictions, which paint a more complex and truthful picture than Zuboff's high-contrast one. When the Marxist Internet scholar Christian Fuchs (2014) claims that "Google stands at the same time for the universal and the particular interests on the Internet," representing "the idea of the advancement of the Internet that benefits humanity and the reality of the absolute exploitation of humanity for business purposes" (p. 149), this is arguably no less dramatic a position than Zuboff's, but comes closer to the company's obsessive-neurotic compromise formation.

Language game modelling

In order to trace these conflicts a little further into the programming, I would like to present and discuss another of Google's patent documents. Specifically, Georges Harik and Noam Shazeer's patent, "Method and apparatus for characterizing documents based on clusters of related words" (2003), does not merely show how the separation between organic searches and ads would gradually erode, but also how much the desire for Google Search to be useful and relevant served as a reparative, compensational fantasy with which to counter this erosion. More precisely, the patent shows how ad placement and search were not so much intermixed in this design, but rather sublated on a higher level of virtuousness that became introduced with the gradual refinement of automatic language modelling. When Rieder (2020) remarks critically that "Google nowadays prefers the term 'useful' to 'important'" (p. 288) and attributes this to the workings of the Alpha (damping) value, what can be added from this chapter's perspective is that this solution of "usefulness" is clearly at the heart of Google's ideal of, in Strauss's (2014) words, "a world that holds together without any hole" (n.p.). It is this universal focus on the useful that

I see as driving a utilitarian attitude on the part of Google's users which has been shaping the sociocultural ever since.

Turning to the automation of language modelling, the need for an intelligent way of handling search queries was apparent from the time the service opened to a broader user base. Durham Peters (2015) writes that, already "In their founding paper, Brin and Page 'vehemently' opposed the idea that search queries should be exact and lengthy. They favored demotic entreaties, open access to the inarticulate" (p. 330). Along these lines, the service needed to develop ways of translating people's frequently obscure queries into items that the engine could handle in ways that resulted in meaningful finds. When, in 1999, the freshly hired data engineer Amit Patel was first tasked with the analysis of user data, he was particularly struck by the way people would alter and refine their searches when their first attempts did not bring the hoped-for results. "So someone would say 'Pictures of dogs,' and then they'll say 'Pictures of puppies.' That said that maybe dogs and puppies are inter-changeable," Amit Singhal, another engineer, explained to Levy (2011, 46), "We were learning semantics from humans, and that was a great advance" (ibid). But not only interchangeabilities and synonyms needed to be learnt, also contextual differ-ences. "Hot," for example, meant something different in "Hot Water," "Hot Dogs," or "Hot Girls," and the system had to be programmed to tell these apart. "New," "New York," "New York Times," and "New York Times Square" again referred to distinct phenomena, even though there was a significant degree of overlap between them.

In his interview with Levy (2011, 48), Singhal credits Ludwig Wittgenstein's language philosophy for Google's breakthrough in language modelling. And like Vaidhyannathan and Durham Peter's references to pragmatism, Wittgenstein's take on language holds that the 'essence' of language resides in concrete use scenarios and in what he called "language games" (Wittgenstein 1953; Moi 2017). The chal-lenge for Google Search was – and is – that countless different language games are being played every second of each day (at the time of writing, about 350.000 per second), so that the establishing of what each game is about and what context it ap-plies to became key. Importantly, then, next to building a usefully ranked index of the World Wide Web, another main challenge pertaining to Google Search was to build a machine-learning system that would be able to 'understand' what language games people were attempting to play when embarking on a web search.

In this way, a focus on language modelling, understood as "language-game modelling," or the modelling of concrete language uses, already casts a light on the relevance of personalisation and the use of personal data that is at least partly different from Zuboff's interpretation. To a colleague, Page once explained that "[w]e are not really interested in search. We are making an AI" (Kelly in Fisher 2018, 278), and this suggests that the obsessive stowing of user data could always be attributed to the continuous need for more data with which to train the AI to dis-ambiguate the use contexts of people's searches. Since queries were typically brief, the more information the system had about the individual user (and other users like them), the better it could associate the words in their query to use scenarios. In this perspective, then, use data could be seen as merely an extension, qualification, and contextualisation of the general language model that Google was building. And as much as the possibilities for surveillance that the company was thus creating started to shift the balances of social power in its favour, this could still be seen as being done in the name of serviceability and the greater public good.

Compulsions of usefulness and relevance

This, then, is the context in which Harik and Shazeer's (2003) patent makes sense; it defines and constructs relationships between users, language (games), search queries, and advertisements. In elegant and (relatively) accessible prose, the authors describe here a system that, once trained sufficiently, would automatically identify, characterise, and suggest contexts for various kinds of information: new webpages being crawled, new advertising being pitched, or new search queries being entered. All of these would be – and are now – handled as "sets of words" for the task of determining the highest probabilities of how a particular set might be related to already learned clusters of concepts and contexts. Rieder discusses the "Bayes Classifier as interested reading of reality," so the title of his article from 2017, emphasising just how widespread this ordering device, which calculates "the fit between [an existing] word list for a category and the word list for each incoming document," is in "the larger field of contemporary machine learning techniques" (p. 108). Correspondingly, Harik and Shazeer (2003) give a detailed description of how their system relates to Bayesian Networks, categorising their variation as a "Bayesian Network with noisy-or combination functions" (n.p.) – meaning that context probabilities are created based on whether, and if so, which of the possible root contexts for an incoming document display what degrees of fit between them.

When towards the end of the patent application the authors list the "possible uses of our model," the motivations driving the patent become more concretely graspable. "Guessing at the concepts behind a piece of text" is the most general one, followed by "Comparing the words and concepts between a document and a query," which in turn is followed by the disambiguation of search queries. "For example," the patent states, "a query for the word 'jaguar' is ambiguous. It could mean either the animal or the car" (Harik and Shazeer 2003, n.p.). Then, however, and sandwiched between the above and a wide range of further applications such as detecting misspelled words and filtering out pornography, the uses for advertising are specified as: "Comparing the words and concepts between a document and an advertisement" and "Comparing the words and concepts between a query and an advertisement" (ibid).

In this way, the word and concept clusters to which increasingly more "sets of words" are added become the vassals within which users, their searches, webpages, and ads are pooled together and then elevated. Since language here essentially comes packaged in language games which only make sense in the specific scenarios in which they are being used, everything for Google becomes interesting from the perspective of such usefulness. Webpages become interesting for their potential uses for users and advertisers, ads for their relevance for users' searches, searches, in turn, for what webpages and ads users find appealing. Users themselves become interesting in this context for the light they can shine on all those uses. In this way, the image of Google that emerges is not one of turning from a Dr. Jekyll to a Mr. Hyde, but rather a wild conflation of different kinds of roles and interests – private/corporate as well as common, public, and universal – which all flow into applications tied together in language modelling and intent on identifying the pragmatics entailed in its various articulations.

What the analysis of Harik and Shazeer's (2003) patent indicates is that, while Zuboff is clearly right to critique Google's vast expansion of its ad business all across the web, the company nevertheless remained tied to their compromise formation of relevance and usefulness. The more obsessive energy the company has invested in the aggregation of data to feed the ad system, the more it has sought to make this data improve the overall usefulness of its service. Yes, ads, websites, search words, and user data have all been thrown into the 'same pot' and intermixed, but this brew has nevertheless been refined to a significant degree by virtue of its contribution to an overarching sense of usefulness and serviceability. This brew, then, could still be conceived as virtuous, even if it optimised ad targeting at the same time. As Patel and Ahmad (2023) state about Google Search: "relevance is the hyper-optimized parameter" (n.p.). Paradoxically, then, this usefulness itself has taken on something compulsive, and it is in this compulsive form that it has been exuding a formative effect on Google's users. This formative effect, I argue, is best described along the lines of Herbert Marcuse's (1986 [1964]) notion of "repressive desublimation."

Usefulness and the repressive desublimation of knowledge

"[S]ociety emerges as *a lasting and expanding system of useful performances*," states Marcuse in *Eros and Civilisation* (1987 [1956], 89, emphasis added), in an attempt to flesh out, in sociologist Philip Walsh's (2008) terms, "the tendency towards technocracy and an all-pervasive culture of utility within contemporary society" (p. 242). Whereas this expansion of utility and usefulness refers to Marcuse's notion of the "performance principle," the tendency towards technocracy points ahead to the concept he has become best known for, namely, that of "repressive desublimation" (in his later *One-Dimensional Man*, Marcuse 1986).

Regarding this notion of "repressive desublimation," Marcuse (1986) observes the loss of a utopian and imaginative dimension of consciousness. Due to swift technological advances, modern society, Marcuse argues, has become increasingly capable of realising and materialising its existing ideals. By the same token, however, these technological advances and capabilities "are progressively reducing the sublimated realm in which the condition of man was represented, idealized, and indicted" (1986, 58). Put differently, when phenomena which used to be conceivable only in the realm of ideals become achievable, obtainable, control- and manageable and then rapidly seep into everyday life, they tend to be befallen by a structure of feeling characterised by disinterest, indifference, and entitlement, and it is this disinterest which unfolds a repressive trajectory.

In such a social reality, ideals do not lose their efficacy and truth value because they need to be rendered taboo; rather, they lose this vitality because they have been rendered mundane and unexciting, or, as Walsh (2008) puts it, they become, if not trivial, then *de-differentiated* (cf. p. 249). According to Marcuse, this de-differentiation is importantly facilitated by the commercial interests attaching themselves to technological advances. He writes: "If mass communications blend together harmoniously, and often unnoticeably, art, politics, religion and philosophy with commercials, they bring these realms of culture to their common denominator – the commodity form" (Marcuse 1986, 57). Along these lines, repressive desublimation defines a process of continuous devaluation by commodification leading to states of perpetual sameness and loss of vital tensions and life energies in the dialectic play of the synthesising and destructive forces of human-being (i.e., the Life and Death drives).

Rigid object relations

While it would take another 35 years before Google was invented, Marcuse's conception of repressive desublimation strongly resonates with what I see as its central psychosocial effect. In this respect, particularly Marcuse's diagnosis of a flattening out of the human faculty of imagination and a subsequent de-differentiation of human relations with the world are characteristic of what Vaidhyannathan (2011) has warned against as the Googlisation of Everything. This Googlisation, I argue, can be traced in contemporary social relations in the form of two opposing yet inherently related tendencies in user interactions which both display obsessive traits. On the one hand, one can find in the uses of Google the tendency to intuitively co-opt the objects that are being returned by a web search. On the other, one can find a general tendency towards a spectacular form of estrangement that conceives of an object as an absolute other. Put differently, Google's repressive desublimation effect and its flattening out and de-differentiation of the sociocultural sphere is one that either suggests – and thus normalises – the seamless availability, obtainability, and controllability of objects and people in the world. Or it suggests – and thus normalises – these objects' status as absolute others – others, that is, who no longer share any common ground with us (see also Johanssen and Krüger 2022, 125ff). Flippantly put, what the act of Googling has helped bring into the world as a new, compulsively tinged common-sense is that others can be known, can be controlled and have wielded power over, because they are literally offered to us on webpages and social media profiles and made digestible as well as reduced in complexity through what other pages have captured about them on the web.

In shrill colours this co-optation effect is brought to the fore in David Eggers's novel The Circle (2013), with the novel's ending poignantly emphasising the slippery slopes between knowledge, control, ownership, and drive to power so prevalent in communicative and informational capitalism. The book's protagonist, Mae, who climbs the ranks of a digital technology firm by being instrumental to this firm's massive extension of data capture and surveillance practices, ends up sitting at the side of the hospital bed where her friend and colleague, Annie, lies in a coma:

> What was going on in that head of hers? It was exasperating, really, Mae thought, not knowing. It was an affront, a deprivation, to herself and to the world. She would bring this up with [the heads of the company] at the earliest opportunity. They needed to talk about Annie, the thoughts she was thinking. Why shouldn't they know them? The world deserved nothing less and would not wait.
>
> (Eggers 2013, 258)

I agree with the book's critics, who accused it of demonising digital platforms; yet, what the quoted scene shows in abundant clarity is an attitude that, in less spectacular form, has become central to a Googlised common sense. Returning to the scene that Leta Jones (2016) discusses in her study on The Right to be Forgotten (see beginning of this chapter), a variation of this attitude can be found in the French school's official reasoning for letting its arts teacher go. "[T]he Internet had ushered the 'erotic portion of [the teacher's] career into the present'" (p. 4), it stated, thus putting its argumentation onto the basis of a primary-process-like thinking that knows no time – no past, no history, no change – only the present. This is an argument that obsessively clings to its truths and that cannot let the past go but instead makes it play out in the present again and again.

In a more general but related context, Wendy Chun (2021) writes that: "Correlation is complicated. [...] It condenses, displaces, multiplies" (p. 244). Indeed, Chun's argument about the ideology of programmed "homophily," the creation of neighbourhoods of like-minded people, points to the same othering mechanisms that I am discussing here. Chun brings these mechanisms into the picture by returning to 20th-century practices of "eugenics" and "segregation" (p. 239). Eugenics aimed at 'pruning' people so that they would meet similar 'quality standards,' while those who would not meet these standards were to be kept separate from those who did.

A less political scenario than Chun's, related by the psychoanalytic therapist Aaron Balick (2014), shows how compulsive acts of othering can unfurl, not from a position of power and a feeling of being powerful, but, to the contrary, from a position of vulnerability and powerlessness. When, one night, Balick found a large, dangerous looking centipede in his home, he caught it and handed it over to the Natural History Museum, where the uncanny curiosity of his find was affirmed. The museum's monthly magazine published a short article on the hair-raising centipede and, soon after, the story had gone viral (2014, 33), becoming one of the most read and reposted stories around the globe in 2005. This virality, however, fed Balick's name into Google's database, with many different pages linking his name to the curious story, thus creating an online version of himself that inalienably tied him to the centipede. While there are surely much worse stories one can imagine going viral about oneself, this relatively innocent one nevertheless had an impact on Balick's professional life. Long after he had forgotten about the event, one of his patients, in a weak moment and in need of a feeling of safety, searched him on Google and found the centipede story. Balick writes:

> While we can only presume that in his search [the patient] was unconsciously seeking what he knew of me from our sessions together, what he found was a completely disproportionate representation of me that seemed utterly alien to what he knew of me and felt like a betrayal.
>
> (Balick 2014, 39)

This notion of betrayal again gestures towards the tendency for the acquisition of knowledge to become infested with a more regressive leaning towards ownership, control, and the wielding of power. And frequently it is not the case that we regress towards a drive to gain power over others because we feel powerful, but because we are afraid of what we might learn.

Conspicuously, the notion of betrayal flares up again in the title of Seth Stephens-Davidowitz's popular-science book, *Everybody Lies* (2017). Enthusiastically, the book builds on the thesis that investigating accumulated Google search data "can tell us a lot more about what [people] really think, really desire, really fear, really do than anyone might have guessed" (2017, 4). While, according to the author, we all lie to each other in order to keep up conventional appearances, our 'true selves' can be revealed in quantified Google searches. However, giving credence to this argument, I think, would amount to shifting all epistemic authority to a cultural unconscious that is significantly formed by the overall process I am seeking to describe here. Hence, when the author, by way of a flabbergasting example, points out that, "On Obama's first election night, [...] roughly one in every hundred Google searches that included the word 'Obama' also included 'kkk' or 'nigger(s)'" (p. 6–7), this markedly primitive stance is not simply a 'truth' that is 'out there.' Rather, it ties directly in with the play of inhibition and disinhibition that Jacob Johanssen (2019; 2021) has fruitfully identified with digital modes of relating. When Johanssen writes together with Bonnie Rambatan, that "[b]odies and networks are trained to habitually act in particular ways which are fundamentally dis/inhibited, clustering with those who are like them and forming lines of segregation" (Rambatan and Johanssen 2021, 39), this brings Chun's (2021) programmed "homophily" argument closer to a psychoanalytic understanding and fleshes out one of the forms that the repressive desublimation of consciousness has taken.

In a study on social media and human development, Kate Eichhorn (2019) writes that, "[b]y the end of the first decade of the new millennium, the realm once known as 'cyberspace' [...], which had promised to help us forget who we really were, had become, instead, an obstacle to forgetting and being forgotten" (p. 64). Examples abound for this rigid mode of 'unforgetting'; Google CEO Eric Schmidt, for example, advised people that, if they do not want to accumulate unwanted information in their search histories, they should not do these unwanted things in the first place. Likewise, Mark Zuckerberg claimed with an eye on the fake-name profiles on Facebook, that not being the same person in every context would amount to lying. While the CEOs' statements might have been taken back and even regretted to a degree, structurally, they have remained in place – by virtue of databases and analytics that do not forget and do not forgive.

The notion of forgiveness (or lack thereof), in turn, has become key in the obsessional-neurotic streak of digital modes of information management. Meg Leta Jones introduces the notion of "digital redemption" into the discussion: "As we watch search engines and social networks shift their societal roles, we must wonder if forgiveness and reinvention can and should move into the Digital Age, when information lingers indefinitely and restricts individuals to their pasts" (Jones 2016, 12). When she refers to psychological literature that discusses lack of forgiveness as a public health issue, she once more points us to the potential implications of Google's 'compromised formation' of consciousness. Holding on to one's grudges and encrypting them within oneself can thus seamlessly be facilitated with the Internet and a personalised Google search, with the searchable web taking on a melancholic structure (cf. Balick 2014, 113ff). Hayat (2005) writes about obsessions in the clinic that they "are experienced as morbid inasmuch as they temporarily deprive the individual of freedom of thought and action" (p. 1179), and, in many cases of 'Googling and Being Googled,' this morbidity is brought upon people from the outside – by a search engine that compulsively and upon request repeats and reproduces the same injuries over and again, because a well-linked webpage bearing the hurtful information has proven powerful in drawing clicks towards itself. At the very end of his chapter on Google, Durham Peters (2015) asks: "Could our storage-crazy moment grasp the lesson that the worst thing to happen would be to lose loss?" (p. 376). And indeed, losing the ability to lose is the foremost characteristic of a compulsion.

Conclusion – *the lesser evil*

Freud (1913a) states that "obsessional neurotics have to develop a super-morality in order to protect their object-love from the hostility lurking behind it" (p. 325), and, dialectically, it is this super-morality that Google achieved with an immoral proposal – an ad system that would also start to protect the company itself against critique. In the past two decades, whenever critique was directed at Google, it could point to the virtuousness of its arrangements. For the USA, Vaidhyannathan (2011) writes rightly that the platform stepped into the void left by neoliberal politics and orientations that led to a retreat "from any sense of *public* responsibility" (p. 43; emphasis in the original). In light of the present analysis, one can say that this public calling is what is at the heart of Google's self-understanding. In other words, it has been the company's very persuasion of its own goodness that now works as the constituent fantasy to which it holds on compulsively.

In their *Playboy* (2004) interview, Brin and Page defined what the then-company motto "Don't be evil" meant. "[A]lways do the right, ethical thing," Brin offers, and: "It's not enough not to be evil. We also actively try to be good" (Playboy 2004, n.p.). This moral stance, which the company clings to (even though it let go of the motto), has increasingly been flying in the face of the antitrust cases that the US Department of Justice opened against Google, claiming the company illegally monopolised the online advertising industry. As US Assistant Attorney General, Jonathan Canter, explained in an interview (Swisher and Galloway 03/02/2023)[3]: "Google has the dominant position as the exchange. They represent the buyers, they represent the sellers, and then they buy and sell on their own exchange." As Galloway explains further: "if everybody has to pay an organization and [...] it's impossible to establish differentiation, it's not a service, it's a tax" (ibid).

This notion of a tax seems particularly fitting in Google's case – a private company that wants to be a public utility in corporate guise. When Canter goes on to say that Google, through their ad system, has built "a moat" around their business, this is the exact term that Google's engineers themselves used when they implemented this system. Levy (2011) quotes Gokul Rajaram, the AdSense product manager, saying that AdSense "was kind of a moat that protects the king's castle" (p. 104). To be fair, with the "king" Rajaram meant the search engine; and, if one can trust official numbers, this system of implementing a quasi-tax to protect the purity of search seems to be taken very seriously still. Dylan Patel and Afsal Ahmad (2023) from the tech analysis firm Semianalysis write that:

> On average, over the past four years, 80 percent of searches on Google haven't had any ads at the top of search results. Further, only a small fraction of searches – less than 5 percent – currently have four top text ads.
>
> (Patel and Ahmad 2023, n.p.)

And yet, even if these numbers hold, a private company can never be fully and entirely 'of the people and for the people,' and can never be a genuinely altruistic operation, no matter how much it tries *not* to be evil. "Would you prefer to have the government running innovative companies or would you rather have the private sector running them?" Schmidt asked rhetorically at a public Q&A in 2009, with Schmidt clearly landing on the latter (in Vaidhyannathan 2011, 45). However, even though one can see in individual cases how a company can be virtuous and protect people from authoritarian forces, such as when Google deletes abortion-related searches from people's search histories to protect them from government surveillance,[4] such virtuous policies can darken quickly in the course of an executive board meeting.

"Power corrupts, absolute power corrupts absolutely," goes the old saying. With Google having entrenched itself ever deeper in its justification of virtuousness, it has obsessively sought to protect its compromise(d) formation with a morality that, paradoxically, it has given itself to protect the people it serves from the powers it has amassed through this very service. Now it holds on to its immense powers, not in the name of its discarded "Don't be evil" motto, but because it sees itself as a *lesser evil*.

As for the people Google serves, they have become the inheritors of the company's tense relation to usefulness. While usefulness is surely a quality for a company to strive for, the compulsive form in which it is offered is geared to transmit traces of a process of desublimation that generally orients people's thirst for knowledge towards a wielding of power. With this, I do not argue that knowledge is ever without personal interest; in the case of Google Search, however, utilitarian motives are so thoroughly worked into its design that they become normalised in a way that seems pre-, even nonideological. As I have established in this chapter, Google tends to do this by moving the objects of our interest so close to us as to suggest they are ours, or so far from us as to imply they have nothing to do with us. This ease in relating to objects is part and parcel of the seamlessness and effortlessness with which corporate digital media have generally been offering to relieve us from the pressures of everyday life. In the case of Google Search, its formative power lies in the implicit invitation for users to inhabit projective identificatory modes of thinking and acting – an invitation to swiftly find, identify, select and use, or discard objects. Thus easing the burdens of self-responsibility and self-management, this relief comes with the risk of an overall regression in our forms of self-conduct. Assisting us with the many things we need to control in our lives, Google has also helped us establish a form of control that is uncontrolled and unruly itself.

Notes

1 https://app.podscribe.ai/episode/84679380, 00:35:40 (accessed 09/02/2023).
2 https://about.google/ (accessed 14/09/2023).
3 Find the transcript here: https://app.podscribe.ai/episode/84778159 (accessed 16/03/2023).
4 https://www.cnbc.com/2022/07/01/google-will-delete-location-history-for-visits-to-abortion-clinics.html (accessed 15/03/2023).

Chapter 5

The joke that isn't funny anymore – Twitter, aggression, and the perfect shitstorm

There are many names for the act of people ganging up on and attacking someone on the Internet in retaliation for what this someone has said and/or done to someone else on one of the corporate media platforms. Especially the term "firestorm," defined as "the sudden discharge of large quantities of messages containing [...] complaint behavior against a person, company, or group in social media networks" (Pfeffer et al. 2014, 118), has been a popular handle, both in academic circles and in wider cultural discourses. More recently, "digital vigilantism" has been introduced to point not only to a digital-media genre but also to a general social orientation and its moral dimension (Trottier 2020). Other alternatives circulating in academic discourse are "moral contagion" (Brady et al. 2020), or "negative word-of-mouth" (Stich et al. 2014).

In both popular and academic discussions, the word "shitstorm" has also been widespread (e.g., Pastore 2019). Though less palatable, the latter seems the more precise term, since the practice of hostile and vitriolic complaint by large numbers is closely related to well-established trolling strategies, such as "shitposting" and "crapflooding" (Coleman 2014). In these latter cases, online forum pages or discussion threads are literally flooded with repulsive imagery. Another trolling inspiration of the shitstorm are Distributed Denial of Service (DDoS) attacks, in which a website is bombarded with such a high number of (coordinated and automated) requests that it stops functioning and can no longer be reached. That these practices indeed bear a strong sadomasochistic dimension rooted in anal sexuality I have detailed elsewhere (Krüger 2020; 2021). Importantly, the psychosexual constellation of the shitstorm points to the proximity of humour and aggression, creativity and violence, inhibition and disinhibition, self-assertion, aversion, and self-deprecation, and, in this chapter, I will unfold these tense relationships in the context of what, until mid-2023, was known as Twitter, then renamed "X". The shitstorm pairs a dynamic of "crapflooding" with the aim of overwhelming a person, group, institution, or firm with a drive towards "naming and shaming" them (Favarel-Garriguez et al. 2020, 190) and dragging them in front of the eyes of others so as to effectively ruin their social existence. When Daniel Trottier (2020) writes about digital vigilantism that it is "not simply problematic or deviant," but that it may rather "be understood as a standardised mode of communication" (p. 198), it is this

DOI: 10.4324/9781003307044-6

sense of standardisation that I want to turn productive for my analysis. Hence, in this chapter, I unfold the shitstorm as a ritualised process as well as an inherent, structural dimension of social media platforms and their uses.

As regards the shitstorm and its neighbouring theorisations, it is Twitter/X that has inevitably and invariably been pointed to in the research literature as the foremost space for such assaults. Trottier (2020), for one, argues that "it stands to reason that a reliance on platforms like Twitter to air social grievances may exacerbate categorical forms of discrimination" (p. 201). In a similar vein, Rost et al. (2016) write that, in the light of the platform's affordance for users to be short and quick, "[i]t is less astonishing that Twitter has been involved in most of the recent cases of online firestorms" (p. 4). And that Pfeffer et al. (2014) deem it necessary to remind their readers that Twitter "is not the only platform which can serve as a hotbed for online firestorms" (p.119) can well be read as symptomatic for Twitter's reputation as the platform for trading aggressive charges (see also Murthy 2013). While the platform's relaunch as "X" might have been an attempt – albeit misguided (e.g., Kircher 2023[1]) – to shake off its poor reputation, it is becoming increasingly clear that the platform's use cultures are regressing further into primite modes of defence. Hence, with the future of "X" being ever more uncertain, I simply keep referring to "Twitter" in this chapter, since my focus lies on the original conception of the platform as a microblogging service.

The pointing towards Twitter as a 'primary suspect' has tied in with a wider orientation, in and outside academia, that has identified the platform with the troubling undersides of communicative connectivity. As a rough point of indication, a search for the platform combined with the search word "hate" on the University of Oslo's digital library portal brings more than 1,200 finds, compared with about 1,100 for the significantly more 'colossal' Facebook. To put these numbers further in perspective: Google and "hate" returns about half of Twitter's results, namely 650 hits; YouTube about 450; Instagram 130; and Tumblr as a more fan-specific platform a mere 33.[2] Hence, Twitter has long been perceived as a machine for hate and aggression – within academia and outside. And while the platform had been attempting to counter this perception through building in minor guardrails, such as the "read before retweet" prompt in 2020 (see Johanssen and Krüger 2022, 256), its new owner, the multi-billionaire and tech-entrepreneur Elon Musk, who acquired the company for 44 billion dollars in late 2022, has initiated a vast roll-back of such caution and embraced the phallic aggressiveness that has characterised – and haunted – Twitter since its inception.

Zooming further in on research on Twitter, studies have attempted to *map* hate speech on the platform (Lingiardi et al. 2020), looked into the instigators of hate speech and their victims (ElSherief et al. 2018) into the moving boundaries between free speech and hate speech (Enarsson and Lindgren 2019), and inquired into automatic and artificially intelligent ways of detecting and characterising aggressive users (Ribeiro et al. 2018) as well as the predictive features that might make such detection more feasible (Waseem 2016). As practised throughout this book, this chapter again sides with the relational and design-oriented approaches towards the formation of subjective dispositions in the social. In the words of Luke Munn (2020), what I seek to understand is "how hate might be facilitated in particular ways by hate-inducing architectures" (p. 2) – even though Munn's formulation here seems a little too eager to locate hate and aggression purely on the side of the architecture, thus leaving the intricacy of the human response and the entanglement of this response with both the rational and the irrational, as well as the moral and amoral, out of the picture (Bereswill et al. 2010).

Consequently, I seek to tease out and unfold the intimate connection between Twitter and aggression by conceiving of the shitstorm as a paradigmatic, "standardised mode of communication" (Trottier 2020, see above), as well as a contradictory form of *moral action*, on – and of – Twitter. Hence, in what follows I want to flesh out and corroborate this intimate, yet highly contradictory, connection between tweeting and 'aggressing' by digging into the platform's history: the people building it, its influences and forerunners, its design choices and programming. In this respect, historical and generative aspects (i.e., those pertaining to how things become) play a central role in my assessment – aspects that have recently been captured wittily in Jean Burgess and Nancy Baym's *Twitter: A Biography* (2020). The most substantial contribution to this perspective, however, has come from Nick Bilton's in-depth study, *Hatching Twitter* (2013), in which the author reconstructs in vivid – sometimes romanticised – prose the platform's development, as well as that of the people who created and ran it, based on a wealth of interviews, internal communications, company protocols, and papers. When Bilton observes with respect to Twitter's early phase that "Companies often take on the traits of their founders and first employees" (2013, 92), this resonates with this chapter's analysis, which brings to the fore how the mix of affordances, preferences, and orientations arose that would make the shitstorm a psychosocial constellation structurally inherent to the platform.

In what follows, I will first reconstruct the cultural, design, programming, and biographical histories of Twitter and those who have contributed to its rise. These characteristics, which still inform interaction on the platform today, I argue, are fundamentally based on the social logic of the joke. In psychoanalytic and particularly Freudian theory, the joke is closely connected to aggression. It amounts to a small instance of persuasive communication – a mild act of seduction – in which the teller makes themselves vulnerable by attempting to bring their audience to spontaneously join in a mutual moral transgression that often entails an aggressive stance against another. This aggressively seductive/seductively aggressive element is one of Twitter's central affordances. It has become the core feature of "tweeting," where it is amplified through related – yet highly conflicting – motivations, intentions, and layers of meaning, most importantly that of moral watchfulness, which is diametrically opposed to the moment of seduction. In a sentence, I argue that Twitter taps into human aggression by inviting aggressive assertions of the self but at the same time triggering defences against such assertions.

Hence, the central moment in (the ignition phase of) a shitstorm is when an act of persuasion fails to prompt agreement (in laughter) on the part of its audience and comes into breach of the morality it evokes. While this act of persuasion is afforded by the platform, the hostile defence which sets in against it, once it is identified as in breach of moral norms, is so, too. In other words, what I claim is at the heart of a shitstorm – as well as baked into Twitter's interaction design – is *an attempt at seduction as well as its response in the form of the indignant feeling of:* '*Someone is trying to seduce me into something immoral*'. Since this latter realisation always comes *après coup*, i.e., after the seduction has already been attempted and after one has already been included inside its sphere, the counterreaction is all the more hostile, taking on hysterical aspects in the narrow psychoanalytic sense of the term, namely as the appropriation of another's desire by identifying with them (Evans 1996, 79). It is this identification and the defence against it that are afforded through the dynamic of tweeting and, paradoxically, both are again being performed with the very means that the platform affords: small acts of seduction along the lines of jokes.

Now, with the strictly formal and formative reading that I am unpacking here, I do not want to suggest that 'all shitstorms are equal,' or that there are no variations in them. As Jacob Johanssen rightly interjects (in private communication), there are, for example, shitstorms *by* as well as those *against* right-wing extremism which then have vastly different moral outlooks. However, the core of my project is to work out a *general dynamic*, baked into Twitter's design and use cultures, which holds true for, and becomes a productive tool of analysis for, a vast majority of cases. In this respect, it is a further point of my argument that *all* moral outlooks in a shitstorm swiftly regress to the group-psychological one of prohibition, retaliation, and annihilation (Freud 1921). Building thus on the social dynamic of a joke failing to seduce its audience, I complement this understanding of the shitstorm with psychoanalytic theories of mass psychology and group processes to make perceivable how Twitter's architecture and its multiple orientations facilitate a quasi-contagious dynamic in which increasingly large numbers of people unite behind a common moral ideal. With Twitter being centred on the distribution of small acts of seduction, users participating in a shitstorm ritually sacrifice one such seducer so as to expel this common element from their midst. Yet, as psychoanalytic theory holds rightly, "to kill the 'Father' is to remain within and reaffirm the law of the Father" (Adams and Girard 1993, 27). Put differently, *to retaliate against someone on Twitter is to reaffirm the law of Twitter*.

"Hatching Twitter" (Bilton) – assembling the building blocks of the shitstorm

In *Twitter and Society* from 2013, the first in-depth, academic study of the platform, Katrin Weller and colleagues write:

> While Twitter, Inc. has occasionally changed the appearance of the service and added new features – often in reaction to users' developing their own

> conventions [...] – the basic idea behind the service has stayed the same: users may post short messages (tweets) of up to 140 characters and follow the updates posted by other users.
>
> (Weller et al. 2013, xxix)

Apart from the doubling of the character limit to 280 in November 2017 – a relaxation of standards that did not receive a *unisono* welcome – Weller et al.'s assertion still holds true in the 2020s. Even with more space at users' disposal, the limitation of characters to what amounts to *brief communiqués* reminiscent of the classic telegram functions as the defining rule of the 'Twitter language game.'

As company lore has it, the character limit was derived from the app's main programmer, Jack Dorsey, and his fascination with dispatch and messenger services, such as truck couriers and bike messengers, emergency service communications – police, ambulance, fire brigades – GPS (Global Positioning System), and CB radio, as well as SMS (short message system) text messaging (Sarno 2009; Rogers 2013, x), which in the USA in the second half of the 2000s was still not a widespread practice. Dorsey's fascination dated back to the time before joining the team of the podcast development company, Odeo – a company whose main bid to podcasting was doomed to failure when tech giant Apple made podcasts an integral part of their iTunes service in 2005. The idea for Twitter was taken up when the Odeo team was literally faced with finding 'the next best thing' to develop so as to keep the company afloat (cf. Bilton 2013).

Other influences feeding into the creation of Twitter mentioned in existing documents are AOL's instant messenger, designed in 1997 mainly to give people the ability to post short away-from-keyboard (Afk) messages; LiveJournal, a blogging service which offered the possibility to write short status updates and was instrumental in giving shape to the whole online status-update genre; and Dodgeball, a location updating app similar to Foursquare, which had started in 2000 (Bilton 2013, 136ff). Furthermore, some of the Odeo staff had also been involved in creating TXTMob, an SMS-based, mobile phone application for coordinating political protest 'on the go,' which was an inspiration, too (Fisher 2018, 393).

The vision that emerged from these influences was to focus exclusively on short messages of a strict character limit, and this technological constraint would come to add a playful restraint and scarcity to the activity of tweeting – a constraint that has been the defining trait of tweeting ever since. And while there is something brusquely aggressive in the dispatch genre already, Twitter's character limitation has nevertheless been prompting an outpour of creativity and artistry – although mostly of an ephemeral kind. The name Twitter, a combination of "twitch" and "jitter", meaning "Bird song," "light, tremulous speech or laughter," "agitation and excitement; flutter", and "short bursts of inconsequential information" (cf. Bilton 2013, 158–9; Rogers 2013, xi; Sarno 2009), points to both this ephemeral creativity and the brusqueness. As Zizi Papacharissi (2012) found in a study on how individuals "perform the self through the use of Twitter trending hashtags," play proved a:

dominant performative strategy and pointed to the reordering of grammar, syntax, and literary conventions as prevalent ways through which play is performed. Affect, redaction, and deliberative improvisation frame performances that become part of the ongoing storytelling project of the self on Twitter.

(Papacharissi 2012, 1989)

Whereas I will turn to issues of selfhood and subjectivity later in the chapter, what is central in Papacharissi's (2012) article are the creative and artistic aspects in the improvisational play with linguistic and literary conventions. In this context, the forced brevity of the message suggests and brings about the kind of symbolic transformation in the descriptions of the everyday that is a core function of art – akin to Berthold Brecht's *Verfremdungseffekt* (the V-effect). This function has held an important place in Twitter culture and remains a key promise and attraction of the platform and its core service. While the company has taken various steps over the years to gradually introduce the circulation of more visual content, the artistry of tweets was originally – and is still very much – based on written language (albeit with an oral orientation).

The ephemerally artistic orientation of the service could further be found in the adoption of 'txtng speak', in which vowels would be dropped and words shortened or drawn together into acronyms, which again had emerged as conventions in "courier messaging protocol" (Rogers 2013, x), constructed along the lines of Short-Message-System code on mobile phones. Initially, this affinity was also captured in the first iteration of the Twitter spelling "Twttr" – a fashion of the mid-2000s that was set in motion by the then well-known photo-sharing platform *Flickr* (2004–) and which lives on in the dating app *Grindr* (2009–). However, already in the first test tweets, sent amongst the team, one can find the buddings of what would later expand into wide varieties of (mildly) creative renderings of the tweet genre: "Wishing I had another sammich", Biz Stone, Twitter's co-founder, wrote in one of the trials, and the approximation of 'sandwich' to the childishly munching pronunciation of 'sammich' can well be seen as the first attempt at creating a merciful counterweight to the spectres of banality and brusqueness that have been haunting Twitter use ever since – especially thanks to the many food-related messages clogging early users' feeds (before moving on into Instagram images). "Eating a vegan peanut butter cookie. Mmm," Ev Williams blogged to see what could be done with status updating as an idea, and: "Eating a vegan burger in Salt Lake airport" (Bilton 2013, 67). The food focus emerging from his attempts would soon set the mood for the "ambient intimacy" the service would become linked with (Rogers, 2010, xii).

While Twitter's basic idea of a messaging service with many-to-many functionality did not appear as markedly different from text messaging – a circumstance which caused a sense of unease amongst some of its stakeholders (Bilton 2013) – the introduction of the first iPhone in 2007, just a few months after the official launch of Twitter in mid-2006, and the service's strikingly smooth functioning on the iPhone's pre-installed web browser gave the platform a competitive edge over its rivals in the field. Yet, as became clear through the many food tweets, the transfer of dispatch messaging and CB radio chatter into a more general messaging application had a major weakness. Mostly, 'tweeters' were *not* on courier runs, and, mostly, the recipients could not be expected to be waiting on dispatches. In the mundanely intimate atmosphere that resulted from this original lack of purpose, tweets turned into updates on the things people ate and drank, the places they sat, the work being done or not, to watching, listening, hanging out. Hence, as with advertising, which frequently uses humour as an apology and in exchange for its intrusion into people's lives, the users' vague awareness of the redundancy, superfluousness, and, not least, intrusiveness of a fair number of their tweets made them turn towards the comedic and jocular, ironic, witty and clever, in large numbers so as to offer a reward, or remuneration, to those who would pay them attention. And again, the limited number of characters helped facilitate this, because brevity and an economical, reticent attitude towards words lends itself to jokes and their punchlines. "A new joke acts almost like an event of universal interest; it is passed from one person to another like the news of the latest victory", Freud (1905b, 15) observed about the inherent 'mediality' of jokes in his study *Jokes and Their Relation to the Unconscious*. On early Twitter, this held very much true; witty tweets were copied and retweeted repeatedly and thus showed a tendency of leaving their creators behind and started leading lives of their own.[3]

Theories of jokes and the comic – excursus

Fleshing out the role of wit, jokes, and the comic on Twitter and the shitstorm, a short excursus into the theory of the comic is in order. As regards jokes and the comic, the theory that has found most acceptance and uptake amongst scholars is the "incongruity theory" (Morreall 2020). The incongruity theory holds that jokes and other comic phenomena force things together that appear impossible to combine or think in relation with one another. Through its often twisted, faulty, and absurdly elliptical logic, the comic suggests visions of the world that are incongruous with people's intuitive and common-sensical understandings of what is normal, ordered, 'natural,' and right. Yet, in case of the joke being successful in prompting laughter, people's attempts at fitting the wittily incongruous claims of the joke into established understandings result in a renewed – and sometimes critically liberatory – appreciation of such understandings, including their cultivated, as well as *contingent*, character.

Indeed, frequently the insight offered in jokes and laughter holds the potential of a modification, recalibration – even recreation (which makes jokes *recreational* in the deepest cultural sense; Kris 1938) – of an aspect of reality which proves the putatively faulty logic of the joke to be true on a higher level of reasoning. For example, the one-liner characterising the internet as a place "where men are men, women are men, and children are the FBI," dryly and compactly, moves some of the aberrations of male sexuality, misogyny, and child pornography, which have been thriving online, into the centre of what characterises the space. It is this realisation of an elevated sense of paradoxical congruity in the midst of a wittily incongruous statement that connects the joke to the distancing, or V-effect of art, and further to the central modality of tweeting. As the Twitter account @NeinQuarterly puts it: "Tweet like nobody's reading. Because they're not" (01/06/2022).

Whereas the incongruity theory supplies a convincing view of what jokes and the comic do in the context of social reality, it is less powerful in allowing us to understand why people would want to meddle with their reality in this way. In this respect, the notion of recreation seems productive in that it points to the idea of a mode of relaxed, unfocused thinking that, uninhibited by logical restrictions, can lead to a heightened state of cognitive-affective functioning. Along these lines, the ego-psychologist Ernst Kris (1936) put forward the idea of the "regression in the service of the ego" as a formula that he extracted from Freud's (1905b) study of jokes. People can never give up on sources of pleasure they once have tapped into, psychoanalysis holds, and jokes and the comic offer a pleasurable means to re-enter a mental state in which the play with sounds, shapes, and forms trumps the logical differentiation of these forms' contents and conventional meanings. Kris held that this disorganising and reorganising along freely associative lines is not merely the source of the comic but that of creativity and problem solving at large.

Yet, Freud and Kris went further in their conception of the intra- and interpsychical motivations of jokes. Jokes and the comic, they held, are not merely artfully veiled invitations to the audience to harmlessly regress to more creative forms of thinking; rather, these regressions entail and make possible small acts of aggression and transgression and thus serve to circumvent established super-ego structures in the form of widely held morals and norms. By artfully bringing into play social prohibitions and cultural taboos, jokes suggest their trespassing without fully and openly committing to it (see also Dundes 1987). Hence, by cunningly lifting a ban, suspending moral taboos, and thus making the guarding of repression temporarily unnecessary, the energy that subjects otherwise use to keep up their guard suddenly becomes superfluous and is released in laughter. "Do you come here often," asks one male donor another at a sperm bank; "Only when the Internet is down at my place," replies the other. And whereas sexual themes do not activate grave cultural defences anymore, this joke still goes some way to show how aggression and transgression can flow into the mildly funny point of the internet as the go-to place for jerking off.

Within the psychoanalytic field, while most theories of the comic depart from Freud, they do not use his theory as a central point of reference. Lacan, for example, states that:

> the element in comedy that satisfies us, the element that makes us laugh, that makes us appreciate it in its full human dimension, not excluding the unconscious, is not so much the triumph of life as its flight, the fact that life slips away, runs off, escapes all those barriers that oppose it.

(Lacan 1997, 314)

This definition of the comic as residing in the *indomitability* of life connects to some extent with Freud's view of unconscious wishes and desires breaking their way through social and cultural obstacles; yet, Lacan's take also moves away from Freud's social concerns here. In turn, when Slavoj Žižek argues that the comic form makes it possible for us to, in Joseph Newirth's (2006) words, "faithfully symbolize the emotional, unconscious experience of the real" (p. 562), this still harks back to Freud, if more to the later Freud of the essay on "Humour" (1927), in which he conceived of the super-ego as taking on supportive functions in the ego's task of facing reality (cf. Critchley 2002).

Scholars in the Lacanian and Žižekian tradition, such as Todd McGowan (2017) or Alenka Zupančič (2008), have again built on Lacan's positions rather than on Freud's.[4] A red thread running through these post-Freudian theories of the comic is that they embrace inadequacy, failure, regression, and irrationality. In so doing, what they see as central in humour is human vulnerability. This vulnerability too becomes relevant for my understanding of Twitter. Nevertheless, I argue that, if one wants to adequately bring into view the techno-social dynamic of the platform, Freud's original statement and especially his formulations on "the joke as a social process" (1905b, 140) are still key.

This centrality of Freud's theory for the case of Twitter shitstorms can easily be demonstrated. For example, when Trottier (2020) outlines the communicative situation of the shitstorm as "a largely unidirectional relation, with one party acting, others mediating (or mitigating), and another being acted upon, and possibly reacting" (p. 201), this builds a strong parallel with what Freud sees as the dynamic of a joke. According to Freud (1905b), jokes again require three parties: the teller of the joke, the butt of the joke, and the "laughing third" as the joke's audience and judge. When he writes that it seems as though this third person "has the decision passed over to [them] on whether the joke-work has succeeded in its task – as though the self did not feel certain in its judgement on the point –" (p. 144), we encounter the vulnerability that post-Freudian theories emphasise once more. Here it comes in the form of an uncertainty that makes the joke teller turn towards others and in this way making themselves dependent on the acceptance and laughter of the audience to complete the process and validate the joke. That this uncertainty of judgement does not merely concern the formal qualities of a joke but is also heavily dependent on the context in which it is placed becomes clear when Freud turns to the "subjective determinants in the case of the third person" (1905b, 144). In this respect, Freud observes that "an audience composed of my opponent's devoted friends would receive my most successful pieces of joking invective against him not as jokes but as invective, and would meet them with indignation and not with pleasure" (p. 145).

Running somewhat ahead of myself here, what Freud works out as the joke's psychosocial dynamic is key to my understanding of the shitstorm. Specifically, by wrapping into elliptical form a measure of aggression and by inviting others to join in on this aggression and legitimise it with their laughter, jokes are not merely small transgressions of widely held morals and norms, but they are always also attempts (although half-conscious or unconscious ones) at establishing new moral frameworks by seducing others to legitimise these frameworks through their laughing consent. They are suggestive attempts at shaping "public opinion," since, after all, in the triangular situation of the joke, all depends on the reaction of the third. In their efforts to create 'critical mass' for a certain attitude, jokes must be seen to belong to the field of persuasive communication (cf. Krüger 2011). In this respect, however, the joke teller always makes themselves vulnerable in that they come to depend on others for the decision on whether they can be counted as part of the in- or the out-group and on whether they stand alone with their transgression or together with others in holding a new moral truth.

This dependency on the third can thus be encountered again in another, later text by Freud, "Group Psychology and the Analysis of the Ego" (1921), and this encounter, paired with the distributed social dynamic of a joke, forms the core of my psychoanalytic theory of the shitstorm. Freud refers here to McDougall's (1926) "principle of direct induction of emotion"[5] and unfolds it in the direction of his own theory, writing that:

> A group impresses the individual as being an unlimited power and an insurmountable peril. For the moment it replaces the whole of human society, which is the wielder of authority, whose punishments the individual fears, and for whose sake he has submitted to so many inhibitions. It is clearly perilous for him to put himself in opposition to it, and it will be safer to follow the example of those around him and perhaps even 'hunt with the pack.' *In obedience to the new authority he may put his former 'conscience' out of action, and so surrender to the attraction of the increased pleasure that is certainly obtained from the removal of inhibitions.*
>
> (Freud 1921, 84–85, emphasis added)

To a relevant degree, a joke can bring about the "removal of inhibitions" that Freud refers to and, for those laughing, such a mutually disinhibited state can indeed replace societal authority with a new one for a while. By the same token, such disinhibition can result from the agitated rejection of a joke's proposition. The moment at which a group of people starts aggregating around a joke – in its favour or in defence against it – is when the *virality* of the social Internet switches from a networked mode of distribution, circulation and contagion to a congregational mode of concentration, massification, and retaliation, resonant of crowd-psychological dynamics of the late 19th and early 20th century (cf. Baxmann, Beyes and Pias 2014). Hence, in the field of tension between a joke as a social process and the socialisation of the individual in a group of jesters (or as the butt of their jokes), Twitter shitstorms are born. The key moments from Freud's theory that feed into them are (a) an initial aggression that, in joke form, circumvents individual conscience functions, (b) a fundamental uncertainty of judgement that inheres in the joke's address, (c) the vulnerability inhering in its dependency on a third party, (d) a moment of suggestion and seduction that arises from the former two, and (e) the audience as an, albeit ephemeral, moral authority which promises disinhibition in the form of a mutual regression. As such, these elements are foundational for Twitter as a digital medium and a communication platform.

Twitter, wit, and aggression

Referring the theory of the comic to Twitter in general, one can see how already the atmosphere in which it was conceived was suffused with jocular transgressions reminiscent of Freud's theorised play between inhibition and disinhibition. Co-Founder Evan Williams, who was bankrolling the ragtag team of programmers and designers that would eventually develop Twitter, could already claim a measure of Silicon-Valley fame for having created the successful *Blogger* platform, which was bought by Google in 2003. By way of an anecdote, Bilton (2013) illustrates just how salient Williams's penchant for the jocular-transgressive was. In 2002, a new Blogger recruit was made responsible for the customer-service e-mail. Faced with the deluge of user complaints about the often-extreme contents of other users' blogs coming in, he asked Williams what to do and how to respond. To the amusement of the co-workers in the office, Williams simply answered by reciting Blogger's unofficial corporate motto: "Push-button publishing for the people." As Bilton (2013) explains, this basically meant "that anyone should be able to publish whatever they wanted" (p. 31). This attitude would carry over into Twitter; hence when Elon Musk, after having bought Twitter, rescinded the ban of ex-US president Donald Trump from the platform, this must be seen as merely reviving an approach to speech (be it free, volatile, hateful, dangerous, or extreme) that has informed the service from the first.

Furthermore, the 'anything-goes' attitude that is linked to such a disinhibited atmosphere has been widespread amongst Silicon Valley developers and entrepreneurs. Telling from the existing accounts about Twitter's development and early years, the transgressive outlook on how to do business online and run a social media company quickly became part of the platform. It is at work, for example, when Williams (quoted in Fisher, 2018) distinguishes between two production cultures in Silicon Valley, hackers and engineers, reserving the hacker label for his team of programmers and the engineer label for Google, the company to which he had turned his back soon after selling Blogger. It is also prevalent in Fisher's *Valley of Genius* (2018), which, like Bilton's (2013) account, is enmeshed in the heroic tradition of tech-company founding myths. In an assemblage of – "uncensored"[6] – interview statements by the people involved in Twitter's making, the platform emerges as one conceived by nerdy, anarchistic, anti-establishment, white men in their 20s. Evan Henshaw-Plath, aka Rabble, one of the anarchistic programmers on the Odeo team, who clearly served as a blueprint for some of the dramatis personae of the HBO show *Silicon Valley* (2014–9), had helped to develop TXTMob, one of the first applications that connected mobile phones for the distribution of messages to groups of people with the aim of organising street protests – "a social network for bringing down governments," as Rabble himself dubbed it (in Fisher 2018, 393).

This tool, too, served as a source of inspiration for Twitter and suggests just how deep a rebellious, transgressive spirit had been built into its code. Programmers of Rabble's ilk on the team felt little loyalty, or responsibility towards the service and worked on it with at least one eye on the expected pay-off of their stock options and with a good measure of contempt for the pedestrian use scenarios they helped facilitate. "I was waiting around for my stock options and ready to move on and had enough of the dot-com thing. I felt I wasn't changing the world enough," Rabble is quoted in Fisher's book (2018, 395).

As Bilton (2013) sums up the platform's early years, Twitter was very much operating "as an anarchist-hacker collective with no rules" (p. 92). But while it might have been more permissible to harbour admiration for its developers' deadpan refusal of editorial and social responsibility in the early 2010s, the radically anarcho-populist strain, which becomes aligned with the economic interests and profit strategies of social media platforms, has long since shown its anti-democratic potentials.

World News and Twitter r/evolution

As quoted above, Freud (1905b) likens the circulation of jokes to "the news of the latest victory" (p. 15), and this approximation of jokes to news points towards another of Twitter's central formative characteristics. Competing visions for the service had created tensions amongst the developer team from the start, particularly between Ev Williams, the CEO and owner of Odeo, and Jack Dorsey, one of Williams's more recent hires (Bilton 2013). It was during a brainstorming session that Dorsey introduced the idea of brief status-messages to his colleagues. While Dorsey saw Twitter's main usage to lie in such personal updates, Williams, true to his background in blogging, saw the service rather as a "mini blogging product," oriented towards "what was happening in the world" and, hence, towards news (Bilton 2013, 93).

Williams's more worldly orientation was at least in part fed by concerns about the relevance and respectability of Twitter as a communication tool – a concern that was surely better addressed with the service being associated with 'newsiness' than with the intimate banalities that it was accused of circulating (Kelly 2009, quoted in Burgess and Baym 2020, 14). Faced with the need for a fresh round of venture capital and under the pressure of financiers demanding their say on the Twitter supervisory board, Dorsey, who had been made CEO of the company months before, was replaced by Williams, who subsequently initiated a change in the platform's orientation towards news in 2009.

According to Jean Burgess and Nancy Baym (2020), the Twitter headboard constructed "a narrative of progress from a me-centered, personal, and intimate Twitter, to a world-centered, public and newsy one" (p. 13). Biz Stone, who had advanced to the spokesperson and PR manager of the company officially announced this change during 2009s South by Southwest festival, bragging that: "The fundamentally open model of Twitter created a new kind of information network and it has long outgrown the concept of personal status updates" (in Burgess and Baym 2020, 13). Even Dorsey himself admitted in an interview in the same year that Twitter was doing well at "… disasters, events, conferences, presidential elections" (Rogers 2013, x) – i.e., some of the mainstays of news. Hence, in 2009, Twitter's original prompt, which had asked "What's your status" and which shortly after, had been replaced with the more personal "What are you doing?'" (Burgess and Baym 2020, 12), was now again revamped into the more event and news oriented "What's happening?"

The San Diego wildfires in 2007, the Sichuan earthquake in 2008 and particularly the 'Miracle on the Hudson' in 2009, the first news story that had broken on Twitter (Rogers 2013, xvii), in which a passenger plane miraculously made a successful emergency landing on the Hudson River – these and other events had already indicated how Twitter could, and was made to, function as a grassroots news ticker. When civic unrest broke out in the wake of the 2009 election in Iran and anti-government activists partly turned to Twitter for organising, exchanging information, reaching out to the outside world, and drawing attention to the situation inside the country, this made a strong impression on Twitter's developers and their sense of the service's relevance for matters of top political priority. "There is quite literally a Twitter Revolution going on in Iran right now," announced a US State-Department email addressed to Twitter headquarters (quoted in Bilton, 2013, 209) and thus coined a phrase that, for a brief historical moment, would capture the techno-utopian hopes and dreams for Twitter stakeholders, academics, users, and laypeople alike.

Faced with such an acute sense of the platform's own relevance, not only as a news source but as a tool for democracy, the paradigm change from personal updates to current affairs, which Stone had announced the same year, must have appeared complete and irrevocable: "[A] technology that just three years earlier people had used to say when they were going to the toilet or to figure out where to get free beer at a party, was now being used in the streets of Tehran to try to overthrow the government", Bilton (2013, 209) evokes the mood of this historical juncture. However, after the first rush of enthusiasm had subsided and the first authoritarian leaders proven non-disposable by digital communication tools (with the search- and traceability of social media having unfolded its counterrevolutionary potential, too – by enabling authoritarian governments to track the revolutionaries), it became apparent that Twitter was not quite the unambiguous enlightenment tool that one might have been excused to take it for while the revolutionary dust had not yet settled. As Ulysses Mejias (2012) has rightly pointed out in his farsighted, early critique, protest movements abroad, such as the Arab Spring, served as boosts for the reputation of social media services at home: "Activists 'over there' are using these tools not just to talk about commercial choices, but about things that *really matter*: the overthrow of injustice, the plight of the poor, etc." (2012, 13). Retranslated into the context of Twitter, the idea of a "Twitter Revolution" offered a distinctly virtuous use scenario and a new type of user that could be imagined as someone, again in Mejias's words, "who applies these tools not for the frivolous ends of consumerism, but for the betterment of the world" (ibid).

The interrelated ideas of Twitter Revolutions in the Middle East and of Twitter as the facilitator of the democratisation of news turned out to be fantasies. Indeed, Twitter, in its reorientation towards the "betterment of the world," never managed to shake off its origins in the "frivolous" and mundane. Rather, a psychoanalytic understanding of these developmental stages points towards a complex entanglement of both and an uncomfortable afterlife of the frivolous in the newsworthy. As a result, Twitter's mundaneness has become more news-like, and its newsiness has frequently turned out to be more mundane than the fare being served by legacy news outlets.

Furthermore, on Twitter, the mundane and the newsy can frequently be seen to converge on the comical again. As stated, jokes on Twitter serve regularly as pay offs for the mundane. News, in turn, if it does not have an immediate impact on one's own life, can have similarly seductive effects: the short flashes of elation, scandalisation, or relaxation that particularly sports and entertainment news offer,[7] but that, by way of the trend of personalisation, have also found their ways into political news. The numerous celebrities who were early to turn on to Twitter, such as Ashton Kutcher, Oprah Winfrey, Drake, Zoe Deschanel, and Kim Kardashian, promised exactly such a kind of news – short, telegraphic, and excitingly punchy. As the pop singer Pink put it in her first tweet: "I have officially entered the 20th century. I mean the 21st" (@Pink 03/04/2009).

News, jokes, and aggression

But news and jokes also share an affinity with aggression, which plays an important role in both their dynamics. This importance is related to the role that aggression plays in human subject formation. From a clinical perspective, the psychoanalyst T. Wayne Downey (1984) has suggested that "aggression may be theoretically conceptualized as a positive force in psychological development and subsequent functioning" (1984, 101). He points towards the importance of aggression in early formative development, such as object seeking and ego constitution: "The aggressive drive serves the overall purpose of self differentiation and the establishment of an individual sense of identity" (p. 111). Otto Kernberg (1991), in an article on "Aggression and Love," makes a similar point in the context of sexuality when claiming that, while "the recruitment of love at the service of aggression" may define perversity, "sexual excitement incorporates aggression in the service of love" (p. 45–6). James Fosshage (1998), in turn, is more careful in his analysis of the function of aggression for a person's sense of self. He sees self-assertion and aversion to represent two different motivational systems regulating "a positive cohesive sense of self," with aggression falling under the second system, aversion. However, under felicitous conditions, he holds, aggression can still offer support to a positive sense of self by *augmenting* assertive acts

In augmenting exploration and assertiveness in overcoming obstacles, aggression can increase our sense of efficacy. This includes, for example, the aggressively tinged effort to be "heard" by the other. Aggression as one pole of aversiveness can serve multiple functions. In regulating our interactions and attachments with others, aggression serves vitally necessary self-protective, self-delineating, and self-restorative functions.

(Fosshage 1998, 47)

Ultimately, Fonagy, Moran, and Target (1993) summarise rightly that it is "generally recognised that aggression is not inherently pathological, and may be part of a healthy mental state. It has a pervasive influence on many everyday activities, such as professional rivalry, humour, sports and fantasy" and "It can also be protective" (Fonagy et al. 1993, 472).

This formative potential of aggression has bearings on the conception of news. Particularly, when Downey emphasises the connection between vision and aggression, this evokes very plausible psychic dynamics and economies of news production and consumption: "To see is to make contact, to take in, to possess in certain ways. Vision may pierce, glare, fasten on" (Downey 1984, 109). Likewise, particularly the theory of news frames (de Vreese 2005) has drawn critical attention to such proto-aggressive acts of object constitution in which news are created by selections and cuts and by deeming certain aspects to be within or without the frame of news, to belong or not belong to an object whose outlines come into view through culturally scripted interests and genre expectations. At the same time, a relational, psychoanalytic perspective would emphasise that we ourselves, the viewers and readers of news, emerge as acculturated beings through its particular framings in that we are interpellated as people who expect such news *as* news. Just as Laura Mulvey in her famous article on "visual pleasure in Hollywood cinema" (1975) sees maleness to be produced and reproduced in the "male gaze," news nudges both its objects and its spectators into their predefined places.

Fake news medium

The mixture of aggression, the comic, and news, as well as the idea of news being delivered from a perspective of a vernacular joke culture had already been in the air at the time Twitter was conceived, specifically, in the form of what from the mid-2000s became known as "fake news shows" – first and foremost *The Daily Show with Jon Stewart* (1999–2015) and its spin-off, *The Colbert Report* (2005–2014). These shows offered popular blueprints, not only for further spin-offs, such as *Full Frontal with Samantha Bee* (2016–2022) and *Last Week Tonight with John Oliver* (2014–), with both presenters again former contributors to the *Daily Show*, but comedy news shows around the world.[8] They also popularised and made palpable the mode of *gate-watching* that became a topical variation of online political commentary at the time (Bruns 2011). When Daniel Trottier (2020), in his "conceptual model of digital vigilantism," describes what he calls "mediated policing" – a constant alertness and state of being on the lookout – as a "general resting place for digital media users" (p. 204), I am wondering whether also these shows of the 2000s and 2010s were forebodings and early forerunners of this sociocultural attitude of vigilance. Stewart's hilarious performances of himself as an 'Average-Joe' member of the television audience became paradigmatic for an active and critical viewership in the context of digital convergence culture (Jenkins 2006, particularly p. 217ff). Steward would demonstratively watch news clips from other channels, coffee cup in hand, ritualistically spraying mouthfuls of its contents over his desk in – only half comedic – shock and bewildered disbelief at what these clips entailed. Many of those, however, who stepped into his shoes and sprayed their dismay over social media were not as endearingly funny and civil as Stewart's persona. Rather, they frequently adopted a 'voting-out' attitude that could be learned from the many Reality TV shows which flooded the niche television markets of the early 2000s (Ouellette and Hay 2008).

Yet, it is important to mark that it is not merely comedy and Reality TV shows that drove the trend towards mediated policing and gate-watching. Rather, such shows were themselves articulations of, and counter-reactions to, a political-communication culture that, in the wake of the success of neoliberalism, parted with the intimate connection between news and genuine reality testing that most had taken for granted. As Favarel-Garrigues, Tanner, and Trottier (2020) write about the ideological ground upon which digital vigilantism has grown:

> Liberal and neo-liberal politics have deputised citizens by rendering them responsible for their own security and fate, and for social order, thus leading to a multilateralized regulatory network rather than strictly top-down governance of society. Yet deputised citizens are not only following their authorities' recommendations; they are also self-directed in what they consider the good march of society. […] [S]uch a transformation in societal participation led to a shift from a deputisation to an autonomization paradigm, referring to the voluntary, or self-appointed, involvement of citizens in the regulatory gatekeeping network. This refers to grassroot mobilisation, rather than governments mobilising the public, with groups of citizens spontaneously aligning themselves with authorities' aims and objectives.
>
> (Favarel-Garrigues, Tanner, and Trottier 2020, 189).

With making news its priority, Twitter steered the usage of its service towards forms of gate-watching that both the comedy and Reality TV shows had coined, thus opening out and widening the field of play in which gate-watching could gradually become reworked into deputising and mobilising, regulating and retaliating. And why not? A PEW research report from 2014 stated that at least the viewers of the "fake news shows" were younger, higher educated, and more knowledgeable about politics than average cable news audiences. In other words, the people who watched fake news shows seemed to be exactly those users that Twitter was seeing to feed successful hashtags such as "CNNFail" (a hashtag protesting what was perceived as CNN's lack of coverage of the 2009 national election in Iran) on their platform. Hence, while these shows were no 'real' news shows but were nevertheless seen by a particularly highly educated segment of the US population to offer higher-quality news than dedicated news channels,[9] Twitter, which had likewise no claim in the established news business, could plausibly wager that it had enlisted the shows' audiences as its content producers.

The "fake news" label was never a very fortunate one for the shows in question. Regardless of the quality of the news made fun of in them, these shows themselves were seldom feigning or faking news. Instead, what they offered were satirical takes on the news, and this approach made them *shows about news,* which made the alternative label, "meta-news show," a better fit. However, the "fake news show" label circulated regardless and made it into a significant number of academic publications (e.g., Amarasingam 2011; Brewer et al. 2013). It is revealing from a historical viewpoint in the early 2020s, how connotations of "fake news" gradually shifted away from satire and notions of media critique that were tending towards the left of the political spectrum, to the more conspiratorial and antidemocratic connotations that became linked first and foremost with the Trump administration in the USA and, following Trump's example, populist leaders and governments across the globe.

In his study of satire television and political engagement, *Entertaining Politics,* Jeffrey P. Jones (2010) plays with the categories of "fake" and "real," and it is striking how his historically still innocent semantic operations evoke the more sombre cultural turns of these words that were waiting to be fleshed out a few years later:

> [W]hat if the fake is actually just a mode for accessing reality in different ways? What if the fake can actually produce a more realistic picture of the world by stepping outside the traditional (and accepted) means of encoding reality that were established through the conventions of news?
>
> (Jones 2010, xi)

While these musings seem to encapsule some of Twitter's ambitions at the end of the 2000s, in the early 2020s they must at least partly be understood along the lines of the political paradoxes that the platform has become entangled and complicit in.

Relevant in this respect is how, in his account of the various metamorphoses of Twitter, Rogers (2013) collocates the service's turn to "newsiness" with the gradual emergence of a use culture that saw it become a *gossip machine*: "The South by Southwest conferences in 2007 and 2008 in Austin, Texas," Roger writes, "established Twitter as an event backchannel, a kind of gossip machine for commenting on what one thinks of speakers' talks" (McCarthy & Calore 2008, in Rogers 2013, xvii). This was not so much the news themselves than, in Jon Stewart's words, "a comedic interpretation" of the news (quoted in Jones 2010, 76).

The push-button communiqué

Let me break down the chapter's findings so far and bring them together in a compressed image of the ambivalences and ambiguities that Twitter worked into the overall direction of its service. Due to the conflicting visions that both developers and users harboured about the platform and the various shifts and turns the service had taken in response to one or other such vision, Twitter created a space where gossip and rumours, jokes and fun, as well as intimate ambience coexisted, mingled and merged with news – a space between an informational and a social-relational network, and between the political consequence of news and the inconsequentiality of a me-me-me-chirping 'ego-machine' (cf. Seymore 2019). Therefore, Nathan Rambukkana (2015) might be right to a degree when claiming that Twitter and the media ecologies it created can take various kinds of forms: "communities, publics, discourses, discursive formations, *dispositifs*" (p. 2). At the same time, however, the intentions, desires, and motivations for the service, the conflicts around and politics behind it, have made some of those forms decisively more plausible than others. For example, the core idea of the brief personal update combined with the basic functionality of following and being followed does not automatically lend itself to dialogical structures of communication. In an early article, Marwick and boyd (2011) pick up on this as a "disconnect between followers and followed. [...] [M]usician John Mayer (johncmayer) is followed by 1,226,844 users, but follows only 47" (p. 117). And even if technology writer Steven Johnson ventures that "… that's fine. Not everything has to be a conversational medium" (in Fisher 2018, 401), this technological limiting of the dialogical has been haunting the platform and must be seen as having played its part in many of the political challenges it has faced over the past decade, with the most substantial one unfolding as I am writing this, under the spell of what has been called Musk's "cultural vandalism" (Newton 2023).[10]

What the structural features discussed so far *do* suggest, however, is the production of brief, punchline-like communiqués – announcements and declarations – that filter news items and commentary through the seductively charged perspectives of (mildly) transgressive attitudes, shot through with primary-processual thinking, which in the context of Blogger had been stamped as "push-button publishing for the people." To be clear, this disposition that the platform itself creates does not mean that no other form of interaction or social formation is possible on the platform; however, it means that these alternate formats must then be established through creative, at times appropriating uses that go at least partly against the platform's orientations.[11] By contrast, what the service itself suggests, affords, and channels on its platform is what might be called the *push-button communiqué*.

Hashtag-mindset – Twitter's core affordances and their formative powers

This unguarded and, at the same time, highly vigilant form of interaction which arises as the core communication genre on Twitter becomes yet more defined and salient when approached in the context of the main "technological affordances" (Stanfill 2015) that the platform added throughout the years. These are specifically the personal address "@username" (since late 2006), which makes it possible to address another user directly; the hashtag "#" (incorporated in 2008), which allows tweets to be ordered and categorised into thematic clusters and groups; and the "retweet" ("RT"; as a button since 2010) function that allows a tweet to be redistributed by other users. As Burgess and Baym (2020, 36) observe, all three features were first introduced by users in search for conventions that would achieve basic communicative effects: addressing someone, gesturing towards something, and sharing someone else's contribution.

All through its history, the company would move to incorporate features into its interface and algorithms once they had become widespread amongst users. In this way, the platform acknowledged "the needs the users sought to fulfill with the feature" while at the same time "serving their emerging business model, seeking to make Twitter more seamless for new users, in pursuit of growth, and more datafied, in pursuit of opportunities to monetize that growth" (Burgess and Baym 2020, 36). While the "@" function might have bettered Twitter's lack of dialogical structures and helped it become more conversational, it also gave the company new data sets and an entirely new "way of observing connections" (Burgess and Baym 2020, 44) beyond the basic affordances of "following" and "followed." Likewise, the rendering of the emerging use convention of "retweeting" prompts users to follow a solid conversational etiquette by automatically repackaging an original tweet and including information on the original author when another user recirculates it. Again, however, this same change in the programming also made activities and connections on the platform more visible, trackable, and commodifiable:

> Just as the @, once embedded, provided a metric that could be used to determine and amplify 'value,' the RT offered a new metric more in line with advertising and media business logics than social networking site logics. Before long, that metric, along with the number of likes and replies, were affixed by design to every tweet.
>
> (Burgess and Baym 2020, 91)

By increasingly tying content to its originators, what both the "@" and the "retweet" have been driving towards is the individuation (Simondon) of Twitter users who are now time and again identified as *creators*. The affixing of user metrics, in turn, which is fed by a promotional logic, to the user interface likewise served as a prompt for users to 'individuate' and start orienting their interactions towards the self-promotional. As Marwick and boyd (2011) were early to point out, Twitter's introduction of the logic of metrics passed ideas of self-promotion on to the users, who adapted their interactions to the audiences that would become visible through these very metrics. Users learned how to formulate, assemble, and spin their tweets so as to 'amp up' their popularity, learned how to create and differentiate between various audiences through strategic modes of address, and how to play to and lead a following.

The hashtag, as the last of the major additions to 'tweeting,' has been praised as the platform's "killer-app" (Bruns and Burgess 2015, 13). By building the hashtag function into its architecture, Twitter gave users the possibility to create discussions on certain themes and issues and make them search- and retrievable. Hence, what the "@" function achieved at the interpersonal, micro level, and the RT at the meso level (i.e., the making traceable of connections beyond users' immediate followings), the "#" achieved at the macro level of issues and trends (Bruns and Burgess 2015, 15). All three made it possible to order and categorise increasingly vast user numbers into 'interest' and target groups. In the latter case of the hashtag, however, the sheer quantity of tweets and users that can spontaneously be gathered around an issue has added unforeseen qualities to the phenomenon of tweeting.

The hashtag function moved Twitter a decisive step closer to its goal of becoming a new type of news medium. The speed and near instantaneity with which a public can be formed around an emerging issue through the simple creation of a Twitter hashtag can turn any event into a media event. As Bruns and Burgess (2015) explain:

> Even online, news stories must be written, edited and published; commentary pages must be set up; potential participants must be invited to join the group. Twitter's user-generated system of hashtags condenses such processes to an instant, and its issue publics can indeed form virtually ad hoc, the moment they are needed. [... I]t is this very flexibility of forming new hashtag communities as and when they are needed, without restriction, which arguably provides the foundation for Twitter's recognition as an important tool for the discussion of current events.
>
> (Bruns and Burgess 2015, 23)

Again, the notions of speed and "ad hoc," I argue, have bearings on users' attitudes towards the praxis of tweeting, which in turn have implications on how users experience themselves as social beings. In this respect, the notions of speed and spontaneity coming to the fore here are closely aligned with many of the characteristics already discussed, especially the quick-wittedness that is part of the comic, but also the absence of a degree of reflection, elaboration, and qualification, which once more points to the dimensions of aggression and regression in tweeting, as well as the more *risqué* aspects of the push-button communiqué.

Weapons of mass inflammation

At this point I have gathered all relevant functions, affordances, tendencies, orientations, and implications of Twitter, as well as the most central motives, intentions, conflicts, and contradictions that went into its design and development. Let's line them up once more so as to bring them into view in condensed form. Twitter's central and simple idea has been the publishing of brief status updates that, due to their rigid space limitations and to avoid coming across as trivial and banal, have from the first been evocative of creative uses. When Sarah Frier (2020) in her insider story of Instagram writes that "Filters on Instagram was like if Twitter had a button to make you more clever" (p. 45), this drives home the central importance of wit and cleverness for the service. In this way, the service was also from the first bent towards the comic and jokes, which entail a substantial, though more or less sub-limated, amount of aggression and primary-processual thinking. The presence of aggression has been nurtured further by the characteristics of speed and spontane-ity, as well as the particular gate-watching positioning of Twitter users who, upon the service's turn towards current affairs and newsiness, were prompted to filter commentary on "what's happening" in the world through their own, trivia-defying, personal artistic lens – a process that had already been on offer as a blueprint in Reality TV and the so-called "fake news shows," which had reached the pinnacle of their popularity in the course of the Bush (Jr.) US-presidency, which again coin-cided with Twitter's rise. Furthermore, while Twitter's reorientation towards news bore a potential for – and requirement of – a certain measure of aggressiveness (as inherent in the process of turning real life into newsworthy events), its gravitating towards dominant modes of advertising-dependent profit generation through the analysis of user data also played into this potential for aggression. This trend would see the service becoming ever more focused on individuals and their metrics – i.e., the number of followers, mentions, likes/hearts and retweets – which, in turn, sug-gested for users to also start integrating the platform's interest in scale and network reach into their practices. Faithful to a more general, neoliberal drive towards self-marketing, users were thus led to apply the platform's promotional logic to them-selves; at the same time, a cultural reflex of "mediated policing" had also long been established and, frequently, shitstorms come about when Twitter-savvy attempts at self-marketing through mildly transgressive jokes activate a vigilant "resting state" (Trottier 2020, 204) and trigger retaliation and "altruistic punishment" (Rost et al. 2016, 4).

Marwick and boyd's (2010) excerpts from interviews with Twitter users indi-cate how the jocular self-promotional logic exacerbated an increasing orientation towards the current, explosive, witty and instantly gratifying: "… my stream 1/3 humors, 1/3 information, 1/3 genial and unfiltered, transparency is so chic. try to tweet the same way"; "… when I tweet sumthin contrvsial or interesting I find a get a cple more followers"; "My tweets are news broadcasts ala NYTimes or Stum-bleUpon with Alltop plugs" (in Marwick and boyd 2010, 121+122).[12] Oriented towards strengthening one's personal brand on Twitter, forms of comic aggression have been serving users as a media-logical mode of building one's following on the platform and, as one of the interviewees stated, controversy and unfilteredness – a kind of 'mental ad-hocness' – have often helped this endeavour.

When the Twit hits the fan – jokes in the heart of the shitstorm

… At least, that is, when the joke is successful and finds its audience to respond with laughter. However, when this laughter does *not* follow, and a positive, benign, and affirmative reaction stays out, then there is a good chance that the originator of the tweet will experience repercussions, as a significant number of platform-dependent self-promoters have done over the years. The person at the heart of the perhaps most famous instance in the history of Twitter shitstorms, Justine Sacco, had clearly intended to make a joke when, on route to South Africa in 2013, she posted "Going to Africa. Hope I don't get AIDS. Just kidding. I'm white!" (in Ronson 2015, ebook, n.p.). "It was a joke about a dire situation that does exist in post-apartheid South Africa, that we don't pay attention to," she told culture critic Jon Ronson in an interview three weeks after the incident, and: "Living in America puts us in a bit of a bubble when it comes to what is going on in the Third World. I was making fun of that bubble" (Sacco in Ronson 2015, n.p.). Having posted this – admittedly harsh – one-liner shortly before switching off her phone, upon switching her phone back on in Cape Town Sacco found herself the "number-one worldwide trend on Twitter" (ibid), with tens of thousands of tweets already posted in retaliation. A few days later she was let go by her employer.

Johnen et al. (2018) discuss an online promotion by the beer brand Bud Light from 2015, "#UpForWhatever," which caused a similar backlash. Having printed the slogan "The perfect beer for removing 'no' from your vocabulary for the night" on their beer cans, a Reddit user had taken a photo of the can and posted it on the platform. Soon:

> [O]ther users started blaming Bud Light for promoting date rape. The outrage spread over to other social media platforms such as Twitter, where more people joined the bandwagon and attacked Bud Light indignantly. At some point, media reported on the issue, increasing its publicity and fostering more indignation on social media.
>
> (Johnen et al. 2018, 3141)

What this – stunningly misguided – promotion shares with a joke is that it aimed for a generally disinhibited atmosphere, inviting people to use alcohol in general and their product in particular to let down their guard. How the creative team behind the ad failed to see the highly problematic gender dynamics suggested in their motto remains a mystery.

Yet, by contrast to *people* coming into the eye of a shitstorm, *brands* frequently fare reasonably well; in the case of Bud Light "within two or three days after the initial post, indignation subsided" (Johnen et al. 2018, 3141). John Roderick, a US-American musician and podcaster, was less lucky with the aftermath of his Twitter shitstorm. Being in Corona lockdown in early January 2021, he turned his nine-year-old daughter's demand for something to eat into a "teachable moment," challenging her to open a can of beans without his help. This set in motion a struggle between daughter and bean can that Roderick documented in a string of tweets wittily formulated in a style reminiscent of a scientific experiment: "I said, 'The little device is designed to do one thing: open cans. Study the parts, study the can, figure out what the can-opener inventor was thinking when they tried to solve this problem.'"[13]

While Roderick deleted his Twitter account soon after the backlash began, what is preserved of his tweets in entertainment news articles online displays an irreverence towards his own child that is easily recognisable as performed and comedic. In a later statement, Roderick specified that: "I didn't share how much laughing we were doing, how we had a bowl of pistachios between us all day as we worked on the problem."[14] The tweets written in retaliation, however, insisted on Roderick's behaviour being abusive, misogynist (because it was his *daughter*), and self-absorbed, as well as framing him as a bad parent and poor role model.

And the retaliation did not remain limited to the bean can. Rather, as is now a widespread practice of 'moral entrepreneurialism' (cf. Favarel-Garrigues et al. 2020, 193), older tweet-jokes were unearthed on Roderick's account. A non-supportive reading could easily frame these as racist and antisemitic, thus cementing the judgement of him as a thoroughly evil person. Additionally, several people informed child-protective services, which then visited Roderick's home and interviewed his daughter: "Turns out she doesn't like the fact he gets tired of playing Legos faster than she does," an online article summed up the outcome of the interview.[15] "If this reassures anyone, I personally know John to be (a) a loving and attentive dad who (b) tells heightened-for-effect stories about his own irascibility on like ten podcasts a week. This site is so dumb," a colleague posted in Roderick's defence – only to be called out for some joking tweets on his own account.[16]

Around the mid-2010s, dynamics similar to the one in Roderick's case could be found to unfold continuously across the platform. As another case in point, US comedian Trevor Noah found himself the target of moral indignation after a reporter from the news site BuzzFeed, specialising in highly personal news and curiosities, had found a number of tweets in the backlog of Noah's account. A reading of these tweets that denied the comic in them could interpret them as antisemitic and misogynist, as for example: "Almost bumped a Jewish kid crossing the road. He didn't look b4 crossing but I still would hav felt so bad in my german car!"; or: "Originally when men proposed they went down on one knee so if the woman said no they were in the perfect uppercut position" (in Gambino 2015). As a colleague commented rightly in defence of Noah: "Given the kind of racist jokes I've had to see and hear over the years that nobody objected I'm not bothered by @Trevornoah jokes" (ibid).

Another case points to a general political orientation in this variation of the shitstorm. In mid-2018, Marvel director, James Gunn, who had written and directed the first two *Guardians of the Galaxy* films, was let go by Disney, because of old tweets that had been dug up. "This shower is the weakest ever. Felt like a three year old was peeing on my head," gives a good indication of the provocative, but ultimately comic play with the taboo of paedophilia Gun offered on his account. "I viewed myself as a provocateur, making movies and telling jokes that were outrageous and taboo," he is quoted by the BBC.[17] Gunn's tweets, however, had not merely resurfaced by accident, but were recirculated by the US conspiracy theorist Mike Cernovich, who had made the resurfacing of old tweets in retaliation to people's outspoken opposition to then-president Donald Trump a standard practice (Bishop 2018). "The Expendables was so manly I fucked the shit out of the little pussy boy next to me! The boys ARE back in town!" goes another unappetising tweet by Gunn. However, while the film *Gunn* refers to, *The Expendables* (2010), has become symbolic of a proto-fascist hypermasculinity (cf. Johanssen 2022) that Trump also represents, the latter merely seemed to thrive under the resurfacing of statements made by him in this direction. Satirical and ironically overblown takes on this masculinity, as those by *Gunn*, by contrast, have tended to force their progressive originators out of their jobs. It is that which the Lacanian media scholar Scott Krzych (2021) has called the weaponisation of hysterical discourse on the part of conservative political media (p. 18).

Already in 2014, US satirist Stephen Colbert intentionally tapped into and exposed this weaponisation of the Twitter shitstorm by satirically imitating the bad-faith virtue signalling towards ethnic minorities on the part of white US politicians and lobbyists. Exaggerating the latter's rhetoric of care, he promised in a tweet that "I am willing to show #Asian community I care by introducing the Ching-Chong Ding-Dong Foundation for Sensitivity to Orientals or Whatever." Whereas the progressive merits of such satire have become questionable indeed (Burges and Brugman 2022), the inevitable Twitter backlash followed promptly, with the "CancelColbert" hashtag soon trending. "Who would have thought a means of communication limited to 140 characters would ever create misunderstandings," Colbert asked naively on his show for good comedic effect. Having intentionally outraged hashtag activists whose outrage then fed legacy news media with fresh content, Colbert concludes: "The system worked."[18]

Despite the tendency to hold conservative and progressive actors to different standards, the strategic exploitation of the aggressive charge of the comic on Twitter/X has long since crisscrossed political borders. When in late 2022, Queen Elisabeth II died, tweets veered between the harmlessly witty and the morbidly hilarious. The pun on a Prince song, "Purple Reign," for example, anchored a picture of the late queen in her beloved violet coat. In another tweet, the German news weekly, *Der Spiegel*'s frontpage title "Die Queen" ("The Queen") is intentionally misread as/in English, with the comment reasoning that: "Wow the Germans hate her as much as the Irish apparently."

However, when a US academic tweeted that "I heard the chief monarch of a thieving raping genocidal empire is finally dying. May her pain be excruciating," this predictably resulted in an outcry of indignation – and not without some justification. Arguably, a jocular dimension is still traceable in the tweet's radically disinhibited mode of speech. And yet, the absence of secondary elaboration, wit and artifice unfolds an undigested and indigestible aggressive charge. It is my worry that such a regressive trait – this rendering primitive of symbolic play – has become significantly more widespread and normalised on "X" under Musk's nihilistically libertarian stance (cf. Slobodian 2023). While pre-Musk Twitter still had substantial rail guards in place to defend the very standards of civility that its design had proven so ambivalent towards, "X" has now wilfully abandoned these (Gallagher 2022).[19] And whereas my point in relation to Twitter shitstorms is that they need to be seen as – albeit heavily regressive – moral acts (see below), I am increasingly concerned about the state of morality on "X." Here the aggressive charge emanating from Twitter's classic design features becomes increasingly uncoupled from the aesthetic elements that turn aggression into seduction. At such a stage, barely veiled acts of assault directly ask to be sanctioned by a tribalistic dynamic of celebration and support vs. opposition and counterattack.

The platformed morality of Twitter

In light of the above, it is significant that the question of morality has advanced to a central point in works on the shitstorm and digital vigilantism. Particularly the work by Johnen, Jungblut, and Ziegele (2018) is useful in this respect. When they draw on the notion of "moral panic" (Goode and Ben-Yehoda 1994; Cohen 1972) as a fertile means to capture the relevant aspects of a shitstorm, this aligns well with the psychoanalytic stance taken in this chapter. As the authors outline, there are five key characteristics of moral panics:

> (1) concern (about a seemingly threatening behavior of a person or group against moral values), (2) hostility (toward the accused), (3) disproportionality (the concern is exaggerated regarding the objective threat), (4) consensus (in terms of a perceived agreement about a threat by a group of people), and (5) volatility (a moral panic emerges and subsides quickly).
>
> (Johnen et al. 2018, 3142)

These characteristics, I argue, need to be read in close coordination with Freud's (1905) theory of the joke and what I have defined as the push-button communiqué. From this angle, already the notion of "concern" takes on a wider significance. Specifically, it needs to be understood as an amoral offer made however in a way that is difficult to refuse. This form of seduction finds its complementary in the high intensity of the "hostility" of individual articulations of the shitstorm. When Lacan defines hysteria as the appropriation of another's desire by identifying with them (Evans 1996), such appropriation is what participants in a shitstorm enact: an unconscious identification with something that has half-consciously been proposed. Like the unconscious male strategy to disperse homoerotic feelings and connotations in all male relationships by using homophobic slurs against outsiders, the plausible response to a failing joke is not merely *concern*, but, indeed, retaliation and hostile defence. Intuitively, this becomes exploited in populist communication strategies that drive the polarisation of political discourse (cf. Bruns 2020).

Yet, the "disproportionality" of the response is also an effect of the emerging group dynamic, with a myriad of responses warranting a wide circulation of the sentiment '*I have been betrayed*' in which the hysterical reaction to the seduction inherent in the comic expresses itself. This response is contagious – i.e., is highly attractive to others – since as a reaction formation it is built into Twitter itself. Where seduction is everywhere it can be defended against anywhere. In this respect, what might be offered as consolation to many of those having been 'shitstormed' is that, at least partly, they need not take it personally. Rather, no matter whether shitstorms arise spontaneously or are strategically arranged, they must be seen as systemic, with their dynamics being inherent parts of the plat-*form* (sic). Hence, the moral "consensus" forming around the aggressive rejection of a tweet is fed by the status of this reaction as the *switch phenomenon and dialectical counterpart* to the tweet's seductive dimension. From this perspective, the Twitter shitstorm is first and foremost a matter of form, with its moral core being without concretely discernible content. Put differently, I argue that it is not the perceived racism in Sacco's tweet, the presumed cruelty in Roderick's bean can experiment, or the breached taboos in Gunn's paedophilia provocations *per se* that have triggered these shitstorm – even though it is obviously these things that are attacked and retaliated again. Rather, these surface phenomena offer a way for the retaliatory energy that Twitter's seductiveness affords people to build up to flow. In a sentence, what has made the shitstorm an inherent part of Twitter is that its "procedural rhetoric" (Bogost 2007) invariably invites users to perform acts of aggression and seduction, but – also and by the same token – creates an arena in which people are driven to avert these acts by the same means.

When ex-president Donald Trump states that the recipe for "a really good tweet" is "just the right amount of crazy" (Panetta and Lahut 2022[20]), this ties in well with most of the platform's characteristics that I have sought to bring to the fore: artistry with which to defend against triviality, quick-wittedness, self-promotional provocativeness, newsiness, and a transgressive streak paired with a sensitisation towards public opinion (gate watching). While these are subjective qualities that are in high demand in neoliberal capitalist Western societies, they should not so much be seen as intrinsic to these subjects, but as 'extimate' (Miller 1988; see Engley 2022 for a similar argument): i.e., baked into Twitter's programming and use culture. Hence, the characteristics of a "moral panic" that Johnen et al. (2018) see as resonating with the shitstorm need to be read as the formation of a structural defence in kind. Furthermore, when Johnen et al. argue that participation in online shitstorms is driven by a "moral compass" (p. 3144), this is only partly borne out by the theoretical perspective developed in this chapter. Rather than users entering a shitstorm with a pre-set moral compass, such morality follows primitive group-psychological premises (Bion 2004 [1961]; Freud 1921, see above) and is derived in large parts from the formal structuring of interaction on the platform.

The scapegoating mechanism

Shitstorms thus unfold and draw their strength from the rejection of an attempt at seduction. The circumstance that this rejection quickly takes on seductive form again points to the structural similarity and parallelism between the shitstorm and any other trending topic/hashtag on Twitter, as well as each individual shitstormer's complicity in the platform's logic of seduction. "[I]t's an impressive rise for a dude who three years ago was replying to Uberfacts tweets with dick jokes," reads a tweeted joke in retaliation to Trevor Noah's jokes (in Gambino 2015). Or: "Bean dad being cancelled for being a jerk to his daughter and people then finding out he's basically a Nazi is like when they got Capone for tax evasion."[21] Both are examples of tweets retaliating against a joke by making another joke. Even the dry: "Cheers for Death of The Queen On Twitter – Your typical leftist," in response to the harsh "May her pain be excruciating" tweet can be seen along those lines. And while these latter tweets do not grant the ones they respond to any benefit of the doubt (of non-seriousness), they all wrap themselves in a coat of non-committal wit themselves. Creating a moment of ambiguity as to whether their critique of the original tweet is serious or not thus seems to point to a degree of fetishistic disavowal. The structural similarities between what I perceive as a threat in another and what I do myself seemingly impossible to acknowledge.

"Whatever that pleasurable rush that overwhelms us is – group madness or whatever – nobody wants to ruin it by facing the fact that it comes with a cost," writes Ronson (2015, 92) in picking up on such mutual acts of disavowal. What is ultimately rendered unconscious in these disavowals is the primitive form of sacrifice and scapegoating that inheres in the firestorm and that makes this kind of digital vigilantism so fierce. In a parallel to Freud's *Totem and Taboo* (1913b), one could say that those who become devoured by the 'band of brothers' (and sisters) in a Twitter firestorm function as stand-ins for the "primal father," a "feared and envied model of each" (Freud 1913b, 142) – a totemistic being of the platform itself. "[I]n the act of devouring him they accomplished their identification with him, and each one of them acquired a portion of his strength," writes Freud (ibid) about the violent origins of totemism. In so doing, he offers a vivid sense of the reproductive function of the Twitter shitstorm, which, paradoxically, stabilises the social in an unstable, polarised form. Before implementing any concretely moral norms, this form of vigilantism enacts the renewal of the specific sociality that the platform affords – the sociality of the push-button communiqué, in which all are prompted to declare their transgressive personal politics while being vigilant of the declarations of others. In this respect, the butts of the jokes in Twitter shitstorms have a contradictorily conservative function; they are sacrificed and devoured so that the rest of the platform can continue its self-cannibalising work.

Appendix: further problems and lines of work

Having reached the formal end of this chapter's argument here, I would like to emulate Freud's "Group Psychology" text (1921) and add an appendix to make two further contributions to wider debates within scholarly work on social media that the distinct procedural form of the Twitter shitstorm suggests. These relate to questions pertaining to what has been framed as "social contagion" (e.g., Sampson 2013) and, relatedly, to the question of how – or better: at which level – users are being addressed on/by social media. Put briefly, while the notion of contagion has been suggesting pre-individual, pre-subjective modes of address and interpellation, the phenomenon of the shitstorm seems to offer evidence to the opposite.

Due to the omnipresence of Internet-connected devices and their ability to inter-link dispersed populations, there has been a lively debate throughout the 2000s and 2010s concerning the form and socio-political significance of 21st-century crowd phenomena. A general consensus that seems to have formed has centred on the work of Gabriel de Tarde, with its emphasis on mimesis and contagion and its theoretical proximity to Gilles Deleuze (1994) and Bruno Latour (2012) (cf. Bax-mann, Bayes, and Pias 2014, 11). Following in Latour's and Deleuze's footsteps, scholarly inquiries into the ways in which digital media *organise masses* (Baxmann et al. 2014, 11) have drawn upon Tardeian notions of contagion and imitation. In this respect, the belief in media relating to people at the pre-individual and pre-subjective level[22] – through the distribution and circulation of affects – has been paradigmatic of media studies of the past 15 years.

However, whereas Tarde and his current followers have without a doubt been hugely influential in how to understand the social formations brought about and facilitated by digital media, the phenomenon of the Twitter shitstorm shows that Freud's *Group Psychology and the Analysis of the Ego* (1921) – a work vastly ignored in media studies – is far from irrelevant for such an understanding, not least because it counters the consensus on contagion. As the Internet philosopher Charles Ess (2014) states in his critical appreciation of crowd theories in the context of social media, if one seriously wants to discuss the ethical and normative aspects of digital mass formations, some notion of subjectivity needs to be reintro-duced (p. 356). Along these lines, I claim that psychosocial attempts at understand-ing the impact of interacting in digital media on subject formation and, eventually, identity building – what Deleuze and Guattari frame as the *reterritorialising* effects of the movements of affect – remains of undiminished relevance.

To unfold this relevance, a short aside by Freud in *Group Psychology* (1921) is productive. Here, Freud is interested in how to account for the "mental change" that people undergo when becoming part of a group, crowd, or mass:

> [W]hat we are offered as an explanation by authorities on sociology and group psychology is always the same, even though it is given various names, and that is – the magic word 'suggestion'. Tarde [1903] calls it 'imitation'; but we cannot help agreeing with a writer who protests that imitation comes under the concept of suggestion, and is in fact one of its results (Brugeilles 1913).
>
> (Freud 1921, 88)

In search of an understanding of *social contagion* – translated into the more con-crete question of what it is in a shitstorm that pulls vast numbers of people into contributing to the disciplining and shaming of others – I find myself as dissatisfied as Freud was when presented with "imitation" as an answer. Rather, with Tarde de-fining imitation as "the action at a distance of one mind upon another" (Tarde 1903, xiv, quoted in Borch 2006, 83), my follow-up question in this chapter has been: *what kind of action?* As Eugenie Brinkema (2014) writes: "The turning to affect in the humanities does not obliterate the problem of form and representation. Affect is not where reading is no longer needed" (p. xiv). In my application of Freud's (1905b) study of the joke to Twitter, I have analysed such a form and given such a reading, offering the play with seduction and the violent rejection of this seduction as the interactional source of the shitstorm. As refers to the theme of group formation, both moments in this play are of central importance as they make possible a loosening of inhibitions in the name of a common good. In Freudian terms, both moments, seduction and rejection, break a path for a mutual *regression*. When the accent lies on the first moment of seduction, this can lead to a *regression in the service of the ego*. When the accent lies on the second moment of rejection, it is a *regression in the service of the super-ego* (cf. Kris 1936), or, as Favarel-Garrigues, Tanner, and Trottier (2020) put it with respect to digital vigilantism, a "confluence between justice seeking and entertainment" (p. 191).

In this respect, also Freud's focus on the libidinal ties between the participants in a group proves productive. Freud sees a crowd to be structured by a field of tension between an act of idealisation that is mutual for all members and an identification of all members with one another on the point of the mutually held ideal. Members of a crowd approximate and imitate one another because they can identify with each other on the basis of what they all idealise. And while Freud's crowd psychology is mostly known for the importance it grants to the existence of a leader as the receiver of such idealisation, it is significant that also a "leading idea" can function as the central "libidinal factor" in the formation of a crowd (Freud 1921, 95). In the case of Twitter shitstorms, this leading idea is invariably the reassertion of a moral norm. Paradoxically, this norm is built along the lines of a *seduction into not being seduced*.

This finding, in turn, points to the second problem that I would like to raise here in relation to theories of contagion and viral spread in social media, namely, the belief in the pre-individual grasp that mediated affectation has on social media users. This notion of the pre-individual is often taken to mean that subjectivity and the individual human being do not play a decisive role in the social formations brought about in the digital. In this respect, the centrality of aggression in the make-up of Twitter opens a markedly different perspective. In her entry on "Aggressiveness/ aggression" in the *International Dictionary of Psychoanalysis* (Mijolla et al. 2005), Jean Bergeret (2005) defines aggression as "the manifestation in fantasy or symptoms of a combination of hostile and erotic affective currents." As such, aggression can be seen as "a common relational occurrence, but one without a unique or even homogeneous origin" (p. 33). Since aggressiveness thus requires "the person to have an imagination capable of integrating a certain level of ambivalence," it presupposes a relatively mature subject. Simply put, for someone to be aggressive, they need to have developed a minimum integral sense of their own subjectivity.

Turning this finding back onto Twitter and the phenomenon of shitstorms, one can see how the notion of the pre-individual needs to be understood in this context. What shows in this light is that it cannot be taken to mean that social media merely affect people at a *non-subjectified* level. Rather, along the lines of Simondon, who holds that "the pre-individual will form a system of relations governing the genesis of the individual" (Bowden 2012, 138), interaction on Twitter demands that this "pre-individual" be already individuated to the degree that enables them to tolerate ambivalence.

But this argument can even be pushed one decisive step further. Specifically, when Bergeret (2005) goes on to delineate the effect that Freud's differentiation between libidinous and narcissistic object relations has on aggression, this again sheds light on subject formation and individuation on Twitter. She writes: "Narcissistic objects result from primary identifications and defensive violence, while with ego objects, ambivalence causes the person to oscillate between love and its equally eroticized opposites: aggressiveness, hate, and sadism" (p. 34). Consequently:

> Aggressive fantasies can involve a simultaneous libidinal satisfaction in attacking an object who represents (consciously or unconsciously) an oedipal rival, whereas in narcissistic conditions, the resulting violent primitive anger (rage) seeks to protect the self without taking into account the injuries inflicted on one who is experienced simply as an external threat and not as a genuine object (other).
>
> (Bergeret 2005, 34)

This differentiation between the libidinal satisfaction of aggressive fantasies at the oedipal level and the rise of violent primitive anger at the narcissistic level, I hold, is key to an understanding of the dynamics of subject formation on Twitter. With regard to the platform's formative logic, what the shitstorm brings to a head is the *instability of the oedipal subject tasked with the integration of constant intensities of ambivalence*. Defined as a regression from the oedipal to the narcissistic level of mental functioning, the shitstorm demonstrates the ease with which Twitter users, who are constantly promised and afforded the libidinal satisfaction of attacking oedipal rivals, resort to violent primitive anger in their attempts to protect themselves from one such attack. Hence, when Johnen et al. (2018) point towards "a desire for social recognition" (p. 3140) as one central motive for participating in a shitstorm, this must again be modified in the light of the psychoanalytic approach taken here. It is not the desire for social recognition that drives people to participate in a shitstorm. Rather, it is the narcissistic desire to protect oneself against others' attempts at attaining such recognition and at elevating themselves from the mass. "Social justice," writes Freud (1921), "means that we deny ourselves many things so that others may have to do without them as well, or, what is the same thing, may not be able to ask for them" (p. 121).

Notes

1 https://www.nytimes.com/2023/07/28/style/x-marks-the-spot.html (accessed 15/09/2023).
2 Last comparative search: 07/06/2022.
3 However, as discussed further below, the technological affordances of such author-effacing circulation have undergone several changes over the years.

4 McGowan develops his theory of the comic based on the formative opposition between lack and excess in Lacan's conception of the subject, writing that: "Comedy reveals that lack and excess can coincide and that this coincidence, though it isn't visible in every-day existence, is constitutive of our subjectivity. In this sense, subjectivity itself is inher-ently comic, but subjects plunge themselves into everyday life and its separation of lack and excess in order to avoid confronting their traumatic intersection. Comedy returns us to the trauma of our subjectivity" (McGowan 2017, 15). We constantly feel that there is something lacking in our lives, and once we get access to such a 'something,' we tend to dig into it excessively – overeating, stuffing, and hopelessly overloading ourselves. This too-much usually will soon leave us empty and hollow and lacking again. Comedy is to acknowledge this inherent impossibility of adequate regulation in laughter.

In a similar vein, Alenka Zupančič conceives of the comic, or more precisely, "comic subjectivity," as not so much residing "in the subject making the comedy, nor in the subjects or egos that appear in it," but in an "incessant and irresistible, all-consuming movement" between these parts (2008, 3). "Comic subjectivity is the very movement of comedy," she writes (ibid). Yet, this movement between the subject and its identi-fications, imagos, desires, and fears – which according to Lacan is where subjectivity itself resides – is hardly ever smooth and uncomplicated, Zupančič holds, but involves "[s]tumbling, interruptions, punctuations, discontinuities, all kinds of fixations and pas-sionate attachments" (ibid). Hence, what defines humans – and what the comic brings to the fore – resides not in what people *think* they are and what they *think* they hold dear, but in a movement that consciously aims for one thing but gets derailed by another.

5 https://brocku.ca/MeadProject/McDougall/1926/1926_03.html (accessed 20/04/2023).

6 The subtitle of Fisher's book is: "The Uncensored History of Silicon Valley" (2018).

7 Numbers for 2020 suggest that, in Norway, Twitter still is the preferred platform for men between 18 and 29 (44%) interested in sports and gaming (Helt Digital, 15/01/2021).

8 Wikipedia's "The Daily Show" page lists 14 «unofficial spin-offs» in other countries, from Algeria, via Germany, to Iraq: https://en.wikipedia.org/wiki/The_Daily_Show (ac-cessed 20/04/2023).

9 https://www.pewresearch.org/short-reads/2015/08/06/5-facts-daily-show/ (accessed 22/09/2023).

10 https://www.platformer.news/p/twitter-becomes-x (accessed 14/12/2023).

11 For example, while major television news channels may have been using Twitter as a simple elongation of their service and brand, they have been doing so by at least partly downplaying and side-lining the personal and informal dimensions that are amongst Twitter's core use characteristics, and it is well plausible that this neglect is at the heart of what frequently amounts to "the inability of such institutional participants to effec-tively channel or dominate the conversation" (Bruns and Burgess 2015, 23).

12 Stumble upon was an advertising engine that recommended web content to its users. It closed in 2018, after a 16-year run (Sawyers 2018). Similarly, Alltop(.com), which is still in existence, is a news curator, aggregating news headlines from top Internet sites, blogs, and social media.

13 https://www.thewrap.com/bean-dad-9-year-old-open-can-6-hours-infuriates-twitter/ (accessed 19/04/2023)

14 https://reason.com/2021/02/16/bean-dad-child-services-john-roderick-can-opener/ (ac-cessed 19/04/2023)

15 https://reason.com/2021/02/16/bean-dad-child-services-john-roderick-can-opener/ (ac-cessed 19/04/2023)

16 https://www.thewrap.com/bean-dad-deletes-twitter-account-anti-semitic-homophobic-tweets-resurface/ (accessed 19/04/2023)

17 https://www.bbc.com/news/world-us-canada-44906019 (accessed 19/04/2023).

18 https://www.youtube.com/watch?v=MBPgXjkfBXM (accessed 18/04/2023).

19 https://www.latimes.com/business/story/2022-12-02/twitter-shrunk-compliance-teams-risks-investigations-fines (accessed 14/12/2023).
20 https://www.businessinsider.com/barr-book-trump-good-tweet-just-the-right-amount-crazy-2022-3?r=US&IR=T (last accessed 16/05/2022).
21 https://www.thewrap.com/bean-dad-deletes-twitter-account-anti-semitic-homophobic-tweets-resurface/.
22 The concept of the pre-individual is central to both Gilles Deleuze and Gilbert Simondon (see Bowden 2012, 138–9).

Chapter 6

Conclusion – 'platforming' the digital subject

"In the consumption-centred commercial internet, there is a very small number of very big corporations that control the access to goods, services and infrastructure," Staab reminds us (2019, p. 20; my translation). These few corporations, he continues, have become the gatekeepers of the commercial internet. It is they that "pull the strings that, from there, continue to run ever further into all economic processes and private life worlds" (p. 21; my translation).

This gatekeeping function has been the point of departure for my study's psychoanalytic inquiry into the social formations shaped by the digital. With our lives increasingly flowing through the platforms and their tacit design principles, it would be naïve not to expect the latter to mould these lives by virtue of their intermediation (cf. Hepp 2013). What I have sought to do is unpack what I see as the central formative principles and figurations of this intermediation and the sociocultural and political directions it has taken. Since digital platforms have shown a marked tendency to venture into each other's territories (e.g., van Dijck et al. 2018), most of them display several of the patterns of affectation I have worked out in the book's chapters to some degree. The platforms' spheres of influence need to be seen as overlapping, complementing, competing, and sometimes countering each other. In this respect, what I want to do by way of a conclusion is condense my study's findings with respect to this patterning, integrating the various moulding processes so as to allow for a more general formative tendency to arise.

This tendency returns me to Dean's (e.g., 2009; 2010; 2015) theory of communicative capitalism and the capturing of subjects in the digital through the shaping of drives. Dean's theory has been helpful for my conception of the platforms' formative a/effects as the crystallisation and establishing of "forms of interaction" (Lorenzer 2022 [1986]). However, Dean is also important in defining the kind of subject arising from such formations, which is one that is not merely characterised by its drives, but one characterised by *drive* in general. Whereas digital platforms might be designed in ways that would bring about *positive* formative effects in the sense of helping people to mature and guiding them out of the dependencies that platforms establish, such exit strategies have so far not been forthcoming, since they would violate and hurt the platforms' business model. In this respect, contemporary corporate platforms must be seen

DOI: 10.4324/9781003307044-7

in the ambivalent light that I have cast them in in the introduction. On the one hand, they fashion themselves as, in Winnicott's (2005 [1971]) words, "transitional objects" and "potential spaces" that offer their users positive opportunities for development and growth. On the other hand, however, they seek to capture people in the positivity of these potential spaces and fixate them through facilitating the very creativity that is characteristic of transitional objects. In this respect, Dean's assessment of communicative capitalism as based on capturing subjects at the level of drive is to the point. Keeping users in repetitive cycles of symbolic engagement with issues relevant to them makes this engagement, as worthy and ethical as it might otherwise be, turn stale and self-referential. Hence, before offering a vision of the overall structure of subjectivity as it arises from the processes of digital platforming that I have observed, I want to briefly establish Dean's theory as a major frame of reference.

Communicative capitalism and subjects of drive

The internet, Dean (2010) holds, is a major driving force of the crisis of the symbolic in late capitalism. Communication, online and offline, has mostly lost its connection to a vital sense of binding power – has lost its sense of obligation and commitment to a socially pervading truth. Under such circumstances, symbolic interactions lose their ties to things and people – i.e., to *objects* – with the relations to such (fading, absent) objects then merely echoing back to the subject enacting them.

Once people's object relations are weakened to the point at which their references to a reality can no longer be taken for granted as shared or binding, desire, which in Lacanian theory is always directed towards objects (although it is never coextensive with them), is reduced to something more auto-erotic, specifically, drive. Hence, in a situation in which the shared fantasy of a binding reality has been significantly weakened and all desire is thrown back onto the subjective play of drive, such drive cannot attain the liberating powers that Žižek, in following Lacan, granted it. While, in his early works on the internet, Žižek (e.g., 1998) found in the often rigidly repetitive rituals that still characterise much of internet culture the very vehicles with which to traverse and transcend ideologically fixating structures of desire, Dean argues that such rituals get stuck in self--perpetuating loops. Desire can no longer be traversed but only serves to keep people in 'holding patterns.' "Communicative capitalism thrives," Dean (2010) writes, "not because of unceasing or insatiable desires but in and as the repetitive intensity of drive" (p. 30).

Decisively, this thriving of communicative capitalism is facilitated by the various modes in which people in the current historical juncture are constantly prompted to reflect upon their interactions and identities (cf. Beck 1992). *What will it say about me if I like this post? How might I come across if I send a friend request to this person? Who will be offended if I share this article on Twitter? Why the hell do I like these 'Love Island' clips YouTube is constantly offering me?* According to

Dean (2010), self-ruminations and doubts such as these are the very fuel that turns our desires into drives. "[T]he endless loop of reflexivity," she argues, "becomes the very form of capture and absorption" (p. 13). Along similar lines, as I have stated for the case of anxious narcissism, Instagram users frequently do not reach the point where (other) objects of desire would come into the picture.

Flisfeder (2021), in his contention with Dean, does not seem to fully realise the central role that reflexivity plays in Dean's argument. He raises the point that "the postmodern subject's recognition of the nonexistence of the big Other," which he sees Dean to claim, might only be "apparent" (p. 86). People, he holds against Dean, might merely pretend that there is no social authority for them anymore. I understand Dean's argument differently – and even closer to what Flisfeder himself holds. I understand her as saying that we are frequently so concerned with how our desires might appear to others – or more precisely: in relation to a potential big Other – that these desires become auto-erotically consumed by people's concerns about how others might judge them. It is not the non-existence of a big Other but the constant anticipation of such an Other's judgement that produces a short-circuiting kind of self-absorption. Ultimately, this self-absorption has become a main driver of the crisis of the socio-symbolic. Hence, whereas Flisfeder insists that, "[w]hile enjoying social media we are still subjects of desire" (p. 87), Dean's reply to this might simply be that this enjoyment hardly ever manages to reach the status of desire in the first place. André Green (2002a), in his article on negative narcissism, makes a point similar to Dean's when he warns that one of the dangers of narcissism might just be that people become preoccupied with themselves to the point that others no longer register – it "impoverishes relationships with objects" (p. 637).

I have already indicated that I tend to side with Dean in this debate. What makes her argument fruitful for my study is her overall suggestion to read structures of desire *as drive*. In continuation I have read this drive as formative of subjectivity and this subjectivity then as formative of the political and social. Likewise, Dean (2015) writes: "As drive designates the plasticity of the objects to which we become attached, [...] it indexes the primary structure of enjoyment for contemporary subjects" (p. 99). Accordingly, Kornbluh (2019) conceives of psychoanalysis per se "as an intervention distinctly concerned with building new social formations" (p. 140).

To repeat my central point, what arises from the synthesis of this book's chapters along Dean's lines is not merely a form of subjectivity characterised by its drives, but also a subjectivity characterised by drive in general. Put differently, what arises is a form of subjectivity that, through its very modes of attachment, fundamentally struggles with establishing relationships in the full sense of the term, with the objects of such relationships – i.e., things and people, animals, plants and other living beings, social and material reality per se – frequently fading from view or becoming blocked by layers of doubts, distinctions, contentions, contradictions, and conflicts.

Pertaining to the subject characterised by its drives, what I argue with respect to the formative forces of the platforms is that the Meta-owned Facebook and

Instagram and the Alphabet-owned Google and YouTube exert distinct yet converging orientations. While the Meta services are based on the logic of what Dean has called the "loop of reflexivity" (see above), capturing users by prompting them to reflect on themselves in light of a constantly increasing net of related nodes, the Alphabet-owned ones, by contrast, embed their users more straightforwardly – i.e., less self-reflexively – into circuits of drive. As I unpack below, the form of flirtation in the case of Facebook and that of anxious narcissism in the case of Instagram both establish an ambiguous state of "having and not-having" (Simmel 1984 [1909]) that is constitutive of socialisation and sociality in corporate digital environments. Conversely, the design of YouTube's recommender system is geared towards a function of the *stilling* of attachments and relational excitations. When assessed in the wider context of the digital ecosystem, YouTube can thus be seen to function as a dependable anti-container with the help of which relational deficits and conflicts – particularly, the feelings of inadequacy that short circuit through us by the Meta platforms – can be precariously abated. Crudely put, while Facebook and Instagram constantly keep users on their toes by distributing small, libidinally charged relational tasks, YouTube offers respite from such relations by seeking to feed us with what is most seamlessly catering to our tastes.

It is in this latter aspect of a seamlessly-pertaining-to-us that also the formative potential of Google Search lies. While the ideally interpellated subject of Facebook and Instagram is always at risk of losing its objects from sight through reflexive self-absorption, that of Google is invited to seamlessly incorporate objects and make them their own, thus again approximating others to themselves. These convergent tendencies – the loops of self-reflexion, of self-abandonment, and of seamless incorporation – are combined in an explosive mix on Twitter, where the indeterminacy of flirtation and the urge to wield power over others become interwoven in the dynamics of seduction. Here the other finally *does* come to the fore – as a challenge and a threat to self-integrity – only, however, to be ritualistically sacrificed in an eruption of communal feeling, specifically, in the shitstorm as "community without community" (Dean 2015, 91). As much as Twitter/X is now aggressively being restructured under the aegis of tech entrepreneur Elon Musk, the microblogging function, which has been at its core from the start, will remain riddled with these problematic dynamics as long as it remains part of the platform and the platform part of the established corporate logic of advertising and promotion. Furthermore, the same dynamics will haunt rival products built on similar premises, first and foremost the Meta-owned Threads, no matter how much they promote themselves as friendly, non-toxic alternatives.

In terms of the subject characterised by drive, then, what emerges as an overriding, general tendency is a fading from view of objects – of others, be they big or small. This is what Byung-Chul Han has dubbed *The Expulsion of the Other* (2018), writing that "[t]otal interconnection and total communication by digital means does not facilitate encounters with Others. Rather, it serves to pass over those who are unfamiliar and other" (p. 3).

Flirting with disaster – the precarious state of having and not-having

Unpacking the platformed subject's relation to drives further, I first return to the theme of flirtation. Along the lines of Freud's Love and Life drives, or Eros, I suggested the social form of flirtation as an alternative for thinking about what digital media studies have sought to theorise as "virality" (e.g., Sampson 2013) and/or "contagion" (Stark 2018). When, in the first chapter, I point to the "cruel optimism" (Berlant) that underlies the constant translation of love into labour – into what Couldry (2012) has called "presencing" and Vincent Miller (2008) "phatic communication" – this is perfectly in line with the principal mode of flirtation that social media takes part in generating. Flirtation, in turn, finds its psychological and sociological counterpart in the form of "anxious narcissism" that I have discussed in the chapter on Instagram. If all communication oscillates around a fundamental insecurity as to my relational status, the logical outcome is an existential anxiety that constantly makes me question myself. Hence, while much on Facebook and other platforms trading in the relationships between people appears to be about formalising and fixating such relationships – *"Steffen and so-and-so are now friends"* – what these formalisations actually achieve is a tendency to render them problematic.

As if anticipating this dynamic, Simmel (1971 [1908]) wrote about the tensions between "Social Forms and Inner Needs" that:

> Our inner life, which we perceive as a stream, as an incessant process, as an up and down of thoughts and moods, becomes crystallized, even for ourselves, in formulas and fixed directions often merely by the fact that we verbalize this life. Even if this leads only rarely to specific inadequacies; even if, in fortunate cases, the fixed external form constitutes the center of gravity or indifference above and below which our life evenly oscillates; there still remains the fundamental, formal contrast between the essential flux and movement of the subjective psychic life and limitations of its forms. These forms, after all, do not express or shape an ideal, a contrast with life's reality, but this life itself.
>
> (Simmel 1971 [1908], p. 352)

Once this life has become verbalised and thus formalised, one might continue Simmel's argument, something in us will revolt against and start moving away from this centre of gravity again.

About flirtation, Simmel (1984 [1909]) observes that it is a play with reality that suspends our commitment to this reality. Oscillating between affirmation and denial, domination and subjugation, ability and inability, jest and seriousness, flirtation "plays off all oppositions against one another and in a certain sense relieves the relationship in which they are situated from every burden of a decision" (p. 147). It is in this function of creating an ambiguous position between "having and not-having" (ibid), writes Simmel, that flirtation "provides the prototype for countless relationships between the individual and the inter-individual life" (p. 149; see also Phillips 1994).

This conception of flirtation as a basis of social relationships has evocative parallels with the ways in which the virtual has been defined with respect to digital culture. As Brian Massumi (2013) argues, "the virtual" should not so much be understood as "*un*reality," i.e., an artificiality or illusion, in the way "virtual reality" has come to signify. Rather, derived from the "Latin word for strength or potency, the base definition of the virtual in philosophy is 'potentiality'" (Massumi 2013, p. 54). Similarly, Rob Shields (2006) sees the virtual not as the opposite of the real but defines it as *that* form of the real which is not (yet) actualised. Quoting from a letter by Marcel Proust, Shields defines the virtual as "real without being actual, ideal without being abstract" (p. 284). "[T]he Virtual itself is a multiplicity which can be actualised in different ways," he writes, "If it is known by its effects, then it is known through a specific instantiation, not as a whole" (p. 285).

This suspended state of reality – of *un*actuality, *un*commitment, and *un*decision – is thus at the core of both flirtation as a social form and the virtual as a central metaphor of digital media culture. In this respect, what Facebook has paradigmatically introduced as a catalyser for the field of "social networking" is flirtation-as-virtuality/virtuality-as-flirtation. In Facebook's notorious accumulation of "weak ties" (Granovetter 1973), the ambiguous and ambivalent state oozing from the resulting relations creates a form of being-real-but-not-actually-real that needs to incessantly be stabilised by way of small 'pokes' – *I am here! I exist! I am real! I belong!* As Bucher (2012) put it more than a decade ago, the real punishment of the social media panopticon is not to be seen at all. Yet, the Likes and comments which one seeks to accrue tend to register not so much as indexes of the 'real world,' but as the stimulus and affective charge that drives self-creation. The cruelty of Facebook's conception of Eros is that it covers over and denies the precarity of the connections it fosters and tacitly leaves us to our own devices when dealing with them. Flirtation demands constant rumination.

When Olga Goriunova (2019), upon being confronted with the profile made of her by an online advertising company, writes that "[i]t is clearly not I, and yet it is no one other than I" (p. 126), this connects Simmel's logic of flirtation as a form between "having and not-having" with the anxious form of narcissism that I see as another invariable of social media socialisation. Robert Graves (2011 [1960]) reconstructs the central dimension of the Narcissus myth in the line of "How could he endure both to possess and yet not to possess?" (p. 520; see Walsh 2015), and this question can indeed be extrapolated to the state of existence in social media in its entirety.

In an elegant reading of Freud's theory of narcissism in the context of the video streaming platform TikTok, my Master student Zhiyuan Hu (2023) has outlined the interplay between the platform's algorithmic sorting of videos and user traits as well as these users themselves. What is formed in this interplay, which again oscillates between having and not-having, is what Hu calls the "algorithmic self." He writes:

[W]e can understand the algorithmic self as an intermediate state, in Freudian terms, between the "baby's thumb" and the newly formed "ego" that emerges when dispersed libido is integrated. It is both a part of the user, in that interactions with it are essentially interactions with oneself, providing compensation for pleasure that is directed outward, and a relatively complete and independent entity that can be objectified by the user.

(Hu 2023, 91)

What Hu brings into the picture is what Kriss Ravetto-Biagioli has referred to as the *Digital Uncanny* (Ravetto-Biagioli 2019), an uncanny that questions "the status of the human" and blurs "the line between the human and the technologies that mediate what it means to be human" (p. 8). However, whereas both Hu and Ravetto-Biagioli seem to agree on the positive formative potentials inherent in this questioning – seeing in them reconfigurations of "our understanding of subjectivity, embodiment, and experience" (Ravetto-Biagioli 2019, 9) – the potential downsides also loom large. When Ravetto-Biagioli writes further that the digital uncanny challenges "subject and object positions and with them our ability to identify a self" (p. 14), this refers me to the risks and dangers of such new forms of subjectivation. Hence, while I agree with both authors in their cautious endorsement of new, virtual forms of subjectivity, in the case of corporate digital platforms as socialisation agencies, the integrity of subjectivity (as far as this is realisable at all) is constantly challenged through the flirtatious ways in which new formations are being suspended in the virtual – permanently made available for paying suitors and interested third parties (cf. Cheney-Lippold 2011) seeking to produce resonances with some of these traits while toning down others. Whereas Flisfeder (2021) is thus right that we ceaselessly respond to the virtual by approaching our data doubles through the eyes of our imagined audiences, Dean is right that this compulsive perspective-taking is often so absorbing that it amounts to solipsism. In this respect, the haunting questions of *Am I ok? Is this good enough?* which I have found at the root of anxious narcissism must be seen as utterly consequential of the communicative-capitalist expansion and delimiting of "the state of the human" (see above). Since this expansion goes hand in hand with a new form of social centralisation – *monopoly markets* rather than *market monopolies* (Mejias 2013) – new media users are more than justified to feel anxious, since this *platformed* digital ecology, with its fully privatised 'public spaces,' poses a palpable thread to democratic modes of government. Furthermore, in case Mark Zuckerberg succeeds with his vision of the metaverse (chances are he might not), the risks of subjectivities becoming radically expanded there but at the same time reterritorialised in ways that serve corporate capital seem staggeringly obvious. Ultimately, with costs of AI-supported services such as Microsoft's ChatGPT-powered Bing still being painfully high, it seems merely a question of time until "sponsored links" are more tightly integrated into these services, too. In this sense, the more relevant question might be what form these sponsored links will take and whether they will still be identifiable as such.

Extracting our own resources – self-absorption and other-incorporation

Turning to Google and YouTube, the capturing of subjectivity in circuits of drive has in their cases been debated via the notions of ideological embedding (e.g., Vaidhyannathan 2014) and addiction (e.g., Tufekci 2018), respectively. In the case of YouTube, one of the neuroscientific terminological pairs that the engineering literature on recommender systems has relied upon is "exploitation" vs. "exploration" (Daw et al. 2006). Whereas in the mode of "exploration" users are offered videos that the system has identified as lying outside their usual consumption patterns, "exploitation" comes to mean the degree to which the recommender system nudges a user to literally *extract their own resources*; it means offering something that is virtually already there, specifically: another that is oneself – a breast that turns out to be one's own thumb.

Entailed in the widespread discourse about online addiction – for which YouTube has become a salient case – is thus an implicit understanding that consuming video clips online is a mindless and asocial form of compensation for something else one should be doing. Surely, this is not a fortunate way of framing many of the online viewing cultures in existence today, since these cultures often prove astonishingly resilient to the platforms' circuitous affordances (e.g., Lüders and Sundet 2022). And yet, the more the recommender system is designed to detect and tap into people's pre-existing dispositions, the more this compensatory logic becomes a sociotechnical reality. A precarious form of (over)compensation is thus designed into the intended usage of YouTube. By containing users in this negative way,[1] YouTube is actively, though tacitly, encouraging users to be subjects characterised and captured by drive.

Similarly, in the case of Google Search, the firm's single-minded focus on usefulness and relevance, in tandem with its wealth of user data, is oriented towards the creation and habituation of a dyadic relationship between users and platform in which users are matched so perfectly with what they desire that this desire again seems to be intended to approximate the autopoietic, thus switching to drive. In this way, search results become endowed with a tendency to be mere retrievals and re-actualisations of what appears to have always already been there. This recursiveness of *The Daily You* (Turow 2011), in turn, affords a conservatism that has imperialist overtones, which Chun (2021) has meticulously analysed under the label of "homophily." At the heart of this conservatism again lies a compensatory logic that finds 'something-like-another' within the sphere of its intimate self. In the case of information retrieval services along the lines of Google, however, this cultural logic no longer seems purely compensational. Rather, in appropriating what Freud (1920) described as the Fort/Da game, one can say that people in contemporary digital culture frequently seem to accept the reel as preferential to a present, significant other. Put differently, the absence of objects no longer seems a prerequisite for entering into the play of compensation. And while this might be the ultimate vindication of Jean Baudrillard (e.g., 1983), Sherry Turkle (e.g., 2011;

2016) has been tirelessly warning about this shift in people's structure of desire. In her ethnographic studies, Turkle has observed people preferring their phones to other people in the same room, or people texting each other despite being in adjacent rooms, "we look to the network to defend us against loneliness even as we use it to control the intensity of our connections," she writes (Turkle 2011, 13). In this way, the people in Turkle's studies prove to be subjects that constantly become stuck on their way towards one another.

Seducing and eliminating the other

Turning to Twitter, what sets the platform apart from the formative influence of the others is that it has the form of the joke at the core of its functioning. Yet, by virtue of this structure, Twitter becomes a hybrid between the self-reflexive Meta platforms and the power-wielding Alphabet ones. Whereas, in addition, the joke has something flirtatious about it in that it shifts between the humorous and the serious and between play and reality, the triangulation of the joke's social setting – the joke teller, the audience, and the butt of the joke – inevitably makes the joke political. The joke's aim is to shape 'public opinion,' albeit mostly in micro form, through laughter, with the 'laughing third' deciding on the permissibility of the joke teller's proposition. Hence, the form of interaction that Twitter has been coining is not so much that of flirting, stilling, or incorporating, but that of seducing. In terms of its design, Twitter is oriented towards the shaping of social and political reality by persuading others of one's world view. And yet, as has come forth in my exegesis of the shitstorm (Chapter 5), the subject position from which this is done is extremely vulnerable, with the constant ambivalence in user relations inviting users to regress to a narcissistic level of defence against others. In this respect – and despite the group-psychological dynamics it affords – Twitter's political form and efficacy lean heavily towards the individual. For as long as the tweeted jocular attempts at seduction succeed in amusing people, their circulation might be high but remains mostly without consequence. If such a joke and its transgressive suggestion become rejected, however, a moral dynamic is set in motion that aims to identify, punish, and eliminate the offender. Object-oriented action thus tends to be possible mostly in the negative form of retaliation and defending-against. The other thus comes into view as a trespasser of borders that are drawn retroactively.

My habits and I – compensational thoughts on behaviourism

Before making a final attempt at characterising the digitally platformed subject, there is one more issue that I want to shed light on: the challenge of behaviourism. Behaviourism has become a dominant theoretical, if often implicit, perspective in relation to digital media platforms, and this perspective, too, establishes the subject as captured in its drives as a norm and common sense. Indeed, one of the main challenges in studying digital media from a relational, psychosocial/psychoanalytic perspective is that behaviourist viewpoints have suffused cultural consciousness so thoroughly that theoretical advances diverging from behaviourism often appear implausible, impractical, and overly elaborate.

In this respect, the widely read How-to guide for digital start-ups and entrepreneurs, written by Nir Eyal, coined the "Hooked Model" for building "habit-forming products" (Eyal 2019 [2014]), has been a key text for the spread of behaviourist ideas (see also Chun 2016). As Eyal explains in a handy formula, habit formation in the digital initially builds on "external," but then increasingly "internal triggers" geared towards initiating specific actions on part of the users. Once performed, these actions lead to variable rewards, which ideally lead to renewed user investments, which then function as internal triggers initiating the next round of actions (p. 39). In other words, what Eyal describes is again an increasing interiorisation of stimuli – the rendering of desires into drives.

In his work on recommender systems, the anthropologist Nick Seaver (2019) rightly points out that Eyal's line of thought emanates from Stanford University's Persuasive Technology Lab, headed by B. J. Fogg, of which Eyal is an alumnus (p. 424). Fogg's science of "Captology" – with "capt" being an acronym for "computers as persuasive technologies" (Fogg 2003, eBook version; n.p.) as well as a pun on 'captivation' – "focuses on the design, research, and analysis of interactive computing products created for the purpose of changing people's attitudes or behaviors" (ibid). Whereas both Fogg and Eyal claim that their intention is to, in Fogg's (2019) words, "help us be happier and healthier" (in Fogg and Euchner 2019, 14), the application of their principles on the part of commercial start-ups and big corporate platforms has made it more than doubtful that the inclusive sounding "us" actually entails the normal user.

While understanding and critiquing algorithmically driven persuasive design in terms of Skinner boxes "is now commonplace," as Seaver rightly observes (2019, 431), what is relevant in the present context is how this understanding informs widespread conceptions of social media use per se. In this respect, the behaviouristic model tends to frame this use and its ensuing problems as mere disturbances in solipsistic self-creation. In this view, the spectre of addiction, for example, merely resides in the *quality of the habits* that people acquire. This becomes clear when both Fogg (2019) and Eyal (2019), in their recent turns away from consulting tech companies and towards the users of these companies' products, suggest for the latter to empower themselves through simple habit-changing regimes. As Fogg (2019) writes: "After seeing the power of these methods to successfully design business solutions, I shifted my focus to the personal: How do we change our own behavior?" (eBook version, n.p.). At bottom, what he suggests is for his readers to take a habit they consciously want to acquire, "make it tiny, find where it fits naturally in your life, and nurture its growth" (n.p.). In this way, Fogg assures his readers, unwanted habits will increasingly become replaced by virtuous ones.

In line with Fogg, the secret ingredient of Eyal's "recipe" for human behaviour change (eBook version, n.p.) is a mixture of what in the idiom of mentalisation is called "urge surfing" (Kober 2014, 439) – "noticing the sensations and riding them like a wave" (Eyal 2019, n.p.) – and conscious habit change brought about by identifying and eliminating distractions, defining one's goals and entering into "precommitments," i.e., small pacts with oneself.

I do not claim that these suggestions are wrong per se. Research has shown that such cognitive regimes can and *do* help a significant number of people to bring about positive changes in their lives. And yet, what becomes lost in this behaviourist common sense is the importance of the relational origins of our most troubling habits, with our relations being compensated by and buried under them. What becomes squeezed out when behaviourist models seep into the norms of our thinking, both within and without academia, is an understanding of the necessity for people to *mourn and work through* their losses and life changes and to mourn themselves as the people they were in relation to what they have lost (Freud 1917; Leader 2008). Richard Seymore (2019) rightly critiques behaviouristic learning models by asking:

> How to educate the part of us that stubbornly entertains unrealistic fantasies and unreasonable passions, regardless of reality, cleaving to self-destruction in the face of all warning? Behaviourism blithely overlooks this everyday reality, or treats it as an inconvenience to work around.
>
> (Seymore 2019, 61)

... Or, as one could continue Seymore's thought, behaviourism, especially in its digital renderings, treats people's conflicts as 'energy sources' and *drives* with which to capture these people ever more firmly in circuits of compensatory habits. In this respect, what becomes difficult to discern in the face of the pervasive spread of behaviourist ideas is how communicative capitalism feeds off the very weakening of people's awareness of themselves as the products of their relationships. Being given to understand that we are the products of our self-formed habits, we again turn to self-reflexion and self-work and attempt to 'pull ourselves up by our own bootstraps.'

Platformed subjectivity – the digital under our skins

But what about the subject in the era of formative media? What are its salient characteristics and relational styles? In answering these questions, what comes to the fore are both the problems and potentials of the digital for human life and sociality per se. Facebook's emphasis on the erotic and flirtatious *might* have the power to bind people to others and might even be advanced into a community-building and strengthening tool, but its commercially motivated denial of the death drive as the constant companion of its binding endeavour repeatedly unleashes the immensely destructive powers that, too, can be part of human existence. YouTube's recommender system, in tandem with Alphabet/Google's immense wealth of user data and analytic prowess, might indeed have the potential to provide a nourishing holding environment, simulate a "good enough mother" (Winnicott 2005 [1971]), and provide the optimal distance between gratification and frustration that people need to be well-functioning, well-reasoning, and empathic beings. However, the platform's orientation towards optimal nourishing and holding turns it into a feeding tube that has no realistic strategies of detachment and weaning built into its design. In this respect, users of Facebook and Instagram are driven to constantly disambiguate their relationships, striving for fusion with others in order to gain independence. YouTube's intrusiveness and unwillingness to let people go, in turn, seem to suggest the formation of response patterns along the lines of anorexia nervosa, where feelings of autonomy are paradoxically obtained via the self-denial of needs (Jeammet 2005, 91). In other words, where there is significant eagerness for people to consume and significant (if precarious) care sought to be provided, a logical way to free oneself of such forms of dependence seems to be to flatly deny any kind of care.

This intense polarity between dependence and independence, in turn, continues into Google Search's facilitation of symbolic exchanges, bringing up questions of power, control, and mastery. Responding to the questions we have about the world, Google has a great share in shaping our conception of this world. By bending all its answers towards the useful, however, it collapses what we should know with what is 'on offer' for and available to us. Google's compulsively utilitarian attitude towards knowledge as a currency is most painfully palpable for those users who are at the receiving end of the control that is being facilitated by it, for example, those who are not granted the right to be forgotten. And yet, the logic of automated surveillance (Andrejevic 2019), which has become omnipresent, might work in a generalised subject-formational sense, i.e., in the sense that we all have tools with which to wield power over others. The "measurable types" (Cheney-Lippold 2017) which Google analytics makes of us inevitably rub off on the ways we assess others as well as ourselves. In this way, both the drive towards mastery and control and that towards dependence, subjugation, and conformity have been 'democratised' to the point at which they now appear as fixed parts of people's affective-cognitive horizon. In the context of such anxious controllability, it also becomes conceivable how the pursuits of our wishes and desires become accompanied by constant acts of seduction, in which we seek to bring others to legitimise these desires in the first place – frequently becoming stuck in our scheming.

What thus arises from the era of platformed, formative media is a subject that is constantly stimulated and wrapped in positivity, soothed, calmed, and fed, helped, assisted, and cared for; it is controlled, measured and empowered, held in constant touch with close and likeminded others – self-objects as well as ideal objects (Kohut 1971) – and tuned into the dynamic currents of morality as well as an ever-shifting public opinion. These states and holding patterns are by no means negative or damaging in themselves. What makes them highly problematic is that, due to profit strategies, the formative functions that they are geared to perform are pre-set and, instead of offering paths towards maturation, they seek to arrest subjects within the formative zones and affective forcefields that the services provide. Digital media constantly suggest and initiate formative growth but refrain from bringing it about. In these modes of constant impulsion, corporate platforms provoke responses that are symptomatic of the fixations they create. Hence, what can be found in the subject of the current corporate digital sphere are the insignia of those psychic ailments that are most widespread in society already, particularly depression and bipolar states (Leader 2008; 2013). This subject is prone to prolonged phases of paralysed rumination interspersed by outbursts ranging from the (auto) aggressive to the manically enthusiastic. Attention-deficit/hyperactivity disorder (ADHD) has become the metaphor of the present cultural moment. Endowed with a general tendency towards loosening its ties to other objects, the subject is prone to, on the one hand, fusion-like dependence and, on the other, disinhibited acts of asserting independence, frequently applying to others the exacting gaze that it feels on its own skin.

Note

1 In Dean's (2015) words, "negativity here connotes positive feedback and the excess of an effect in relation to its cause" (p. 98).

Bibliography

Aagaard, J. (2021). Beyond the Rhetoric of Tech Addiction: Why We Should Be Discussing Tech Habits Instead (and How). *Phenomenology and the Cognitive Sciences*, 20(3), 559–72. https://doi.org/10.1007/s11097-020-09669-z.

Aarseth, H. (2016). Eros in the Field? Bourdieu's Double Account of Socialized Desire. *The Sociological Review (Keele)*, 64(1), 93–109. https://doi.org/10.1111/1467-954X.12348.

Abadi, M., Agarwal, A., Barham, P., Brevdo, E., Chen, Z., Citro, C., Corrado, G.S., Davis, A., Dean, J., Devin, M., Ghemawat, S., Goodfellow, I., Harp, A., Irving, G., Isard, M., Jia, Y., Jozefowicz, R., Kaiser, L., Kudlur, M., … Zheng, X. (2016). TensorFlow: Large-Scale Machine Learning on Heterogeneous Distributed Systems. *arXiv Preprint*. https://doi.org/10.48550/arxiv.1603.04467.

Abel-Hirsch, N. (2010). The life instinct. *The International Journal of Psychoanalysis*, 91, 1055–71. https://doi.org/10.1111/j.1745-8315.2010.00304.x.

Abidin, C. (2016). "Aren't These Just Young, Rich Women Doing Vain Things Online?": Influencer Selfies as Subversive Frivolity. *Social Media + Society*, 2(2), https://doi.org/10.1177/2056305116641342.

Abidin, C. (2018). *Internet Celebrity: Understanding Fame Online*. Bingley: Emerald Publishing.

Abraham, K. (1916). Untersuchungen über die früheste prägenitale Entwicklungsstufe der Libido. *Internationale Zeitschrift für Psychoanalyse*, 4(2), 71–97.

Abraham, K. (1994 [1924]). A Short Study of the Development of the Libido, Viewed in the Light of Mental Disorders. In: Frankiel, R. (Ed.), *Essential Papers on Object Loss*. New York and London: New York University Press.

Abraham, N., & Torok, M. (2005 [1987]). *The Wolf Man's Magic Word: A Cryptonymy*. Minneapolis: University of Minnesota Press.

Abram, J. (2007). *The Language of Winnicott: A Dictionary of Winnicott's Use of Words, 2nd Revised Edition*. New York and London: Routledge.

Adams, R., & Girard, R. (1993). Violence, Difference, Sacrifice: A Conversation with René Girard. *Religion & Literature*, 25(2), 9–33.

Adorno, T.W. (1954). How to Look at Television. *The Quarterly of Film, Radio and Television*, 8(3), 213–35.

Adorno, T.W., & Horkheimer, M. (1989). *Dialectic of Enlightenment*. London: Verso.

Aichhorn, T. (2006). Jenseits des Lustprinzips. In: Lohmann, H.M. & Pfeiffer, J. (Eds.), *Freud-Handbuch. Leben – Werk – Wirkung*. Stuttgart: Metzler, pp. 158–62.

Allen, A. (2021) *Critique on the Couch: Why Critical Theory Needs Psychoanalysis*. New York: Columbia University Press.

Alter, A. (2017). *Irresistible: The Rise of Addictive Technology and the Business of Keeping Us Hooked*. New York: Penguin.

Amarasingam, A. (2011). *The Stewart/Colbert Effect: Essays on the Real Impacts of Fake News*. Jefferson, NC: McFarland.

Andrejevic, M. (2019). Automating surveillance. *Surveillance & Society*, 17(1–2), 7–13. https://doi.org/10.24908/ss.v17i1/2.12930.

Angwin, J., Varner, M., & Tobin, A. (2017). Facebook Enabled Advertisers to Reach 'Jew Haters'. *ProPublica*. https://www.propublica.org/article/facebook-enabled-advertisers-to-reach-jew-haters.

Anzieu, D. (1979). The Sound Image of the Self. *International Review of Psycho-Analysis*, 6, 23–36.

Bahney, A. (2006). Don't Talk to Invisible Strangers. *The New York Times*. https://www.nytimes.com/2006/03/09/fashion/thursdaystyles/dont-talk-to-invisible-strangers.html.

Bainbridge, C. (2019). Box-Set Mind-Set: Psycho-Cultural Approaches to Binge Watching, Gender, and Digital Experience. *Free Associations: Psychoanalysis and Culture, Media, Groups, Politics*, (75). https://doi.org/10.1234/fa.v0i75.262.

Bainbridge, C., & Yates, C. (2014). *Media and the Inner World: Psycho-Cultural Approaches to Emotion, Media and Popular Culture*. London: Palgrave Macmillan.

Balick, A. (2014). *The Psychodynamics of Social Networking: Connected-Up Instantaneous Culture and the Self*. London: Routledge.

Banet-Weiser, S. (2012). *Authentic™ the Politics of Ambivalence in a Brand Culture*. New York: New York University Press.

Basu, K., Caspi, A., & Hockett, R.C. (2021). Markets and Regulation in the Age of Big Tech. *Capitalism and Society*, 15(1). https://ssrn.com/abstract=3985585.

Bates, D. (2014). Unity, Plasticity, Catastrophe: Order and Pathology in the Cybernetic Era. In: Lebovic, N., & Killen, A. (Eds.), *Catastrophes: A History and Theory of an Operative Concept*. Boston, MA: De Gruyter Oldenbourg.

Bateson, G., Jackson, D.D., Haley, J., & Weakland, J. (1956). Toward a theory of schizophrenia. *Behavioral Science*, 1, 251–64. https://doi.org/10.1002/bs.3830010402.

Baudrillard, J. (1983). *Simulations*. Beichten, P., Foss, P., & Patton, P. (Trans.). Cambridge, MA: MIT Press.

Baudry, J.-L. (1975). The Apparatus: Meta Psychological Approaches to the Impression of Reality in Cinema. In: Cohen, M., & Braudy, L. (Eds.), *Film Theory and Criticism: Introductory Readings*. Oxford: Oxford University Press, pp. 760–77.

Bayer, J., Ellison, N., Schoenebeck, S., & Falk E. (2016). Sharing the small moments: ephemeral social interaction on Snapchat. *Information, Communication & Society*, 19(7), 956–77, https://doi.org/10.1080/1369118X.2015.1084349.

Baxmann, I., & Pias, T. (Eds.) (2014). *Soziale Medien – Neue Massen: Medienwissenschaftliche Symposien der DFG*. Zürich und Berlin: Diaphanes.

Beck, U. (1992). *Risk Society: Toward a New Modernity* (Ritter, M., Trans.). London: Sage.

Beebe, B., & Lachmann, F. (2003). The Relational Turn in Psychoanalysis. Contemporary *Psychoanalysis*, 39(3), 379–409. https://doi.org/10.1080/00107530.2003.10747213.

Benjamin, J. (1988). *The Bonds of Love: Psychoanalysis, Feminism, and the Problem of Domination*. Toronto: Penguin Random House.

Benvenuto, S. (2016). *What are Perversions? Sexuality, Ethics, Psychoanalysis*. London: Karnac.

Bereswill M., Morgenroth C., & Redman P. (2010). Alfred Lorenzer and the depth-hermeneutic method. *Psychoanalysis, Culture and Society*, 15(3), 221–54.

Bergeret, J. (2005): Aggressiveness/Aggression. In: Mijolla et al. (Eds.), *International Dictionary of Psychoanalysis*. Detroit, MI: Macmillan, pp. 33–5.

Bernays, E. (2005 [1928]). *Propaganda*. New York: IG Publishing.

Berlant, L. (2011). *Cruel Optimism*. Durham: Duke University Press.

Bersani, L. (2015). *Thoughts and Things*. Chicago: University of Chicago Press.

Beutel, A., Covington, P., Jain, S., Xu, C., Li, J., Gatto, V., & Chi, E.H. (2018). Latent Cross: Making Use of Context in Recurrent Recommender Systems. *WSDM 2018 – Proceedings of the 11th ACM International Conference on Web Search and Data Mining*, 46–54. https://doi.org/10.1145/3159652.3159727.

Beutel, A., Chen, J., Doshi, T., Qian, H., Wei, L., Wu, Y., Heldt, L., Zhao, Z., Hong, L., Chi, E.H., & Goodrow, C. (2019). Fairness in Recommendation Ranking through Pairwise Comparisons. *Proceedings of the ACM SIGKDD International Conference on Knowledge Discovery and Data Mining*, pp. 2212–20. https://doi.org/10.1145/3292500.3330745.

Bhargava, V.R., & Velasquez, M. (2021). Ethics of the Attention Economy: The Problem of Social Media Addiction. *Business Ethics Quarterly*, 31(3), 321–59. https://doi.org/10.1017/beq.2020.32.

Billig, M. (2006). Lacan's Misuse of Psychology: Evidence, Rhetoric and the Mirror Stage. *Theory, Culture & Society*, 23(4), 1–26. https://doi.org/10.1177/0263276406066367.

Bilton, N. (2013) *Hatching Twitter: A True Story of Money, Power, Friendship, and Betrayal*. London: Sceptre.

Bion, W. (2004 [1961]). *Experiences in Groups and Other Papers*. London: Routledge.

Bion, W. (1962). The Psycho-Analytic Study of Thinking. *International Journal of Psycho-Analysis*, 43, 306–10.

Bishop, B. (2018). Writer-Director James Gunn fired from Guardians of the Galaxy Vol. 3 over Offensive Tweets. *The Verge*. https://www.theverge.com/2018/7/20/17596452/guardians-of-the-galaxy-marvel-james-gunn-fired-pedophile-tweets-mike-cernovich.

Blackman, L., & Walkerdine, V. (Eds.) (2002). *Mass Hysteria: Critical Psychology and Media Studies*. London: Red Globe Press.

Blankenstein, L. (1986). Conscience of a Hacker or, the Hacker Manifesto. Self Published. http://phrack.org/issues/7/3.html

Bogost, I. (2007). *Persuasive Games: The Expressive Power of Videogames*. Cambridge, MA: MIT Press.

Borch, C. (2005). Urban Imitations. *Theory, Culture & Society*, 22(3), 81–100. https://doi.org/10.1177/0263276405053722.

Borges, J.L. (1999 [1944]). *Collected Fictions*. New York: Penguin.

Boulton, C. (2007). Facebook Refreshes Ad System after Privacy Protest. *eWEEK*. https://www.eweek.com/enterprise-apps/facebook-refreshes-ad-system-after-privacy-protest/.

Bowden, S. (2012). Gilles Deleuze, a Reader of Gilbert Simondon. In: de Boever, A., Murray, A., Roffe, J., & Woodward, A. (Eds.), *Gilbert Simondon – Being and Technology*. Edinburgh: Edinburgh University Press.

Bowlby, J. (1979). *The Making and Breaking of Affectional Bonds*. London and New York: Routledge.

Brady, W.J., Crockett, M.J., & Van Bavel, J.J. (2020). The MAD Model of Moral Contagion: The Role of Motivation, Attention, and Design in the Spread of Moralized Content Online. *Perspectives on Psychological Science*, 15(4), 978–1010. https://doi.org/10.1177/1745691620917336.

Braidotti, R. (2013). *The Posthuman*. Cambridge, UK: Polity Press.

Bratton, B. (2015a). *The Stack: On Software and Sovereignty*. Cambridge, MA: MIT Press.

Bratton, B. (2015b). Outing Artificial Intelligence: Reckoning with Turing Tests. In: Pasquinelli, M. (Ed.), *Alleys of Your Mind: Augmented Intelligence and Its Traumas*. Lüneburg: Meson Press, pp. 69–80.

Brewer, P.R., Young, D.G., & Morreale, M. (2013). The Impact of Real News about "Fake News": Intertextual Processes and Political Satire. *International Journal of Public Opinion Research*, 25(3), 323–43. https://doi.org/10.1093/ijpor/edt015.

Brinkema, E. (2014). *The Form of the Affects*. Durham, NC: Duke University Press.

Bröckling, U. (2018). The subject in the marketplace, the subject as a marketplace. In: King, V., Gerisch, B., & Rosa, H. (Eds.), *Lost in Perfection: Impacts of Optimisation on Culture and Psyche*. London: Routledge.

Brugeilles, R. (1913). L'essence du phénomène social: la suggestion. *Revue Philosophique de La France et de l'Étranger*, 75, 593–602.

Bruns, A. (2011). Gatekeeping, Gatewatching, Real-Time Feedback: New Challenges for Journalism. *Brazilian Journalism Research*, 7(2), 117–36. https://doi.org/10.25200/BJR.v7n2.2011.355.

Bruns, A. (2020). *Are Filter Bubbles Real?* Cambridge, UK: Polity Press.

Bruns, A., & Burgess, J. (2015). Twitter Hashtags from Ad Hoc to Calculated Publics. In: Rambukkana, N. (Ed.), *Hashtag Publics: The Power and Politics of Discursive Networks*. New York: Peter Lang, pp. 13–28.

Bosworth, A. (2018 [2016]). "The Ugly" Memo, June 18, 2016. In: Mac, R., Warzel, C., & Kantrowitz, A. (2018). *BuzzFeed News*. https://www.buzzfeednews.com/article/ryanmac/growth-at-any-cost-top-facebook-executive-defended-data#.upw3jdyR8.

Bown, A. (2018). *The Playstation Dreamworld*. Cambridge, UK: Polity Press.

boyd, d. (2006). Friends, Friendsters, and MySpace Top 8: Writing community into being on social network sites. *First Monday*, 11(12). http://www.firstmonday.org/issues/issue11_12/boyd/.

boyd, d. (2008). Facebook's Privacy Trainwreck: Exposure, Invasion, and Social Convergence. *Convergence*, 14(1), 13–20. https://doi.org/10.1177/1354856507084416.

boyd, d., & Ellison, N. (2007). Social Network Sites: Definition, History, and Scholarship. *Journal of Computer-Mediated Communication*, 13(1), 2007, 210–30. https://doi.org/10.1111/j.1083-6101.2007.00393.x.

Bucher, T. (2018). *If...Then: Algorithmic Power and Politics*. Oxford: Oxford University Press.

Bucher, T. (2020). The Right-Time Web: Theorizing the Kairologic of Algorithmic Media. *New Media & Society*, 22(9), 1699–714. https://doi.org/10.1177/1461444820913560.

Bucher, T. (2021). *Facebook*. Cambridge, UK: Polity Press.

Burch, S. (2018). Mark Zuckerberg "Strongly" Disagrees with Leaked "Ugly" Memo from Facebook VP. *TheWrap*. https://www.thewrap.com/mark-zuckerberg-strongly-disagrees-leaked-memo-facebook-vp/.

Burgers, C., & Brugman, B. (2022). How Satirical News Impacts Affective Responses, Learning, and Persuasion: A Three-Level Random-Effects Meta-Analysis. *Communication Research*, 49(7), 966–93. https://doi.org/10.1177/00936502211032100.

Burgess, J., & Baym, N. (2020) *Twitter: A Biography*. New York: New York University Press.

Burnham, B. (Director) (2018). *Eighth Grade* [film]. A24.

Butkowski, C.P., Dixon, T.L., Weeks, K.R., & Smith, M.A. (2020). Quantifying the Feminine Self(ie): Gender Display and Social Media Feedback in Young Women's Instagram Selfies. *New Media & Society*, 22(5), 817–37. https://doi.org/10.1177/1461444819871669.

Butler, J. (1990). *Gender Trouble: Feminism and the Subversion of Identity*. London: Routledge.

Caldeira, S., Van Bauble, S., & De Ridder, S. (2020). 'Everybody Needs to Post a Selfie Every Once In A While': Exploring the Politics of Instagram curation in Young Women's Self-Representational Practices. *Information, Communication & Society*, 24(8), 1073–90. https://doi.org/10.1080/1369118X.2020.1776371.

Caliandro, A., & Graham, J. (2020). Studying Instagram Beyond Selfies. *Social Media + Society*, 6(2), 2056305120924779. https://doi.org/10.1177/2056305120924779.

Campbell, W.K., & McCain, J.L. (2018). Narcissism and Social Media Use: A Meta-Analytic Review. *Psychology of Popular Media Culture*, 7(3), 308–27. https://doi.org/10.1037/ppm0000137.

Casserly, M. (2012). Inside the Social Network: Facebook Staffer No. 51 Cashes Out, Tells All. *Forbes*. https://www.forbes.com/sites/meghancasserly/2012/07/25/inside-the-social-network-katherine-losse-boy-kings-facebook/?sh=429022a476c0.

Cassirer, E. (2013 [1930]). Form and Technology. In: Lofts, S.G., & Calcagno, A. (Eds.), *Ernst Cassirer, The Warburg Years (1919–1933) Essays on Language, Art, Myth, and Technology*. New Haven, CT: Yale University Press, pp. 262–316.

Chen, M., Beutel, A., Covington, P., Jain, S., Belletti, F., & Chi, E.H. (2019). Top-k off-policy correction for a reinforce recommender system. *WSDM 2019 – Proceedings of the 12th ACM International Conference on Web Search and Data Mining*, pp. 456–64. https://doi.org/10.1145/3289600.3290999.

Chen, A.Y., Nyhan, B., Reifler, J., Robertson, R.E., & Wilson, C. (2023). Subscriptions and External Links Help Drive Resentful Users to Alternative and Extremist YouTube Videos. *Science Advances*, 9(35), eadd8080. https://doi.org/10.1126/sciadv.add8080.

Cheney-Lippold, J. (2011). A New Algorithmic Identity: Soft Biopolitics and the Modulation of Control. *Theory, Culture & Society*, 28(6), 164–81. https://doi.org/10.1177/0263276411424420.

Cheney-Lippold, J. (2017). *We are Data: Algorithms and the Making of Our Digital Selves*. New York: NYU Press.

Chevant, L. (N.D.). How to Develop Link Building without Receiving an Algorithmic Penalty from Google Penguin? *SmartKeywords*. https://smartkeyword.io/en/seo-google-algorithm-google-penguin/.

Chmielewski, D., & Sarno, D. (2009). Once-Trendy MySpace Hits an Awkward Stage. *Los Angeles Times*. https://www.latimes.com/archives/la-xpm-2009-jun-17-fi-ct-myspace17-story.html.

Chun, W. (2016). *Updating to Remain the Same: Habitual New Media*. Cambridge, MA: MIT Press.

Chun, W. (2018). Querying Homophily. In: Apprich, C., Chun, W., Cramer, F., & Steyerl, H. (Eds.), *Pattern Discrimination*. Minneapolis: University of Minnesota Press.

Chun, W. (2021). *Discriminating Data: Correlation, Neighborhoods, and the New Politics of Recognition*. Cambridge, MA: MIT Press.

Cohen, S. (1972) *Folk Devils and Moral Panics: The Creation of the Mods and Rockers*. London: Routledge.

Coleman, G. (2014) *Hacker, Hoaxer, Whistleblower, Spy – The Many Faces of Anonymous*. London and New York: Verso.

Constine, J. (2017). Facebook Changes Mission Statement to 'Bring the World Closer To-gether'. https://techcrunch.com/2017/06/22/bring-the-world-closer-together/.

Copjec, J. (2015 [1994]). *Read My Desire: Lacan against the Historicists*. London: Verso.

Couldry, N. (2012). *Media, Society, World: Social Theory and Digital Media Practice*. Cambridge, UK: Polity Press.

Courtwright, D. (2019). *The Age of Addiction: How Bad Habits Become Big Business*. Cambridge, MA: Harvard University Press.

Covington, P., Adams, J., & Sargin, E. (2016). Deep Neural Networks for YouTube Recommendations. In: *Proceedings of the 10th ACM Conference on Recommender Systems (RecSys'16)*. Association for Computing Machinery, New York, pp. 191–8. https://doi.org/10.1145/2959100.2959190.

Cramer, F. (2018). Crapularity Hermeneutics: Interpretation as the Blind Spot of Analytics, Artificial Intelligence, and Other Algorithmic Producers of the Postapocalyptic Present. In: Apprich, C., Chun, W., Cramer, F., & Steyerl, H. (Eds.), *Pattern Discrimination*. Minneapolis: University of Minnesota Press, pp. 23–58.

Critchley, S. (2002). *On Humor*. London: Routledge.

Cross, K. (2015). The Lost of Found Photography. *Photographies*, 8(1), 43–62. https://doi.org/10.1080/17540763.2014.974285.

Daw, N.D., O'Doherty, J.P., Seymour, B., Dayan, P., &Dolan, R.J. (2006). Cortical substrates for exploratory decisions in humans. *Nature*, 441, 876–9. https//doi.org/10.1038/nature04766.

Dahlgren, P. (2020). *Media Echo Chambers: Selective Exposure and Confirmation Bias in Media Use, and its Consequences for Political Polarization*. Gothenburg: University of Gothenburg.

Daudi, A. (2022). The Culture of Narcissism: A Philosophical Analysis of "Fitspiration" and the Objectified Self. *Physical Culture and Sport Studies and Research*, 94(1), 46–55. https://doi.org/10.2478/pcssr-2022-0005.

De Zeeuw, D., & Tuters, M. (2020). Teh Internet is Serious Business: On the Deep Vernacular Web and Its Discontents. *Cultural Politics (Biggleswade, England)*, 16(2), 214–32. https://doi.org/10.1215/17432197-8233406.

Dean, J. (2009). *Democracy and Other Neoliberal Fantasies: Communicative Capitalism and Left Politics*. Durham, NC: Duke University Press.

Dean, J. (2010). *Blog Theory: Feedback and Capture in the Circuits of Drive*. Cambridge, UK: Polity Press.

Dean, J. (2015). Affect and Drive. In: Hillis, K., Paasonen, S., & Petit, M. (Eds.), *Networked Affect*. Cambridge, MA: MIT Press.

Dean, J. (2016) *Crowds and Party*. New York and London: Verso.

Deleuze, G. (1994). *Difference and Repetition*. (Patton, P., Trans.). New York: Columbia University Press.

Deleuze, G., & Guattari, F. (1983). *Anti-Oedipus: Capitalism and Schizophrenia*. (R. Hurley, M. Seem, & H. Lane, Trans.) London and New York: Penguin.

Deleuze, G., & Guattari, F. (1987). *A Thousand Plateaus: Capitalism and Schizophrenia*. (B. Massumi, Trans.) Minneapolis: University of Minnesota Press.

Dodes, L.M. (1996). Compulsion and Addiction. *Journal of the American Psychoanalytic Association*, 44(3), 815–35. https://doi.org/10.1177/000306519604400307.

Dodes, L.M. (2002). *The Heart of Addiction*. New York: Harper Collins.

Dolata, U. (2015). Volatile Monopole. Konzentration, Konkurrenz und Innovationsstrategien der Internetkonzerne. *Berliner Journal für Soziologie*, 4, 505–29. https://doi.org/10.1007/s11609-014-0261-8.

Downey, T.W. (1984). Within the Pleasure Principle: Child Analytic Perspectives on Aggression. *The Psychoanalytic Study of the Child*, 39, 101–36. https://doi.org/10.1080/00797308.1984.11823422.

Duffy, B. (2017). *(Not) Getting Paid to Do What You Love: Gender and Aspirational Labor in the Social Media Economy*. New Haven, CT: Yale University Press.

Dundes, A. (1987). *Cracking Jokes: Studies of Sick Humor Cycles & Stereotypes*. Berkeley, CA: Ten Speed Press.

Eagleman, D. (2021). *Livewired: The Inside Story of the Ever-Changing Brain*. New York: Pantheon.

Eggers, D. (2013). *The Circle*. New York: Knopf.

Eichhorn, K. (2019). *The End of Forgetting: Growing Up with Social Media*. Cambridge, MA: Harvard University Press.

Elias, N. (1991). *The Society of Individuals*. London: Basil Blackwell.

Elise, D. (2019). *Creativity and the Erotic Dimensions of the Analytic Field*. New York and London: Routledge.

ElSherief, M., Nilizadeh, S., Nguyen, D., Vigna, G., & Belding, E. (2018). Peer to Peer Hate: Hate Speech Instigators and Their Targets. *Proceedings of the International AAAI Conference on Web and Social Media*, 12(1). https://doi.org/10.1609/icwsm.v12i1.15038

Enarsson, T., & Lindgren, S. (2019). Free Speech or Hate Speech? A Legal Analysis of the Discourse about Roma on Twitter. *Information & Communications Technology Law*, 28(1), 1–18. https://doi.org/10.1080/13600834.2018.1494415.

Engley, R. (2022). The Social Sinthome. *CLC Web – Comparative Literature and Culture*, 24(4), 8. https://doi.org/10.7771/1481-4374.4101.

Ess, C. (2014). "Zwischen zwei Stühlen sitzen – oder drei, oder... Ein Kommentar zum Zweiten Medienwissenschaftlichen Symposium der DFG, 'Soziale Medien – Neue Massen. In: Baxmann, I., & Pias, T. (Eds.), *Soziale Medien – Neue Massen: Medienwissenschaftliche Symposien der DFG*. Zürich und Berlin: Diaphanes., pp. 353–9.

Estevez, A., Jauregui, P., Sánchez-Marcos, I., López-González, H., & Griffiths, M.D. (2017). Attachment and Emotion Regulation in Substance Addictions and Behavioral Addictions. *Journal of Behavioral Addictions*, 6(4), 534–44. https://doi.org/10.1556/2006.6.2017.086.

Evans, D. (1996). *An Introductory Dictionary of Lacanian Psychoanalysis*. London: Taylor & Frances/Routledge.

Eyal, N. (2017). Nir Eyal (hooked): Technology is Distracting and Addictive, TNW Conference 2017. *YouTube*. https://www.youtube.com/watch?v=0pxwGzPOHYI.

Eyal, N. (2019 [2014]). *Hooked: How to Build Habit-Forming Products*. New York: Portfolio.

Faddoul, M., Chaslot, G., & Farid, H. (2020). A Longitudinal Analysis of YouTube's Promotion of Conspiracy Videos. *arXiv Preprint*. https://doi.org/10.48550/arxiv.2003.03318.

Fan, J. (2017). China's Selfie Obsession: Meitu's Apps Are Changing What It Means to Be Beautiful in the Most Populous Country on Earth. *New Yorker*. https://www.newyorker.com/magazine/2017/12/18/chinas-selfie-obsession.

Fardouly, J., Willburger, B.K., & Vartanian, L.R. (2018). Instagram Use and Young Women's Body Image Concerns and Self-Objectification: Testing Mediational Pathways. *New Media & Society*, 20(4), 1380–95. https://doi.org/10.1177/1461444817694499.

Favarel-Garrigues, G., Tanner, S., & Trottier, D. (2020). Introducing Digital Vigilantism. *Global Crime*, 21:3–4, 189–95. https://doi.org/10.1080/17440572.2020.1750789.

Fenichel, O. (1939). The Counter-Phobic Attitude. *International Journal of Psycho-Analysis*, 20, 263–74.

Ferarra, A. (2019). Narcissism and Critique: On Kohut's Self Psychology. In Allen, A., & O'Connor, B. (Eds.), *Transitional Subjects: Critical Theory and Object Relations*. New York: Columbia University Press, pp. 75–106.

Figlio, K. (2006). The Absolute State of Mind in Society and the Individual. *Psychoanalysis, Culture & Society*, 11(2), 119–43. https://doi.org/10.1057/palgrave.pcs.2100076.

Fincher, D. (Director). (2010). *The Social Network* [film]. Columbia Pictures.

Finn, E. (2017). *What Algorithms Want: Imagination in the Age of Computing*. Cambridge, MA: MIT Press.

Fisher, A. (2018). *Valley of Genius: The Uncensored History of Silicon Valley (As Told by the Hackers, Founders, and Freaks Who Made It Boom)*. New York: Twelve.

Fisher, H. (2016 [1992]). *Anatomy of Love: A Natural History of Mating, Marriage, and Why We Stray*. New York and London: Norton.

Fiske, J. (1989). *Reading the Popular*. New York and London: Routledge.

Fleming, O. (2017). 'Why Don't I Look Like Her?': How Instagram Is Ruining Our Self Esteem. *Cosmopolitan*. https://www.cosmopolitan.com/health-fitness/a8601466/why-dont-i-look-like-her-how-instagram-is-ruining-our-self-esteem/.

Flisfeder, M. (2021). *Algorithmic Desire: Toward a New Structuralist Theory of Social Media*. Evanston, IL: Northwestern University Press.

Flisfeder, M. (2022). Platform Psychoanalysis: What Does the Algorithm Want? *CLCWeb: Comparative Literature and Culture*, 24(4), 1. https://doi.org/10.7771/1481-4374.4273.

Fogg, B.J. (2003). *Persuasive Technology: Using Computers to Change What We Think and Do*. Burlington, MA: Morgan Kaufmann.

Fogg, B.J. (2019). *Tiny Habits: The Small Changes That Change Everything*. Boston, MA: Houghton Mifflin Harcourt.

Fogg, B.J., & Euchner, J. (2019). Designing for Behavior Change—New Models and Moral Issues. *Research-Technology Management*, 62(5), 14–9, https://doi.org/10.1080/08956308.2019.1638490.

Fonagy, P., Moràn, George, S., & Target, M. (1993). Aggression and the Psychological Self. *International Journal of Psychoanalysis*, 74(3), 471–85.

Fosshage, J. (1998). On aggression: Its forms and functions. *Psychoanalytic Inquiry*, 18(1), 45–54. https://doi.org/10.1080/07351699809534169.

Foucault, M. (2008). *The Birth of Biopolitics: Lectures at the Collège de France, 1978–1979*. London: Picador.

Fowler, G., & Esteban, C. (2018). Analysis: 14 Years of Mark Zuckerberg Saying Sorry, Not Sorry. *The Washington Post*. https://www.washingtonpost.com/graphics/2018/business/facebook-zuckerberg-apologies/.

Freud, S. (1905a). *Three Essays on the Theory of Sexuality*. In: *The Standard Edition of the Complete Psychological Works of Sigmund Freud (SE), Volume 7*, London: The Hogarth Press and the Institute of Psycho-Analysis, pp. 123–246.

Freud, S. (1905b). *Jokes and their Relation to the Unconscious*. In: *SE, Volume 8*. London: The Hogarth Press and the Institute of Psycho-Analysis, pp. 1–247.

Freud, S. (1909). Notes Upon a Case of Obsessional Neurosis. In: *SE, Volume 10*. London: The Hogarth Press and the Institute of Psycho-Analysis, pp. 151–318.

Freud, S. (1913a). The Disposition to Obsessional Neurosis, a Contribution to the Problem of the Choice of Neurosis. In: *SE, Volume 12*. London: The Hogarth Press and the Institute of Psycho-Analysis, pp. 311–26.

Freud, S. (1913b) *Totem and Taboo*. In: *SE, Volume 13*. London: The Hogarth Press and the Institute of Psycho-Analysis, pp. vii–162.

Freud, S. (1914). On Narcissism. In: *SE, Volume 14*. London: The Hogarth Press and the Institute of Psycho-Analysis, pp. 67–102.

Freud, S. (1915). Instincts and their Vicissitudes. In: *SE, Volume 14*. London: The Hogarth Press and the Institute of Psycho-Analysis, pp. 109–40.

Freud, S. (1917). Mourning and Melancholia. In: *SE, Volume 14*. London: The Hogarth Press and the Institute of Psycho-Analysis, pp. 237–58.

Freud, S. (1920). *Beyond the Pleasure Principle*. In: *SE, Volume 18*. London: The Hogarth Press and the Institute of Psycho-Analysis, pp. 1–64.

Freud, S. (1921). Group Psychology and the Analysis of the Ego. In: *SE, Volume 18*. London: The Hogarth Press and the Institute of Psycho-Analysis, pp. 65–144.

Freud, S. (1925). Negation. In: *SE, Volume 19*. London: The Hogarth Press and the Institute of Psycho-Analysis, pp. 233–40.

Freud, S. (1926). Inhibitions, Symptom and Anxiety. In: *SE, Volume 20*. London: The Hogarth Press and the Institute of Psycho-Analysis, pp. 75–176.

Freud, S. (1927). Humour. In: *SE, Volume 21*. London: The Hogarth Press and the Institute for Psycho-Analysis, pp. 159–66.

Freud, S. (1933). Why War? Letter from Freud (to Einstein). In: *SE, Volume 22*. London: The Hogarth Press and the Institute for Psycho-Analysis, pp. 199–219.

Freud, S. (1933a [1932]). *New Introductory Lectures on Psycho-Analysis*. In: *SE, Volume 22*, pp. 1–182.

Freud, S. (1938). Outline of psychoanalysis. In: *SE, Volume 23*. London: The Hogarth Press and the Institute of Psycho-Analysis, pp. 139–208.

Frier, S. (2020). *No Filter: The Inside Story of Instagram*. New York: Simon & Schuster.

Fromm, E. (1989 [1929]). Psychoanalysis and Sociology. In: Bronner, S.E., & Kellner, D.M. (Eds.), *Critical Theory and Society – A Reader*. New York and London: Routledge, pp. 37–39.

Frosh, S. (2010). *Psychoanalysis Outside the Clinic*. Basingstoke: Palgrave Macmillan.

Fuchs, C. (2012). Dallas Smythe Today – The Audience Commodity, The Digital Labour Debate, Marxist Political Economy and Critical Theory. *tripleC*, 10(20), 692–740. https://doi.org/10.31269/triplec.v10i2.443.

Fuchs, C. (2014). *Digital Labor and Karl Marx*. London: Routledge.

Fuchs, C. (2016). *Social Media: A Critical Introduction*. London: Sage.

Gallagher, R. (2022). Twitter Firings Gutted Its Compliance Teams. Now It Risks Investigations and Big Fines. *Los Angeles Times*, 2 December 2022, https://www.latimes.com/business/story/2022-12-02/twitter-shrunk-compliance-teams-risks-investigations-fines.

Gambino, L. (2015). Daily Show's Trevor Noah under Fire for Twitter Jokes about Jews and Women. *The Guardian*. https://www.theguardian.com/culture/2015/mar/31/trevor-noah-backlash-highlights-jokes-jews-women.

Gammon, E. (2017). Narcissistic Rage and Neoliberal Reproduction. *Global Society: Journal of Interdisciplinary International Relations*, 31(4), 510–30. https://doi.org/10.1080/13600826.2017.1280775.

Garber, M. (2014). Instagram Was First Called "Burbn." *The Atlantic*. https://www.theatlantic.com/technology/archive/2014/07/instagram-used-to-be-called-brbn/373815/.

Gehl, R. (2012). Real (Software) Abstractions: On the Rise of Facebook and the Fall of MySpace. *Social Text*, 30(2), 99–119. https://doi.org/10.1215/01642472-1541772.

Gerlitz, C., & Helmond, A. (2013). The Like Economy: Social Buttons and the Data-Intensive Web. *New Media & Society*, 15(8), 1348–65. https://doi.org/10.1177/1461444812472322.

Gevinson, T. (2019). Who Would Tavi Gevinson be without Instagram?. *The Cut*. https://www.thecut.com/2019/09/who-would-tavi-gevinson-be-without-instagram.html.

Gibson, G. (2023). "Just There For the Fashion, Basically": Politicized Fem(me)ininity in the fat-o-sphere. *Fat Studies*, 12(1), 135–48. https://doi.org/10.1080/21604851.2021.2013051.

Ging, D., Lynn, T., & Rosati, P. (2020). Neologising misogyny: Urban Dictionary's folksonomies of sexual abuse. *New Media & Society*, 22(5), 838–56. https://doi.org/10.1177/1461444819870306.

Gill, R. (2017). The Affective, Cultural and Psychic Life of Postfeminism: A Postfeminist Sensibility 10 Years On. *European Journal of Cultural Studies*, 20(6), 606–26. https://doi.org/10.1177/1367549417733003.

Gill, R., & Orgad, S. (2022). *Confidence Culture*. Durham, NC: Duke University Press.

Gillespie, T. (2010). The Politics of 'Platforms.' *New Media & Society*, 12(3), 347–64. https://doi.org/10.1177/1461444809342738.

Gilroy-Ware, M. (2017). *Filling the Void: Emotion, Capitalism & Social Media*. London: Repeater Books.

Giraud, E. (2015). Subjectivity 2.0: Digital Technologies, Participatory Media and Communicative Capitalism. *Subjectivity*, 8(12), 124–46.

Glatt, Z. (2022). "We're All Told Not to Put Our Eggs in One Basket": Uncertainty, Precarity and Cross-Platform Labor in the Online Video Influencer Industry. *International Journal of Communication*, 16, 3853–71.

Glatt, Z., & Banet-Weiser, S. (2021). Productive Ambivalence, Economies of Visibility and the Political Potential of Feminist YouTubers. In: Cunningham, S., & Craig, D. (Eds.), *Creator Culture: An Introduction to Global Social Media Entertainment*. New York: NYU Press.

Goffman, E. (1967). On Face-Work. In: Goffman, E., *Interaction Ritual: Essays on Face-to-Face Behaviour*. Toronto: Random House, pp. 5–46.

Goldberg, G. (2017). Through the Looking Glass: The Queer Narcissism of Selfies. Social Media + *Society*, 3(1). https://doi.org/10.1177/2056305117698494.

Goode, E., & Ben-Yehuda, N. (1994). Moral Panics: Culture, Politics, and Social Construction. *Annual Review of Sociology*, 20(1), 149–71. https://doi.org/10.1146/annurev.so.20.080194.001053.

Goodrow, C. (2021). On YouTube's Recommendation System. *blog.youtube*. https://blog.youtube/inside-youtube/on-youtubes-recommendation-system/.

Google. (2023). About Google. https://about.google/.

Gori, R. (2005). Eros. In: Mijolla, A., et al. (Eds.), *International Dictionary of Psychoanalysis*. New York: Macmillan, pp. 511–3.

Goriunova, O. (2019). The Digital Subject: People as Data as Persons. *Theory, Culture & Society*, 36(6), 125–45. https://doi.org/10.1177/0263276419840409.

Granovetter, M.S. (1973). The Strength of Weak Ties. *The American Journal of Sociology*, 78(6), 1360–80. https://doi.org/10.1086/225469.

Graves, R. (2011 [1960]). *The Greek Myths: The Complete and Definitive Edition*. London and New York: Penguin.

Green, A. (1999). *The Work of the Negative*. London: Free Association.

Green, A. (2000). *The Chains of Eros: The Sexual in Psychoanalysis*. London: Karnac.

Green, A. (2002a). *Time in Psychoanalysis: Some Contradictory Aspects*. London and New York: Free Association Books.

Green, A. (2002b). A Dual Conception of Narcissism: Positive and Negative Organizations. *The Psychoanalytic Quarterly*, 71(4), 631–49. https://doi.org/10.1002/j.2167-4086.2002.tb00020.x.

Green, A. (2005). *Play and Reflection in Donald Winnicott's Writings*, London: Karnac.

Green, V. (2003), Introduction: Emotional Development—Biological and Clinical Approaches—Towards an Integration. In: Green, V. (Ed.), *Emotional Development in*

Psychoanalysis, Attachment Theory and Neuroscience – Creating Connections. London: Routledge, pp. 1–19.

Greenfield, A. (2017). *Radical Technologies: The Design of Everyday Life*. London: Verso.

Halavais, A. (2017). *Search Engine Society*. Cambridge, UK: Polity Press.

Hall, S. (1980). Introduction to Media Studies at the Centre. In: Hall, S., Dobson, D., Lowe, A., and Willis, P. (Eds.), *Culture, Media, Language*. New York and London: Routledge.

Han, B-C. (2018). *The Expulsion of the Other: Society, Perception and Communication Today*. Cambridge, UK: Polity Press.

Harik, G., & Shazeer, N. (2003). United States Patent: Method and Apparatus for Characterizing Documents Based on Clusters of Related Words. https://patentimages.storage.googleapis.com/d8/b6/7e/db11e851e53284/US7383258.pdf.

Hayat, M. (2005). Obsessional Neurosis. In: Mijolla et al. (Eds.), *International Dictionary of Psychoanalysis*. London: Macmillan, pp. 1179–80.

Hayles, N.K. (1999). *How We Became Posthuman: Virtual Bodies in Cybernetics, Literature, and Informatics*. Chicago: University of Chicago Press.

He, X., Pan, J., Jin, O., Xu, T., Liu, B., Xu, T., Shi, Y., Atallah, A., Herbrich, R., Bowers, S., & Candela, J. (2014). Practical Lessons from Predicting Clicks on Ads at Facebook. *Proceedings of the ACM SIGKDD International Conference on Knowledge Discovery and Data Mining*, pp. 1–9. https://doi.org/10.1145/2648584.2648589.

Healey, K., & Potter, R. (2018). Coding the Privileged Self: Facebook and the Ethics of Psychoanalysis "Outside the Clinic" *Television & New Media*, 19(7), 660–76. https://doi.org/10.1177/1527476417745152.

Hendrickse, J., Arpan, L.M., Clayton, R.B., & Ridgway, J.L. (2017). Instagram and College Women's Body Image: Investigating the Roles of Appearance-Related Comparisons and Intrasexual Competition. *Computers in Human Behavior*, 74, 92–100. https://doi.org/10.1016/j.chb.2017.04.027.

Hepp, A. (2013). The Communicative Figurations of Mediatized Worlds: Mediatization Research in Times of the 'Mediation of Everything'. *European Journal of Communication*, 28(6), 615–29. https://doi.org/10.1177/0267323113501148.

Hepp, A., & Couldry, N. (2017). *The Mediated Construction of Reality*. Cambridge, UK: Polity Press.

Hogan, B. (2013). Pseudonyms and the Rise of the Real-Name Web. In: Hartley, J., Burgess, J., & Bruns, A. (Eds.), *A Companion to New Media Dynamics*. Chichester, Blackwell.

Honneth, A., & Whitebook, J. (2016). Omnipotence or Fusion? A Conversation between Axel Honneth and Joel Whitebook. *Constellations (Oxford, England)*, 23(2), 170–9. https://doi.org/10.1111/1467-8675.12232.

Hosseinmardi, H., Ghasemian, A., Clauset, A., Mobius, M., Rothschild, D.M., & Watts, D.J. (2021). Examining the Consumption of Radical Content on YouTube. *Proceedings of the National Academy of Sciences – PNAS*, 118(32), 1. https://doi.org/10.1073/pnas.2101967118.

Hu, Z. (2023), Forming the Spectacle of the Body – Analysis of the User-Platform Relationship through Body Performance Videos on TikTok; Master's Thesis. https://www.duo.uio.no/handle/10852/104537.

Jameson, F. (1990). Cognitive Mapping. In: Nelson, C., & Grossberg, L. (Eds.), *Marxism and the Interpretation of Culture*. Urbana: University of Illinois Press, pp. 347–60.

Jameson, F. (1991) *Postmodernism or, the Cultural Logic of Late Capitalism*. London: Verso.

Jardine, B., Romaniuk, J., Dawes, J.G., & Beal, V. (2016). Retaining the Primetime Television Audience. *European Journal of Marketing*, 50(7–8), 1290–307. https://doi.org/10.1108/EJM-03-2015-0137.

Jarvey, N. (2016). How Instagram's Filters Got Their Names. *The Hollywood Reporter*. https://www.hollywoodreporter.com/news/general-news/instagram-filters-history-names-explained-910720/.

Javornik, A., Marder, B., Barhorst, J., McLean, G., Rogers, Y., Marshall, P., & Warlop, L. (2021). 'What Lies behind the Filter?' Uncovering the Motivations for using Augmented Reality (AR) Face Filters on Social Media and Their Effect on Well-Being. *Computers in Human Behavior*, 128, 107126. https://doi.org/10.1016/j.chb.2021.107126.

Jeammet, P. (2005). Anorexia Nervosa. In: de Mijolla, A. (Ed.), *International Dictionary of Psychoanalysis, Vol. 1. A–F*. Detroit, MI: Macmillan Reference USA, pp. 91–2.

Jefferson, T. (2008). What is 'The Psychosocial'? A Response to Frosh and Baraitser. *Psychoanalysis, Culture & Society*, 13, 366–73.

Jenkins, H. (2006). *Convergence Culture: Where Old and New Media Collide*. New York: New York University Press.

Jiang, L., Miao, Y., Yang, Y., Lan, Z., & Hauptmann, A. (2014). Viral Video Style. *Proceedings of International Conference on Multimedia Retrieval*, pp. 193–200. https://doi.org/10.1145/2578726.2578754.

Johanssen, J. (2019), *Psychoanalysis and Digital Culture: Audiences, Social Media, and Big Data*. London: Routledge.

Johanssen, J. (2021). *Fantasy, Online Misogyny and the Manosphere: Male Bodies of Dis/Inhibition*. London: Routledge.

Johanssen, J., & Krüger, S. (2022). *Media and Psychoanalysis – A Critical Introduction*. London: Karnac Books.

Johnen, M., Jungblut, M., & Ziegele, M. (2018). The Digital Outcry: What Incites Participation Behavior in an Online Firestorm? *New Media & Society*, 20(9), 3140–60. https://doi.org/10.1177/1461444817741883.

Johnson, B. (2003). Psychological Addiction, Physical Addiction, Addictive Character and Addictive Personality Disorder: A Nosology of Addictive Disorders. *Canadian Journal of Psychoanalysis*, 11, 135–160.

Johnson, S. (1994). *Character Styles*. New York & London: Norton.

Steiner, J. (1997). Introduction. In: Segal, H., *Psychoanalysis, Literature and War*, 1–13. London: Routledge.

Jones, E. (1953). *The Life and Work of Sigmund Freud*. New York: Basic Books.

Jones, J. (2010). *Entertaining Politics: Satiric Television and Political Engagement*. Lanham, MD: Rowman & Littlefield.

Jones, M. L. (2016). *Ctrl + Z: The Right to Be Forgotten*. New York: NYU Press.

Kahr, B. (2013). Television as Rorschach: The Unconscious Use of the Cathode Nipple. In: Bainbridge, C., Ward I., & Yates, C. (Eds.), *Television and Psychoanalysis – Psychocultural Perspectives*. London and New York: Routledge, pp. 31–46.

Kaiser, J., & Rauchfleisch, A. (2019). The Implications of Venturing Down the Rabbit Hole. *Internet Policy Review*, 8(2). https://policyreview.info/articles/news/implications-venturing-down-rabbit-hole/1406.

Kennedy, M. (2020). 'If the Rise of the TikTok Dance and e-Girl Aesthetic Has Taught Us Anything, It's That Teenage Girls Rule the Internet Right Now': TikTok Celebrity, Girls and the Coronavirus Crisis. *European Journal of Cultural Studies*, 23(6), 1069–76. https://doi.org/10.1177/1367549420945341.

Kelly, R. (2009). Twitter Study Reveals Interesting Results About Usage – 40% Is Pointless Babble. *Pear Analytics Blog*, 12 August. https://pearanalytics.com/twitter-study-reveals-interesting-results-40-percent-pointless-babble/.

Kernberg, O. (2004 [1975]). *Borderline Conditions and Pathological Narcissism*. Lanham, MD: Rowman and Littlefield.

Kernberg, O. (1991). Aggression and Love in the Relationship of the Couple. *Journal of the American Psychoanalytic Association*, 39(1), 45–70. https://doi.org/10.1177/000306519103900103.

Khantzian, E. (1999). *Treating Addiction as a Human Process*. Lanham, MD: Jason Aronson.

Khantzian, E. (2003). Understanding Addictive Vulnerability: An Evolving Psychodynamic Perspective. *Neuro-Psychoanalysis*, 5(1), 5–56.

King, V., Gerisch, B., & Rosa, H. (Eds.) (2019), *Lost in Perfection: Impacts of Optimisation on Culture and Psyche*. London: Routledge.

Kircher, M.M. (2023). "X" Marks the Spot. *The New York Times*. https://www.nytimes.com/2023/07/28/style/x-marks-the-spot.html.

Kirkpatrick, D. (2010) *The Facebook Effect: The Inside Story of the Company That Is Connecting the World*. New York: Simon & Schuster.

Kirn, W. (2009). Life, Liberty and the Pursuit of Aptitude. *The New York Times*. https://www.nytimes.com/2009/07/05/magazine/05fob-wwln-t.html.

Klein, N. (1999). *No Logo: Taking Aim at the Brand Bullies*. London: Picador.

Kober, H. (2014). Emotion Regulation in Substance Use Disorders. In: Gross, J.J. (Ed.), *Handbook of Emotion Regulation*. New York: The Guilford Press, pp. 428–46.

Kohut, H. (1971). *The Analysis of the Self*. Chicago, IL: University of Chicago Press.

Kohut, H. (2014 [1977]). *The Restoration of the Self*. Chicago, IL: University of Chicago Press.

König, H-D. (2008). *George W. Bush und der fanatische Krieg gegen den Terrorismus. Eine psychoanalytische Studie zum Autoritarismus in Amerika*. Gießen: psychosozial.

Koren, Y., Bell, R., & Volinsky, C. (2009). Matrix Factorization Techniques for Recommender Systems. *Computer (Long Beach, Calif.)*, 42(8), 30–7. https://doi.org/10.1109/MC.2009.263.

Kornbluh, A. (2019). *The Order of Forms: Realism, Formalism, and Social Space*. Chicago, IL: Chicago University Press.

Kramer, A.D.I., Guillory, J.E., & Hancock, J.T. (2014). Experimental Evidence of Massive-Scale Emotional Contagion through Social Networks. *Proceedings of the National Academy of Sciences – PNAS*, 111(24), 8788–90. https://doi.org/10.1073/pnas.1320040111.

Kris, E. (1936). Psychology of Caricature. *International Journal of Psycho-Analysis*, 17, 285–303.

Kris, E. (1938). Ego Development and the Comic. *International Journal of Psychoanalysis*, 19, 77–90.

Kris, E. (1941). The "Danger" of Propaganda. *American Imago*, 2(1), 3–42. http://www.jstor.org/stable/26300880.

Kris, E. (1952). *Psychoanalytic Explorations in Art*. New York: International Universities Press.

Kris, E., & Gombrich, E.H. (1938). The Principles of Caricature. *British Journal of Medical Psychology*, 17, 319–42.

Kris, E., & Kurz, O. (1979 [1934]). *Legend, Myth and Magic in the Image of the Artist*. New Haven, CT: Yale University Press.

Kristeva, J. (2014). Reliance, or Maternal Eroticism. *Journal of the American Psychoanalytic Association*, 62(1), 69–85. https://doi.org/10.1177/0003065114522129.

Krüger, S. (2011). *Das Unbehagen in der Karikatur – Kunst, Propaganda und Persuasive Kommunikation im Theoriewerk Ernst Kris'*. München: Fink.

Krüger, S. (2012). Fresh Brains: Jacques Lacan's Critique of Ernst Kris's Psychoanalytic Method in the Context of Kris's Theoretical Writings. *American Imago*, 69(4), 507–42. http://www.jstor.org/stable/26305035.

Krüger, S. (2020). Anal Sexuality and Male Subcultures Online: The Politics of Self-Deprecation in the Deep Vernacular Web. *Psychoanalysis, Culture & Society*, 26(1), 244–58. https://doi.org/10.1057/s41282-020-00207-z.

Krüger, S. (2021). Beschmutzungen – Anale Sexualität und Anti-Soziale Netzwerke. *texte – psychoanalyse. ästhetik. kulturkritik*, 4(21), 62–90.

Krüger, S., & Johanssen, J. (2014). Alienation and Digital Labour—A Depth-Hermeneutic Inquiry into Online Commodification and the Unconscious. *TripleC*, 12(2), 632–47. https://doi.org/10.31269/triplec.v12i2.548.

Krüger, S., & Ni Bhroin, N. (2020). Your Health is Our Wealth: Self-tracking health insurance deals, privacy and the erosion of solidarity. In: *The European Way of Digital: How to Make Tech Work for Open Societies in Europe*. https://counterpoint.uk.com/the-european-way-of-digital/

Krüger, S., & Spilde, A. (2020). Judging Books by Their Covers – Tinder Interface, Usage and Sociocultural Implications. *Information, Communication & Society*, 23(10), 1395–410, https://doi.org/10.1080/1369118X.2019.1572771.

Krzych, S. (2021). *Beyond Bias: Conservative Media, Documentary Form, and the Politics of Hysteria*. Oxford: Oxford University Press.

Kühn, T. (2019). Leadership in a Digitally Transforming Social World Based on Fromm's Humanistic Approach. In: Funk, R., & Kühn T. (Eds.), *Fromm Forum 23*. Tübingen: Selbstverlag.

Kulwin, N. (2018). An Apology for the Internet – From the Architects Who Built It. *Intelligencer*. https://nymag.com/intelligencer/2018/04/an-apology-for-the-internet-from-the-people-who-built-it.html.

Lacan, J. (1997). The Ethics of Psychoanalysis. In: *The Seminar of Jacques Lacan, book VII*. New York: Norton.

Lacan, J. (1999 [1972–1973). On Feminine Sexuality, the Limits of Love and Knowledge. In: *The Seminar of Jacques Lacan, book XX*. New York: Norton.

Lacan, J. (2006 [1949]). The Mirror Stage as formative of the I Function. In: *Ecrits – The First Complete Edition in English*. Fink, B. (Trans.) New York & London: Norton, pp. 75–82.

Laplanche, J. (1999). *Essays on Otherness*. London: Routledge.

Laplanche, J., & Pontalis, J-B. (1988 [1973]) *The Language of Psychoanalysis*. London: Routledge.

Laporte, D. (2000 [1978]). *History of Shit*. Cambridge, MA: MIT Press.

Lasch, C. (1991 [1979]). *The Culture of Narcissism: American Life in an Age of Diminishing Expectations*. New York: WW Norton & Co.

Latour, B., Jensen, P., Venturini, T., Grauwin, S., Boullier, D. (2012), 'The Whole Is Always Smaller Than Its Parts' – A Digital Test of Gabriel Tardes' Monads. *The British Journal of Sociology*, 63(4), 590–615. https://doi.org/10.1111/j.1468-4446.2012.01428.x.

Layton, L. (2014). Grandiosity, Neoliberalism, and Neoconservatism. *Psychoanalytic Inquiry*, 34(5), 463–74. https://doi.org/10.1080/07351690.2013.846030.

Leader, D. (2008). *The New Black: Mourning, Melancholia, and Depression*. Minneapolis, MN: Graywolf Press.

Leader, D. (2013). *Strictly Bipolar*. London and New York: Penguin.

Leader, D. (2016). *Hands: What We Do With Them and Why*. Penguin Press.

Lear, J. (1996). The Introduction of Eros: Reflections on the Work of Hans Loewald. *Journal of the American Psychoanalytic Association*, 44(3), 673–98.

Leaver, T., Highfield, T., & Abidin, C. (2020). *Instagram: Visual Social Media Cultures*. Cambridge, UK: Polity Press.

Ledwich, M., Zaitsev, A., & Laukemper, A. (2022). Radical Bubbles on YouTube? Revisiting Algorithmic Extremism with Personalised Recommendations. *First Monday*, 27(12), 1. https://doi.org/10.5210/fm.v27i12.12552.

Lee, M., & Lee, H.-H. (2021). Social Media Photo Activity, Internalization, Appearance Comparison, and Body Satisfaction: The Moderating Role of Photo-Editing Behavior. *Computers in Human Behavior*, 114, 106579. https://doi.org/10.1016/j.chb.2020.106579.

Levy, S. (2011). *In the Plex: How Google Thinks, Works, and Shapes Our Lives*. New York: Simon & Schuster.

Levy, S. (2020). *Facebook: The Inside Story*. New York: Blue Rider Press.

Lewis, P. (2018). 'Fiction Is Outperforming Reality': How YouTube's Algorithm Distorts Truth. *The Guardian*. https://www.theguardian.com/technology/2018/feb/02/how-youtubes-algorithm-distorts-truth.

Lewis, P., & McCormic, E. (2018). How an ex-YouTube Insider Investigated Its Secret Algorithm. *The Guardian*. https://www.theguardian.com/technology/2018/feb/02/youtube-algorithm-election-clinton-trump-guillaume-chaslot.

Lewis, J., & West, A. (2009). 'Friending': London-Based Undergraduates' Experience of Facebook. *New Media and Society*, 11(7), 1209–29. https://doi.org/10.1177/1461444809342058.

Lindgren, L. (2021) *Ekko: et essay om algoritmer og begjær*. Oslo: Gyldendal.

Lingiardi, V., Carone, N., Semeraro, G., Musto, C., D'Amico, M., & Brena, S. (2020). Mapping Twitter Hate Speech Towards Social and Sexual Minorities: A Lexicon-Based Approach to Semantic Content Analysis. *Behaviour & Information Technology*, 39(7), 711–21. https://doi.org/10.1080/0144929X.2019.1607903.

Loewald, H. (1951) Ego and Reality. In: *Papers on Psychoanalysis*. New Haven, CT: Yale University Press, pp. 3–20.

Loewald, H. (1988). *Sublimation: Inquiries Into Theoretical Psychoanalysis*. New Haven: Yale University Press.

Lonergan, A.R., Bussey, K., Mond, J., Brown, O., Griffiths, S., Murray, S.B., & Mitchison, D. (2019). Me, My Selfie, and I: The Relationship between Editing and Posting Selfies and Body Dissatisfaction in Men and Women. *Body Image*, 28, 39–43. https://doi.org/10.1016/j.bodyim.2018.12.001.

Lowe-Calverley, E., & Grieve, R. (2018). Self-ie Love: Predictors of Image Editing Intentions on Facebook. *Telematics and Informatics*, 35(1), 186–94. https://doi.org/10.1016/j.tele.2017.10.011.

Lorenzer, A. (1978). Antagonistische Interaktionsformen beim "Double Blind". In: Lorenzer, A., *Sprachspiel und Interaktionsformen*. Frankfurt: Suhrkamp, pp. 58–74.

Lorenzer, A. (2022 [1986]). In-Depth Hermeneutical Cultural Analysis. In: Rothe, K., Krüger, S. & Rosengart, D. (Eds.), *Cultural Analysis Now! – Alfred Lorenzer and the In-Depth Hermeneutics of Culture and Society*, New York: Unconscious in Translation, pp. 21–122.

Losse, K. (2012). *The Boy Kings: A Journey into the Heart of the Social Network*. New York: Simon & Schuster.

Losse, K. (2013a). The Unbearable Whiteness of Breaking Things. *Medium*. https://medium.com/@katelosse/the-unbearable-whiteness-of-breaking-things-521cb394fda2.

Losse, K. (2013b). Feminism's Tipping Point: Who Wins from Leaning In? *Dissent Magazine*. https://www.dissentmagazine.org/online_articles/feminisms-tipping-point-who-wins-from-leaning-in/.

Löchel, E. (1996). "Jenseits des Lustprinzips": Lesen und Wiederlesen. *Psyche*, 50(8), 681–714.

Lüders, M., & Sundet, V.S. (2022). Conceptualizing the Experiential Affordances of Watching Online TV. *Television & New Media*, 23(4), 335–51. https://doi.org/10.1177/15274764211010943.

Lupton, D. (2020), *Data Selves: More-than-Human perspectives*. Cambridge, UK: Polity Press.

Ma, J., Zhao, Z., Yi, X., Yang, J., Chen, M., Tang, J., Hong, L., & Chi, E.H. (2020). Off-Policy Learning in Two-Stage Recommender Systems. *The Web Conference 2020 – Proceedings of the World Wide Web Conference, WWW 2020*, pp. 463–73. https://doi.org/10.1145/3366423.3380130.

MacMillan, A. (2017). Why Instagram Is the Worst Social Media for Mental Health. *Time*. https://time.com/4793331/instagram-social-media-mental-health/.

Macpherson, C.B. (2011 [1962]). *The Political Theory of Possessive Individualism: Hobbes to Locke*. Oxford: Oxford University Press.

MacRury, I., & Yates, C. (2016). Framing the Mobile Phone: The Psychopathologies of an Everyday Object. *CM: Communication and Media*, 38(11), 69.

Maes, C., & de Lenne, O. (2022). Filters and Fillers: Belgian Adolescents' Filter Use on Social Media and the Acceptance of Cosmetic Surgery. *Journal of Children and Media*, 16(4), 587–605. https://doi.org/10.1080/17482798.2022.2079696.

Malseed, M. (2007). The Story of Sergey Brin. *Moment Magazine*. https://momentmag.com/the-story-of-sergey-brin/.

Marcuse, H. (1986 [1964]). *One-Dimensional Man: Studies in the Ideology of Advanced Industrial Society*. London: Routledge.

Marcuse, H. (1987 [1956]). *Eros and Civilisation: A Philosophical Inquiry into Freud*. London: Routledge.

Marikar, S. (2019). You Won't Find Your Self-Worth on Instagram. *The New York Times*. https://www.nytimes.com/2019/11/02/opinion/sunday/instagram-social-media.html.

Marks, L. (2000). *The Skin of the Film: Intercultural Cinema, Embodiment, and the Senses*. Durham, NC: Duke University Press.

Marquard, O. (1982). *Krise der Erwartung – Stunde der Erfahrung: Zur ästhetischen Kompensation des modernen Erfahrungsverlustes*. Konstanzer Universitätsreden.

Marwick, A.E. (2015). Instafame: Luxury Selfies in the Attention Economy. *Public Culture*, 27(1), 137–60. https://doi.org/10.1215/08992363-2798379.

Marwick, A.E., & boyd, d. (2011). I Tweet Honestly, I Tweet Passionately: Twitter Users, Context Collapse, and the Imagined Audience. *New Media & Society*, 13(1), 114–33. https://doi.org/10.1177/1461444810365313.

Massumi, B. (2013). Envisioning the Virtual. In: Grimshaw-Aagaard, M. (Ed.), *Oxford Handbook of Virtuality*. Oxford: Oxford University Press.

Matamoros-Fernández, A., & Farkas, J. (2021a). Racism, Hate Speech, and Social Media: A Systematic Review and Critique. *Television & New Media*, 22(2), 205–24. https://doi.org/10.1177/1527476420982230.

Matamoros-Fernández, A., Gray, J.E., Bartolo, L., Burgess, J., & Suzor, N. (2021b). What's "Up Next"? Investigating Algorithmic Recommendations on YouTube Across Issues and Over Time. *Media and Communication (Lisboa)*, 9(4), 234–49. https://doi.org/10.17645/mac.v9i4.4184.

McDougall, W. (1926). *An Outline of Abnormal Psychology*. New York: Scribners.

McCarthy, M., & Calore, M. (2008). SXSW: Zuckerberg Keynote Descends into Chaos as Audience Takes Over. *Wired*. http://www.wired.com/underwire/2008/03/sxsw-mark-zucke/.

McGowan, T. (2015). *Psychoanalytic Film Theory and the Rules of the Game*. London: Bloomsbury.

McGowan, T. (2017). *Only a Joke Can Save Us: A Theory of Comedy*. Evanston: Northwestern University Press.

McIlwraith, R., Jacobvitz, R.S., Kubey, R., & Alexander, A. (1991). Television Addiction. *The American Behavioral Scientist (Beverly Hills)*, 35(2), 104–21. https://doi.org/10.1177/0002764291035002003.

McRobbie A., & Garber J. (2006 [1975]). Girls and subcultures. In: Hall S., & Jefferson T. (Eds.), *Resistance through Rituals: Youth Subcultures in Post-War Britain* (2nd edn). London: Routledge, pp. 177–88.

Meltzer, D., & Williams, M.A. (1988). The Lobby of Dreams. In: Meltzer, D., & Gosso, S. (Eds.), *Psychoanalysis and Art: Kleinian Perspectives*. London: Routledge.

Mejias, A. (2012). Liberation Technology and the Arab Spring: From Utopia to Atopia and Beyond. *Fibreculture Journal*, 20, 204–17. http://twenty.fibreculturejournal.org/2012/06/20/fcj-147-liberation-technology-and-the-arab-spring-from-utopia-to-atopia-and-beyond/.

Mejias, U. (2013). *Off the Network: Disrupting the Digital World*. Minneapolis, MN: University of Minnesota Press.

Metz, C. (1977). *The Imaginary Signifier: Psychoanalysis and the Cinema*. Bloomington, In: Indiana University Press.

Mezrich, B. (2009). *The Accidental Billionaires: The Founding of Facebook, a Tale of Sex, Money, Genius, and Betrayal*. New York: Doubleday.

Miller, J-A. (1988), Extimité. (Doisneu, E., Trans). *Prose Studies*, 11(3), 121–31.

Miller, L.A., & McIntyre, J. (2022). From Surgery to Cyborgs: A Thematic Analysis of Popular Media Commentary on Instagram Filters. *Feminist Media Studies* (ahead-of-print), 23(7), 3615–31. https://doi.org/10.1080/14680777.2022.2129414.

Miller, V. (2008). New Media, Networking and Phatic Culture. *Convergence*, 14(4), 387–400. https://doi.org/10.1177/1354856508094659.

Milmo, D. (2021a). Facebook Revelations: What Is in Cache of Internal Documents? *The Guardian* https://www.theguardian.com/technology/2021/oct/25/facebook-revelations-from-misinformation-to-mental-health.

Milmo, D. (2021b). Twitter Admits Bias in Algorithm for Rightwing Politicians and News Outlets. *The Guardian*. https://www.theguardian.com/technology/2021/oct/22/twitter-admits-bias-in-algorithm-for-rightwing-politicians-and-news-outlets.

Mitchell, J. (1974). *Psychoanalysis and Feminism: A Radical Reassessment of Freudian Psychoanalysis*. New York: Pantheon.

Möller, J., Trilling, D., Helberger, N., & van Es, B. (2018). Do Not Blame It on the Algorithm: An Empirical Assessment of Multiple Recommender Systems and Their Impact on Content Diversity. *Information, Communication & Society*, 21(7), 959–77. https://doi.org/10.1080/1369118X.2018.1444076.

Moi, T. (2017). *Revolution of the Ordinary: Literary Studies after Wittgenstein, Austin, and Cavell*. Chicago, IL: University of Chicago Press.

Morozov, E. (2013). *To Save Everything Click Here: The Folly of Technological Solutionism*. New York: Public Affairs.

Morreall, John (2020). Philosophy of Humor. In: Zalta E.N., & Nodelman, U. (Eds.), *The Stanford Encyclopedia of Philosophy* (Summer 2023 Edition). https://plato.stanford.edu/archives/sum2023/entries/humor/.

Mowlabocus, S. (2020). 'Let's Get This Thing Open': The Pleasures of Unboxing Videos. *European Journal of Cultural Studies*, 23(4), 564–79. https://doi.org/10.1177/1367549418810098.

Mozilla. (2021). YouTube Regrets: A Crowdsourced Investigation into YouTube's Recommendation Algorithm. https://foundation.mozilla.org/en/youtube/findings/.

Mulvey, L. (2003[1975]). Visual Pleasure and Hollywood Cinema. In: Brooker, W., & Jermyn, D. (Eds.), *The Audience Studies Reader*. London: Routledge.

Munn, L. (2020). Angry by Design: Toxic Communication and Technical Architectures. *Humanities & Social Sciences Communications*, 7(1), 1–11. https://doi.org/10.1057/s41599-020-00550-7.

Murthy, D. (2013). *Twitter: Social Communication in the Twitter Age*. Cambridge, UK: Polity Press.

Newirth, J. (2006). Jokes and Their Relation to the Unconscious: Humor as a Fundamental Emotional Experience. *Psychoanalytic Dialogues*, 16(5), 557–71. https://doi.org/10.2513/s10481885pd1605_6.

Newton, C. (2017). Facebook Just Changed Its Mission, Because the Old One Was Broken. *The Verge*. https://www.theverge.com/2017/2/16/14642164/facebook-mark-zuckerberg-letter-mission-statement.

Newton, C. (2023). Twitter becomes X. *Platformer*. https://www.platformer.news/p/twitter-becomes-x

Ngai, S. (2010). Our Aesthetic Categories. *PMLA, 125*(4), 948–58. https://doi.org/10.1632/pmla.2010.125.4.948.

Nicas, J. (2018). How YouTube Drives People to the Internet's Darkest Corners. *The Wall Street Journal*. https://www.wsj.com/articles/how-youtube-drives-viewers-to-the-internets-darkest-corners-1518020478.

Nieva, R. (2017). Facebook Wants to Save the World. You've Got Work to Do. *Cnet*. https://www.cnet.com/culture/facebook-community-summit-chris-cox-groups-mark-zuckerberg/.

Nitsun, M. (1996). *The Anti-Group: Destructive Forces in the Group and their Creative Potential*. London: Routledge.

Noerr, G.S. (2006). Das Medium spielt sich als Retter auf. In: Prokop, U., & Jansen, M. (Eds.) (2006). *Doku-Soap, Reality-TV, Affekt-Talkshow Fantasy-Rollenspiele – Neue Sozialisationsagenturen im Jugendalter*. Marburg: Tektum, pp. 27–66.

Ohlheiser, A.W. (2021, October 20). TikTok Changed the Shape of Some People's Faces without Asking. *MIT Technology Review*. https://www.technologyreview.com/2021/06/10/1026074/tiktok-mandatory-beauty-filter-bug/.

O'Meara, V. (2019). Weapons of the Chic: Instagram Influencer Engagement Pods as Practices of Resistance to Instagram Platform Labor. *Social Media + Society*, 5(4), https://doi.org/10.1177/2056305119879671.

Orben, A., Przybylski, A.K., Blakemore, S-J., & Kievit, R. (2022). Windows of Developmental Sensitivity to Social Media. *Nature Communications*, 13(1), 1649–49. https://doi.org/10.1038/s41467-022-29296-3.

O'Reilly, T. (2007). What Is Web 2.0: Design Patterns and Business Models for the Next Generation of Software. *Communication Strategies*, 65(1), 17–37.

Osnos, E. (2018, September 10). Can Mark Zuckerberg fix Facebook before it breaks democracy? *The New Yorker*. https://www.newyorker.com/magazine/2018/09/17/can-mark-zuckerberg-fix-facebook-before-it-breaks-democracy.

Ouellette, L., & Hay, J. (2008). *Better Living through Reality TV: Television and Post-Welfare Citizenship*. Oxford: Blackwell.

Özdoyran, G. (2019). The Psycho-Political Economy of New Media: Psychoanalysis and Social Media. In: Doğan, E., & Öze, N. (Eds.), *Debates on Media & Communication Studies*. London and Instanbul: IJOPEC Publication.

Paasonen, S., Attwood, F., McKee, A., Mercer, J., & Smith, C. (2021). *Objectification: On the Difference between Sex and Sexism*. London: Routledge.

Page, L. (2004). United States Patent: Method for Scoring Documents in a Large Database. https://patentimages.storage.googleapis.com/0b/79/8f/5eaeb4a47a50c3/US6799176.pdf.

Page, L., & Brin, S. (2012 [1998]). Reprint of: The Anatomy of a Large-Scale Hypertextual Web Search Engine. *Computer Networks (Amsterdam, Netherlands: 1999)*, 56(18), 3825–33. https://doi.org/10.1016/j.comnet.2012.10.007.

Papacharissi, Z. (2012). Without You, I'm Nothing: Performances of the Self on Twitter. *International Journal of Communication [Online]*, 1989+. https://link-gale-com.ezproxy.uio.no/apps/doc/A298057184/AONE?u=oslo&sid=bookmark-AONE&xid=c56503d4.b

Panetta, G., & Lahut, J. (2022). Trump Told Barr the Recipe for "a Really Good Tweet" is "Just the Right Amount of Crazy". *Business Insider*. https://www.businessinsider.com/barr-book-trump-good-tweet-just-the-right-amount-crazy-2022-3?r=US&IR=T.

Pariser, E. (2014). *The Filter Bubble: What the Internet is Hiding from You*. New York: Penguin.

Pasquinelli, M. (2015). *Alleys of your mind: Augmented Intelligence and its Traumas*. Lüneburg: Meson press.

Pastore, F., 2019. *Not So Global, Not So Compact. Reflections on the Shitstorm Surrounding the Global Compact for Migration*. Italy: Istituto Affari Internazionali. https://www.fieri.it/wp-content/uploads/2019/01/f.pastore-jan2019-iaicom1902.pdf

Patel, D., & Ahmad, A. (2023). The Inference Cost of Search Disruption – Large Language Model Cost Analysis. *SemiAnalysis*. https://www.semianalysis.com/p/the-inference-cost-of-search-disruption.

Peters, J. (2015). *The Marvelous Clouds: Toward a Philosophy of Elemental Media*. Chicago, IL: University of Chicago Press.

Pfeffer, J., Zorbach, T., & Carley, K.M. (2014). Understanding Online Firestorms: Negative Word-of-Mouth Dynamics in Social Media Networks. *Journal of Marketing Communications*, 20(1–2), 117–28. https://doi.org/10.1080/13527266.2013.797778.

Phillips, A. (1994). *On Flirtation*. Cambridge, MA: Harvard University Press.

Pilipets, E. (2019). From Netflix Streaming to Netflix and Chill: The (Dis)Connected Body of Serial Binge-Viewer. *Social Media + Society*, 5(4), 2056305119883426. https://doi.org/10.1177/2056305119883426.

Pine, F. (1994) The Era of Separation-Individuation. *Psychoanalytic Inquiry*, 14(1), 4–24, https://doi.org/10.1080/07351699409533967/.

Pink [@Pink]. (2009, April 3). "I Have Officially Entered the 20th Century. I Mean the 21st". *Twitter*. https://twitter.com/Pink/status/1449214774.

Pinski, G., & Narin, F. (1976). Citation Influence for Journal Aggregates of Scientific Publications: Theory, with Application to the Literature of Physics. *Information Processing & Management*, 12(5), 297–312. https://doi.org/10.1016/0306-4573(76)90048-0.

Playboy. (2004). Google Guys. https://kottke.org/plus/misc/google-playboy.html.

Plessner, H. (1982). *Mit anderen Augen – Aspekte einer philosophischen Anthropologie*. Stuttgart: Reclam.

Pogue, J. (2022). Selling the Metaverse. *The American Conservative*. https://www.theamericanconservative.com/selling-the-metaverse/.

Porter, E. (2018). Facebook Is Creepy. And Valuable. *The New York Times*. https://www. nytimes.com/2018/04/17/business/economy/facebook-regulation-privacy.html.

Prokop, U. (1976), *Weiblicher Lebenszusammenhang – Von der Beschränktheit der Strategien und der Unangemessenheit der Wünsche*. Frankfurt: Suhrkamp.

Prokop, U., Friese, N. and Stach, A. (2009) *Geiles Leben, Falscher Glamour – Beschreibungen, Analysen, Kritiken zu 'Germany's Next Topmodel'*. Marburg: Tectum.

Prokop, U., & Jansen, M. (Eds.) (2006). *Doku-Soap, Reality-TV, Affekt-Talkshow Fantasy-Rollenspiele – Neue Sozialisationsagenturen im Jugendalter*. Marburg: Tektum.

Qin, Z., Cheng, Y., Zhao, Z., Chen, Z., Metzler, D., & Qin, J. (2020). Multitask Mixture of Sequential Experts for User Activity Streams. *Proceedings of the ACM SIGKDD International Conference on Knowledge Discovery and Data Mining*, pp. 3083–91. https://doi. org/10.1145/3394486.3403359.

Radó, S. (1926). The Psychic Effects of Intoxicants: An Attempt to Evolve a Psycho-Analytical Theory of Morbid Cravings. *International Journal of Psychoanalysis*, 7, 396–413.

Rambatan, B., & Johanssen, J. (2021). *Event Horizon: Sexuality, Politics, Online Culture, and the Limits of Capitalism*. Winchester: Zero Books.

Rambukkana, N. (Ed.). (2015). *Hashtag Publics: The Power and Politics of Discursive Networks*. New York: Peter Lang.

Ravetto-Biagioli, K. (2019). *Digital Uncanny*. Oxford: Oxford University Press.

Raymond, C. (2021). *The Selfie, Temporality, and Contemporary Photography*. London: Routledge.

Rettberg, J. (2014). *Seeing Ourselves through Technology: How We Use Selfies, Blogs and Wearable Devices to See and Shape Ourselves*. London: Palgrave Macmillan.

Ribeiro, M., Calais, P., Santos, Y., Almeida, V., & Meira Jr, W. (2018). Characterizing and Detecting Hateful Users on Twitter. *Proceedings of the International AAAI Conference on Web and Social Media*, 12(1). https://doi.org/10.1609/icwsm.v12i1.15057.

Richards, B. (1996). *Disciplines of Delight: The Psychoanalysis of Popular Culture*. London: Free Association Books.

Rieder, B. (2017). Scrutinizing an Algorithmic Technique: The Bayes Classifier as Interested Reading of Reality. *Information, Communication & Society*, 20(1), 100–17. https://doi.or g/10.1080/1369118X.2016.1181195.

Rieder, B. (2020). *Engines of Order: A Mechanology of Algorithmic Techniques*. Amsterdam: Amsterdam University Press.

Rieder, B., Coromina, Ò., & Matamoros-Fernández, A. (2020). Mapping YouTube – A Quantitative Exploration of a Platformed Media System. *First Monday*, 25(8–3). http:// doi.org/10.5210/fm.v25i8.10667.

Rochet, J.C., & Tirole, J. (2003). Platform Competition in Two-Sided Markets. *Journal of the European Economic Association*, 1(4), 990–1029. https://doi.org/10.1162/ 154247603322493212.

Rogers, R. (2013). Debanalising Twitter: The Transformation of an Object of Study. In: K. Weller, A. Bruns, J. Burgess, M. Mahrt, & C. Puschmann (Eds.), *Twitter and Society*. New York: Peter Lang, pp. ix–xxvi.

Ronson, J. (2015). *So You've Been Publicly Shamed*. London: Picador.

Rost, K., Stahel, L., & Frey, B.S. (2016). Digital Social Norm Enforcement: Online Firestorms in Social Media. *PloS One*, 11(6), e0155923–e0155923. https://doi.org/10.1371/ journal.pone.0155923.

Rohr, E. (Ed.) (2014). *Inszenierungen des Unbewussten in der Moderne – Alfred Lorenzer Heute*. Marburg: Tektum.

Rosa, H. (2008). Schrankenloses Steigerungsspiel: Die strukturbildende Einheit hinter der Vielfalt der Kapitalismen. In: Jansen, S.A., Schröter, E., Stehr, N. (Eds.), *Mehrwertiger Kapitalismus*. VS Verlag für Sozialwissenschaften.

Rosenfeld, H. (1971). A Clinical Approach to Psychoanalytic Theory of Life and Death Instincts: An Investigation into the Aggressive Aspects of Narcissism. *International Journal of Psychoanalysis*, 52, 169–78.

Rothe, K., Krüger, S., & Rosengart, D. (Eds.) (2022). *Cultural Analysis Now! Alfred Lorenzer and the In-Depth Hermeneutics of Culture and Society*. New York: UIT Books.

Rouvroy, A. (Ed.) (2011). *Law, Human Agency and Autonomic Computing: The Philosophy of Law Meets the Philosophy of Technology*. London: Routledge.

Rouvroy, A., & Stiegler, B. (2016). The Digital Regime of Truth: from the Algorithmic Governmentality to a New Rule of Law. *La Deleuziana*, 3, 6–29.

Sabshin, E. (1995). Psychoanalytic Studies of Addictive Behavior: A Review. *The Psychology and Treatment of Addictive Behavior*, 79, 3–15.

Sampson, T. (2013). *Virality: Contagion Theory in the Age of Networks*. Minneapolis, MN: University of Minnesota Press.

Sandberg, S. (2013). *Lean In: Women, Work, and the Will to Lead*. New York: Knopf.

Sarno, D. (2009). Twitter Creator Jack Dorsey Illuminates the Site's Founding Document, Part I. *Los Angeles Times*. https://www.latimes.com/archives/blogs/technology-blog/story/2009-02-18/twitter-creator-jack-dorsey-illuminates-the-sites-founding-document-part-i.

Savitt, R. (1963). Psychoanalytic Studies on Addiction: Ego Structure in Narcotic Addiction. *The Psychoanalytic Quarterly*, 32(1), 43–57.

Sawyer, K. (2013). *Zig zag: The Surprising Path to Greater Creativity*. Jossey-Bass.

Schmitt, J.B., Rieger, D., Rutkowski, O., & Ernst, J. (2018). Counter-Messages as Prevention or Promotion of Extremism?! The Potential Role of YouTube: Recommendation Algorithms. *Journal of Communication*, 68(4), 780. https://doi.org/10.1093/joc/jqy029.

Schnabel, T., Bennett, P.N., Dumais, S.T., & Joachims, T. (2018). Short-Term Satisfaction and Long-Term Coverage: Understanding How Users Tolerate Algorithmic Exploration. *WSDM 2018 – Proceedings of the 11th ACM International Conference on Web Search and Data Mining*, 2018, 513–21. https://doi.org/10.1145/3159652.3159700.

Schüll, N.D. (2005). Digital Gambling: The Coincidence of Desire and Design. *The Annals of the American Academy of Political and Social Science*, 597(1), 65–81. https://doi.org/10.1177/0002716204270435.

Schüll, N.D. (2014). *Addiction by Design. Machine Gambling in Las Vegas*. Princeton and Oxford: Princeton University Press.

Seaver, N. (2019). Captivating Algorithms: Recommender Systems as Traps. *Journal of Material Culture*, 24(4), 421–36. https://doi.org/10.1177/1359183518820366.

Seaver, N. (2021). Care and Scale: Decorrelative Ethics in Algorithmic Recommendation. *Cultural Anthropology*, 36(3), 509–37. https://doi.org/10.14506/ca36.3.11.

Seymore, R. (2019). *The Twittering Machine: How Capitalism Stole Our Social Life*. London: Indigo Press.

Shaviro, S. (2014). *The Universe of Things: On Speculative Realism*. Minneapolis, MN: University of Minnesota Press.

Shields, R. (2003). *The Virtual*. London: Routledge.

Shore, A.N. (2003), "The Human Unconscious: The Development of the Right Brain and Its Role in Early Emotional Life". In: Green, V. (Ed.), *Emotional Development in*

Psychoanalysis, Attachment Theory and Neuroscience – Creating Connections. London: Routledge.

Simmel, E. (1929). Psychoanalytic Treatment in a Sanatorium. *International Journal of Psychoanalysis*, 10, 70–89.

Simmel, G. (1971 [1908]). Social Forms and Inner Needs. In: Levine, D. (Ed.), *Georg Simmel on Individuality and Social Forms*. Chicago: University of Chicago Press.

Simmel, G. (1984 [1909]). Flirtation. In: Oakes, G. (Ed.) *Georg Simmel: On Women, Sexuality, and Love*. New Haven: Yale University Press: 1984, pp. 133–51.

Simon, K., & Hurst, M. (2021). Body Positivity, But Not for Everyone: The Role of Model Size in Exposure Effects on Women's Mood, Body Satisfaction, and Food Choice. *Body Image*, 39, 125–30. https://doi.org/10.1016/j.bodyim.2021.07.001.

Simondon, G. (2012 [1958]). *On the Mode of Existence of Technical Objects*. Minneapolis, MN: University of Minnesota Press.

Singh, G. (2016). YouTubers, Online Selves and the Performance Principle: Notes from a Post-Jungian Perspective. *Communication and Media (Novi Sad, Serbia)*, 11(38), 167–94. https://doi.org/10.5937/comman11-11414.

Singh, G. (2019). *The Death of Web 2.0: Ethics, Connectivity and Recognition in the Twenty-First Century*. London: Routledge.

Singh, S., Farley, S.D., & Donahue, J.J. (2018). Grandiosity on Display: Social Media Behaviors and Dimensions of Narcissism. *Personality and Individual Differences*, 134, 308–13. https://doi.org/10.1016/j.paid.2018.06.039.

Slobodian, Q. (2023), Elon Musk's Death Drive. *The New Statesman*, 22–28 Sept. 2023, pp. 38–41.

Snow, S. (2021). The Struggle over YouTube's Recommendation Algorithm. A Sociotechnical Research Paper presented to the faculty of the School of Engineering and Applied Science, University of Virginia.

Softley, I. (Director). (1995). *Hackers* [film]. United Artists.

Soloaga, P.D., & Guerrero, L.G. (2016). Fashion Films as a New Communication Format to Build Fashion Brands. *Communication & Society*, 29(2), 45–61. https://doi.org/10.15581/003.29.2.45-61.

Srnicek, N. (2017). *Platform Capitalism*. Cambridge, UK: Polity Press.

Staab, P. (2019). *Digitaler Kapitalismus:Markt und Herrschaft in der Ökonomie der Unknappheit*. Berlin: Suhrkamp.

Stanfill, M. (2015). The Interface as Discourse: The Production of Norms through Web Design. *New Media and Society*, 17(7), 1059–74. https://doi.org/10.1177/1461444814520873.

Stark, L. (2018). Algorithmic Psychometrics and the Scalable Subject. *Social Studies of Science*, 48(2), 204–31. https://doi.org/10.1177/0306312718772094.

Stephens-Davidowitz, S. (2017). *Everybody Lies: Big Data, New Data, and What the Internet Can Tell Us About Who We Really Are*. New York: Dey Street Press.

Stich, L., Golla, G., & Nanopoulos, A. (2014). Modelling the Spread of Negative Word-of-Mouth in Online Social Networks. *Journal of Decision Systems*, 23(2), 203–21. https://doi.org/10.1080/12460125.2014.886494.

Stokel-Walker, C. (2022). Welcome to the Metaverse. *New Scientist*, 253(3368), 39–43.

Strauss, M. (2014). On Female Obsessional Neurosis. *European Journal of Psychoanalysis*, 1(2).

Sumter, S.R., Cingel, D., & Hollander, L. (2022). Navigating a Muscular and Sexualized Instagram feed: An Experimental Study Examining How Instagram Affects Both Heterosexual and Nonheterosexual Men's Body Image. *Psychology of Popular Media*, 11(2), 125–38. https://doi.org/10.1037/ppm0000355.

Sunstein, C. (2001). *Republic.com*. Princeton: Princeton University Press.

Sweet, S. (2013). Thoughts without a Thinker, Mimetic Fusing and the Anti-Container Considered as Primitive Defensive Mechanisms in the Addictions. *Psychoanalytic Psychotherapy*, 27(2), 140–53. http://dx.doi.org/10.1080/02668734.2013.775181.

Swisher, K. (2018). Zuckerberg: The Recode interview. *Vox*. https://www.vox.com/2018/7/18/17575156/mark-zuckerberg-interview-facebook-recode-kara-swisher.

Swisher, K., & Galloway, S. (Hosts). (2023, March 2). Meta Shakes Off the FTC, and AAG Jonathan Kanter takes on Google [Audio podcast episode]. In *Pivot*. Vox Media Podcast Network. https://app.podscribe.ai/episode/84778159.

Tarde, G. (1962 [1903]). *The Laws of Imitation, 2nd Edition*. (Parsons, E., Trans.). Gloucester, MA: Peter Smith.

Tarde, G. (2003 [1890]). *Die Gesetze der Nachahmung*. Berlin: Suhrkamp.

Tay, Y., Tuan, L.A., & Hui, S.C. (2018). Multi-Pointer Co-Attention Networks for Recommendation. *Proceedings of the ACM SIGKDD International Conference on Knowledge Discovery and Data Mining*, pp. 2309–18. https://doi.org/10.1145/3219819.3220086.

Terranova, T. (2000). Free Labor: Producing Culture for the Digital Economy. *Social Text*, 18(2), 33–5. https://doi.org/10.1215/01642472-18-2_63-33.

Tiidenberg, K., & Gomez Cruz, E. (2015). Selfies, Image and the Re-making of the Body. *Body & Society*, 21(4), 77–102. https://doi.org/10.1177/1357034X15592465.

Tiidenberg, K. (2018). *Selfies: Why We Love (and Hate) Them*. Leeds, UK: Emerald.

Tifentale, A., & Manovich, L. (2015). Selfiecity: Exploring Photography and Self-Fashioning in Social Media. In: Berry, D.M., Dieter, M. (Eds.), *Postdigital Aesthetics*. London: Palgrave Macmillan.

Tiggemann, M., & Zaccardo, M. (2018). 'Strong Is the New Skinny': A Content Analysis of #Fitspiration Images on Instagram. *Journal of Health Psychology*, 23(8), 1003–11. https://doi.org/10.1177/1359105316639436.

Tiggemann, M., Anderberg, I., & Brown, Z. (2020). Uploading your Best Self: Selfie Editing and Body Dissatisfaction. *Body Image*, 33, 175–82. https://doi.org/10.1016/j.bodyim.2020.03.002.

Timberg, C., & Romm, T. (2018). Facebook CEO Mark Zuckerberg to Capitol Hill: 'It Was My Mistake, I'm Sorry'. *The Washington Post*. https://www.washingtonpost.com/news/the-switch/wp/2018/04/09/facebook-chief-executive-mark-zuckerberg-to-capitol-hill-it-was-my-mistake-and-im-sorry/.

Tolentino, J. (2019). The Age of Instagram Face. *The New Yorker*. https://www.newyorker.com/culture/decade-in-review/the-age-of-instagram-face.

Trottier, D. (2020). Denunciation and Doxing: Towards a Conceptual Model of Digital Vigilantism. *Global Crime*, 21(3–4), 196–212. https://doi.org/10.1080/17440572.2019.1591952.

Tufekci, Z. (2018). YouTube, the Great Radicalizer. *The New York Times*. https://www.nytimes.com/2018/03/10/opinion/sunday/youtube-politics-radical.html.

Turkle, S. (2011). *Alone Together: Why We Expect More from Technology and Less from Each Other*. New York: Basic Books.

Turkle, S. (2016). *Reclaiming Conversation: The Power of Talk in a Digital Age*. London and New York: Penguin.

Turkle, S. (2018) Foreword. In Margaret E. Morris, *Left to Our Own Devices: Outsmarting Smart Technology to Reclaim Our Relationships, Health, and Focus*, Cambridge, MA: MIT Press.

Turnbull, O., & Solms, M. (2003). Memory, Amnesia and Intuition: A Neuro-Psychoanalytic Perspective". In: Green, V. (Ed.), *Emotional Development in Psychoanalysis, Attachment Theory and Neuroscience – Creating Connections*. London: Routledge.

Turow, J. (2013). *The Daily You: How the New Advertising Industry Is Defining Your Identity and Your Worth*. New Haven, CT: Yale University Press.

Vaidhyannathan, S. (2011). *The Googlization of Everything (And Why We Should Worry)*. Berkeley, CA: University of California Press.

Vanden Abeele, M.M., & Mohr, V. (2021). Media addictions as Apparatgeist: What discourse on TV and smartphone addiction reveals about society. *Convergence*, 27(6), 1536–57. https://doi.org/10.1177/13548565211038539.

Van Dijck, J. (2013a). *The Culture of Connectivity: A Critical History of Social Media*. Oxford: Oxford University Press.

Van Dijck, J. (2013b). 'You Have One Identity': Performing the Self on Facebook and LinkedIn. *Media, Culture & Society*, 35(2), 199–215. https://doi.org/10.1177/0163443712468605.

Van Dijck, J. (2014). Datafication, Dataism and Dataveillance: Big Data between Scientific Paradigm and Ideology. *Surveillance & Society*, 12(2), 197–208. https://doi.org/10.24908/ss.v12i2.4776.

Van Dijck, J., & Poell, T. (2013). Understanding Social Media Logic. *Media and Communication (Lisboa)*, 1(1), 2. https://doi.org/10.12924/mac2013.01010002.

Van Dijck, J., Poell, T., & de Waal, M. (2018). *The Platform Society*. Oxford: Oxford University Press.

Van Doorn, N. (2010). Keeping it Real: User-Generated Pornography, Gender Reification, and Visual Pleasure. *Convergence*, 16(4), 411–30. https://doi.org/10.1177/1354856510375144.

Victor, D. (2018). How Instagram Rose into a Cultural Powerhouse. *The New York Times*. https://www.nytimes.com/2018/09/25/technology/instagram-celebrities-cultural-powerhouse.html.

Vise, D., & Malseed, M. (2006). *The Google Story: Inside the Hottest Business, Media, and Technology Success of Our Time*. New York: Bantam Dell.

Vreese, C.H. (2005). News Framing: Theory and Typology. *Information Design Journal*, 13(1), 51–62. https://doi.org/10.1075/idjdd.13.1.06vre.

Walkerdine, V. (2007). *Children, Gender, Video Games: Towards a Relational Approach to Multimedia*: London: Palgrave Macmillan.

Walsh, J. (2015). *Narcissism and Its Discontents*. London: Palgrave Macmillan.

Walsh, P. (2008). Herbert Marcuse and Contemporary Social Theory: Beyond the Consumer Society. *Current Perspectives in Social Theory*, 25, 235–60. https://doi.org/10.1016/S0278-1204(08)00007-8.

Waseem, Z. (2016). Are You a Racist or Am I Seeing Things? Annotator Influence on Hate Speech Detection on Twitter. *Proceedings of the First Workshop on NLP and Computational Social Science, Austin, Texas*. Association for Computational Linguistics, pp. 138–42.

Weller, K., Bruns, A., Burgess, J., Mahrt, M., & Puschmann, C. (Eds.). (2013). *Twitter and society*. New York: Peter Lang.

Weston, J., Bengio, S., & Usunier, N. (2010). Large Scale Image Annotation: Learning to Rank with Joint Word-Image Embeddings. *Machine Learning*, 81(1), 21–35. https://doi.org/10.1007/s10994-010-5198-3.

Williams, L. (1989). *Hard Core: Power, Pleasure, and the "Frenzy of the Visible"*. University of California Press.

Williams, R. (1992). Simple Statistical Gradient-Following Algorithms for Connectionist Reinforcement Learning. *Machine Learning*, 8(3–4), 229–56. https://doi.org/10.1023/A:1022672621406.

Winnicott, D. (1958). The Capacity to Be Alone. *The International Journal of Psychoanalysis*, 39, 416–20.

Winnicott, D. (1960). The Theory of the Parent-Infant Relationship. *International Journal of Psycho-Analysis*, 41, 585–95.

Winnicott, D. (1963). Communicating and Not Communicating Leading to a Study of Certain Opposites. In: Caldwell, L., & Robinson, T. (Eds.), *The Collected Works of D. W. Winnicott, Volume 6, 1960–1963*. Oxford: Oxford University Press.

Winnicott, D. (1968). Communication between Infant and Mother, and Mother and Infant, compared and contrasted. In. Joffe, W.G. (Ed.), *What Is Psychoanalysis?* London: The Institute of Psychoanalysis.

Winnicott, D. (2005 [1971]). *Playing and Reality*. London: Routledge.

Wittgenstein, L. (1953). *The Philosophical Investigations*. Oxford: Blackwell.

Wu, T. (2017). *The Attention Merchants: The Epic Scramble to Get Inside Our Heads*. New York: Knopf.

Wurmser, L. (1974). Psychoanalytic Considerations of the Etiology of Compulsive Drug use. *Journal of the American Psychoanalytic Association*, 22(4), 820–43. https://doi.org/10.1177/000306517402200407.

Yates, C. (2015). *The Play of Political Culture, Emotion and Identity*. London: Palgrave Macmillan.

Yates, C. (2019). The Psychodynamics of Casino Culture and Politics. *Journal of Psychosocial Studies*, 12(3): 217–30. https//doi.org/10.1332/204378919X15674406902661.

Yesilada, M., & Lewandowsky, S. (2022). Systematic review: YouTube recommendations and problematic content. *Internet Policy Review*, 11(1), 1–22. https://doi.org/10.14763/2022.1.1652.

Yi, X., Hong, L., Zhong, E., Liu, N., & Rajan, S. (2014). Beyond clicks. *Proceedings of the 8th ACM Conference on Recommender Systems*, pp. 113–20. https://doi.org/10.1145/2645710.2645724.

Yi, X., Yang, J., Hong, L., Cheng, D.Z., Heldt, L., Kumthekar, A., Zhao, Z., Wei, L., & Chi, E. (2019). Sampling-Bias-Corrected Neural Modeling for Large Corpus Item Recommendations. *RecSys 2019 – 13th ACM Conference on Recommender Systems*, pp. 269–77. https://doi.org/10.1145/3298689.3346996.

YouTube Team. (2019a). The Four Rs of Responsibility, Part 1: Removing Harmful Content. *YouTube Blog*. https://blog.youtube/inside-youtube/the-four-rs-of-responsibility-remove/.

YouTube Team. (2019b). The Four Rs of Responsibility, Part 2: Raising Authoritative Voices and Reducing Borderline Content and Harmful Misinformation. *YouTube Blog*. https://blog.youtube/inside-youtube/the-four-rs-of-responsibility-raise-and-reduce/.

Zenaty, G. (2022). *Sigmund Freud lesen: Eine zeitgemäße Re-Lektüre*. Bielefeld: Transcript.

Zhang, S., Tay, Y., Yao, L., & Sun, A. (2018a). Deep Learning Based Recommender System. *ACM Computing Surveys*, 52(1), 1–38. https://doi.org/10.1145/3285029.

Zhang, S., Tay, Y., Yao, L., & Sun, A. (2018b). Next Item Recommendation with Self-Attention. https://doi.org/10.48550/arxiv.1808.06414.

Zhang, Y., Ai, Q., Chen, X., & Croft, W.B. (2017). Joint Representation Learning for Top-N Recommendation with Heterogeneous Information Sources. *CIKM '17: Proceedings of the 2017 ACM on Conference on Information and Knowledge Management*, 1449–58. https://doi.org/10.1145/3132847.3132892.

Zhao, Z., Hong, L., Wei, L., Chen, J., Nath, A., Andrews, S., Kumthekar, A., Sathiamoorthy, M., Yi, X., & Chi, E. (2019). Recommending What Video to Watch Next: A Multitask Ranking System. *Proceedings of the 13th ACM Conference on Recommender Systems (RecSys '19)*. Association for Computing Machinery, New York, pp. 43–51. https://doi.org/10.1145/3298689.3346997.

Žižek, S. (1998) Cyberspace, or, How to Traverse the Fantasy in the Age of the Retreat of the Big Other. *Public Culture*, 10(3), 483–513. https://doi.org/10.1215/08992363-10-3-483.

Žižek, S. (2006). *The Parallax View*. Cambridge, MA: MIT Press.

Žižek, S. (2008 [1989]). *The Sublime Object of Ideology*. London: Verso.

Zuckerberg, M. (2017). Zuckerberg Facebook Post and Photo about Bringing the World Closer Together-pt2. *Zuckerberg Transcripts*, 720. https://epublications.marquette.edu/zuckerberg_files_transcripts/720.

Zuboff, S. (2019). *The Age of Surveillance Capitalism: The Fight for a Human Future at the New Frontier of Power*. London: Profile Books.

Zupančič, A. (2008). *The Odd One In: On Comedy*. Cambridge, MA: MIT Press.

Index

For Product Safety Concerns and Information please contact our EU
representative GPSR@taylorandfrancis.com
Taylor & Francis Verlag GmbH, Kaufingerstraße 24, 80331 München, Germany